THE
Roux BROTHERS

FRENCH COUNTRY COOKING

Albert and Michel Roux

Photographs by
MARTIN BRIGDALE

Quadrille
PUBLISHING

MAMAN

C'est à elle que nous dédions notre ouvrage. Aujourd'hui, bien qu'approchant les 80 ans, elle sait encoure et même souvent, mais jamais trop souvent, nous faire mijoter pour notre plaisir certaines recettes qui sont les siennes et qu'elle nous a léguées pour notre ouvrage.

Native de Normandie, elle nous a imprégné de ce goût pour une cuisine réelle, simple, bien en chair, à l'accent du terroir de norte Belle France. On apprend à cuisiner comme on apprend à bien manger et ceci dés l'enfance, sous la coupelle d'une maman: c'est une vie de bonheur qui vous attend.

This edition first published in 2010
by Quadrille Publishing Limited
Alhambra House
27-31 Charing Cross Road
London WC2H 0LS
www.quadrille.co.uk

Text © 1989 Michel and Albert Roux
Photography © 1989 Martin Brigdale

Translated and edited by Kate Whiteman

Contents

Introduction

FRANCE – THE LAND OF milk and honey, where our love of fine food was born and nourished. Bounded by the North Sea, the Atlantic Ocean and the Mediterranean, the country is veined with a hundred rivers and a thousand streams and studded with an astonishing number of ponds. It is a palette of a myriad colours, with chalk-white plains, the pink stone of Tournus and the grey granite of Morvan and the Brittany shores. The hard-packed earth on the banks of the Loire is brown and the plateau of Châtillon ochre. There are the sombre greens of the Morvan forests and the tender green of the Saône valley, the golden Côte de Beaune, the red and black mining basin and the deep yellow of the plains of Bresse. An aerial view fuses the colours of the countryside into a masterpiece.

With its temperate climate and fertile soil, France offers a unique and inexhaustible range of produce. Its rich and varied provincial cooking reflects the diverse ethnic origins, tastes and cultures of its inhabitants and the abundant resources of the land. It is regional, homely cooking which manages to be both rustic and sophisticated at the same time. This cooking, rooted in tradition, smells and looks wonderful and tastes even better. This is the cooking of our mothers and grand-mothers, who passed on their recipes from one generation to the next, sharing their little secrets and tricks of the trade with their family and friends.

We acquired our love and passion for good food and cooking from our mother. Throughout our childhood, she fed us wonderfully well and many of our recipes come from her; blanquette of veal, fricassee of rabbit, calf's heart with carrots, dandelion salad with fat bacon, duck with turnips. On market day, she would make waffles and oh, such miraculous tarts! Even now, whenever we go to visit her, she concocts our favourite dishes for us.

Our grandfather and father were *charcutiers* in Charolles. For forty years, they beavered away in their little *charcuterie* in the church square. What dishes they prepared for their clients, friends and family! With a twinge of nostalgia, we remember the whitewood tables and pull-out trestles sagging under the weight of cooked meats, Lyonnais tripe with onions, *choucroute*, breaded pigs' trotters and a multitude of sausages, *boudins*, pâtés made from pork, poultry and game and pike quenelles.

We lived above the shop; small wonder that we quickly acquired a well-developed sense of smell! Our noses always told us what day of the week it was – Tuesday was the day for *boudin* and *andouillettes*, Wednesdays was the day for terrines, pâtés and parslied ham and so on.

When, many years later, Michel went to work in the service of Mlle Cécile de Rothschild, we discovered that the owners of the great private houses of France have always been passionate – almost obsessional – supporters of French regional cooking. The dishes Michel was most often asked to cook were such regional classics as *quiche lorraine*, *mouclade d'Aunis*, salad niçoise, lampreys *à la bordelaise*, navarin of lamb, cassoulet, *choucroute*, *pot au feu* and blade of pork with lentils.

This great love for regional food is almost universal in the country houses of France. In the course of our journeys around the country, we are often invited to lunch or dine with local dignitaries, merchants or vineyard proprietors. To our delight, they all love and understand the cooking of their own region. They offer good, honest food, often accompanied by local wines. The sight and smell of the dishes we are served cause the conversation to stop – a mélange of meat or fish in a perfect amber or purple or creamy wine sauce, with fine seasonal vegetables resting on top, simply peeled and never, ever fancily 'turned'.

This traditional style of cookery is as old as cooking itself. It is our aim to use our knowledge and professional experience to inject new life into this ancient craft. We have been helped by friends and colleagues who have given us much support and professional advice.

THE REGIONS OF FRANCE

Our thanks are due to Philippe Olivier, *maître fromager* from Boulogne, and to members of the *Association des Relais et Desserts*, the *Maîtres Pâtissiers de France* and other chefs-patrons. We have thanked each one personally in the ackowledgments section of this book. Selecting the recipes was not easy; French provincial cookery is so full of riches. The recipes we have chosen reflect our own personal taste and preference.

Several regions lay claim to the same recipe with minor variations – we do not wish to fan the flames of old tribal wars! We tried all the different recipes again and chose our own favourite versions.

7

How to use this book

Geography: The introductory chapter to each region lists the seas, rivers and tributaries which bound or cross the area. It also contains information on climate, which in turn influences the type of produce grown in each region, and a list of local produce is also given. All these elements naturally determine the character of the cooking. We believe that the short geographical summaries enable you to understand the recipes more fully and make them more interesting to prepare and cook. You will also find some more general descriptive notes on the countryside and French cooking in general.

Wines: The unique and vast range of French wines is such an enormous subject that in most cases we have ventured only to list the major types of grapes grown in each region.

Cheeses: One of the glories of our country! We mention the most famous cheeses of each region.

The recipes: Many of the dishes in this book are cooked by slow simmering and freeze very well. Most are classic recipes which we have interpreted in our own personal way. We have refined some of the dishes by lightening or simplifying them, but they are all basically uncomplicated recipes. Below we list some advice on using this book which it is important that you read before embarking on our recipes.

THE GOLDEN RULES

1. Prepare and have ready to hand all the equipment needed for the recipe.
2. Weigh, measure and prepare all the listed ingredients before beginning the recipe.
3. Preheat the oven to the required temperature.

MEASUREMENTS

All our recipes have been tested using metric measurements and we suggest that you also use these measurements. Imperial measurements have been rounded up or down to the nearest half ounce. Remember that you must never mix metric and imperial measurements in a recipe; stick to one or the other. All spoon measures are *level* spoons, not heaped.

GENERAL ADVICE

The preparation time given for the recipes has been calculated after all the ingredients have been weighed and measured and all the necessary equipment is ready to hand.

Unless otherwise specified, an egg weighs 55–60g/2oz; sugar is caster sugar; butter is unsalted; flour should be sifted.

Butter used for frying should be clarified; this prevents the forming of little black specks, which stick to the meat and could get into the sauce or gravy.

Casseroles for slow-cooked dishes should be earthenware, stoneware, cast-iron or enamelled cast-iron. We prepare most of our recipes using Le Creuset casseroles and cooking utensils.

OVEN TEMPERATURES

These can vary from oven to oven, so we recommend that you use an independent oven thermometer for perfect results. Do not trust the graduated temperature scale on your oven, which is never as accurate.

INGREDIENTS

Always choose the best possible quality and make sure that your ingredients are absolutely fresh; this is the only way to achieve a really good result.

Authors' Acknowledgments

Many of our friends and colleagues have helped us in preparing this book by giving us traditional recipes from their own region. In particular, we should like to thank our very close friend Mme Aimée Badin and all her family 'à Mouans' for *Daube de supions* and *Panier de legumes*; Gérard Bannwarth, proprietor of the Pâtisserie Jacques at Mulhouse, *Maître Pâtissier* and member of the *Association des Relais et Desserts*, for his recipe for *Tarte flambée*; Louis Berger, from the Pâtisserie Royalty at Tarbes, member of the *Relais et Desserts*, for *Petits poivres limouxin*; our friend Paul Bocuse for *Jambon au foin* from his book *La cuisine du marché* (Flammarion); Michel Favre from Aurillac, member of the *Relais et Desserts* for *Tartelettes à l'Encalat*; Daniel Giraud from Valence, *Meilleur Ouvrier de France*, for *Le Suisse de Valence*; Michel Guérard, *Meilleur Ouvrier de France* and chef-patron of *Les Prés d'Eugénie*, for *Jeune dinde 'ivre d'armagnac'*; Bernard Huguet from Beauvoir-sur-Mer, *Meilleur Ouvrier de France* and member of the *Relais et Desserts* for *Flan maraîchin*; Manuel Lopez from Libourne, member of the *Relais et Desserts*, who introduced us to the famous desserts of his region, like *Millas landais* and *Fichaises*. Our thanks are also due to André Mandion, member of the *Relais et Desserts* from Anglet, for his recipe for *Pithiviers fondant*; to Jean Millet, president of the *Confédération de la Pâtisserie, Confiserie, Glacerie de France*, *Meilleur Ouvrier de France* in pâtisserie for his recipe for puff pastry; Jean-Louis Paul, our first head chef at Le Gavroche in the early seventies; to Jean-Paul Pignon from Lyon, *Meilleur Ouvrier de France* and member of the *Relais et Desserts* for giving us a taste of the past with *Tarte au massepain de Lubeck*, *Balles de neige* and *Tourte des apôtres*; to Michel Pottier, a member of the *Relais et Desserts*, from Saint Germain-en-Laye for his recipe for *Le manceau* and to Jacky Samson from Langeais, *Meilleur Ouvrier de France*, for his *Tarte de Tour au nougat*.

The Authors also wish to thank the following people, without whose help this book would not have been possible: Chris Sellors, *sous chef* at The Waterside Inn, who tested most of the recipes and helped to prepare all the food for photography; Robyn Roux for her constant help and support throughout; Isabelle Ferretjans for collating the information for the introductions to each region; Elaine Partington of Swallow Books for her art direction; Martin Brigdale for his photography; Andrea Lambton for styling the photographs; and Kate Whiteman for her impeccable editing and translation of the French text.

We would also like to thank Le Creuset, France, whose enamelled cast-iron cookware we used in almost all the recipes which needed long, slow simmering. The Le Creuset pans were provided by Elizabeth David Ltd., 46 Bourne Street, London SW1W 8JD.

BASIC RECIPES

Dough

~ PÂTE BRISÉE ~

Shortcrust Pastry

MAKES ABOUT 475G/1LB 1OZ
PREPARATION TIME:
15 MINUTES, PLUS SEVERAL
HOURS RESTING

INGREDIENTS

250g/9oz flour

1 egg

5g/¾ teaspoon salt

10g/1½ teaspoons sugar

160g/5oz butter, diced and
slightly softened

1 tablespoon milk

T HIS LIGHT, DELICATE PASTRY *is excellent for wrapping fish or meat and is used for tartlets,* barquettes *and flan cases. It can also be used as a substitute for puff pastry.*

PREPARATION

Put the flour on a marble or wooden surface and make a well in the centre. Put in the egg, salt, sugar and diced butter and rub the ingredients together with the fingertips of your right hand, drawing the flour into the well with your left hand. When everything is almost completely mixed, add the milk and knead the dough 2 or 3 times with the heel of your hand to make it smooth, but do not overwork it.

STORING

Wrap the dough in clingfilm or greaseproof paper and leave to rest in the fridge for several hours before using. It will keep in the fridge for 3 or 4 days, or for several weeks in the freezer.

———— · ————

~ PÂTE À FONCER ~

Lining or flan pastry

MAKES ABOUT 480G/1LB
PREPARATION TIME: 15
MINUTES, PLUS SEVERAL
HOURS RESTING

INGREDIENTS

250g/9oz flour

125g/4oz butter, at room
temperature and diced

1 egg

10g/1½ teaspoons sugar

5g/¾ teaspoon salt

40ml/3 tablespoons water

T HIS IS THE TRADITIONAL *pastry for use in savoury flans and tartlets, as it is less crumbly than shortcrust pastry.*

PREPARATION

Put the flour on a marble or wooden surface and make a well in the centre. Put the butter in the well and mash it with your fingertips until completely softened. Add the sugar and salt and mix into the butter, then add the egg and mix well, gradually drawing the flour into the mixture. When the dough is well mixed, but still a little crumbly and not quite smooth, add the water and knead the dough 2 or 3 times with the heel of your hand until it becomes completely smooth. Wrap it in clingfilm or greaseproof paper and chill in the fridge for several hours before using.

STORING

The wrapped dough can be kept in the fridge for several days or frozen for at least 3 weeks.

PÂTE SUCRÉE

Sweet short pastry

THIS IS THE CLASSIC *pastry used as a base for sweet tarts and tartlets. It is not as delicate as* pâte sablée *and is therefore easier to work.*

Put the flour on a marble or wooden work surface and make a well in the centre. Put the butter in the well and work with your fingertips until completely softened. Add the sugar and salt, mix well, then add the eggs and mix again. Gradually draw the flour into the mixture. When everything is well mixed, knead the dough 2 or 3 times with the palm of your hand until it is very smooth.

STORING
Roll the dough into a ball, flatten the top slightly and wrap in clingfilm or polythene. Leave to rest in the fridge for several hours before using. It will keep well in the fridge for 3 or 4 days, or can be frozen for several weeks.

MAKES ABOUT 500G/1LB 2OZ
PREPARATION TIME:
15 MINUTES, PLUS SEVERAL
HOURS RESTING

INGREDIENTS

250g/9oz flour

100g/4oz butter, diced

100g/4oz icing sugar

5g/¾ teaspoon salt

2 eggs, total weight 120g/4oz, at room temperature

FEUILLETAGE JEAN MILLET

Puff pastry

ALTHOUGH PUFF PASTRY *takes a long time to prepare, it is not a difficult process, so be bold and give it a try; the end result is well worth the effort.*

PREPARATION
The dough: Put the 500g/1lb 2oz flour on a marble or wooden surface and make a well in the centre. Put in the water, salt, vinegar and melted butter and work together with the fingertips of your right hand, drawing the flour into the centre with your left hand. Mix well, then knead the dough lightly with the palm of your hand until it is very smooth but not too firm. Wrap in polythene or greaseproof paper and refrigerate for 2–3 hours.

Incorporating the butter: Lightly flour the work surface and place the ball of dough on it. Roll it out in 4 places so that it looks like 4 large 'ears' around a small round 'head'. Hit the chilled butter several times with a rolling pin to make it supple, but it must still be firm and very cold. Place the butter on the 'head' so that it covers it completely, with no overhang. Fold the 4 'ears' up over the butter to enclose it completely. Wrap in polythene and chill in the fridge for 30 minutes to bring the dough and butter to the same temperature.

First turn: Lightly flour the work surface, then roll the dough gently and evenly away from you into a 70 × 40cm/27 × 16in rectangle. Fold over the ends to make 3 layers. This is the first turn.

Second turn: On the lightly floured surface, give the rectangle a quarter turn and again roll it gently and evenly away from you into a 70 × 40cm/27 × 16in rectangle. Fold the dough into 3. This is the second turn.

Wrap the dough in polythene or greaseproof paper and place in the fridge for 30 minutes to rest and firm up.

Third and fourth turns: Make 2 more turns as above, then wrap the dough again and place in the fridge for ½–1 hour.

Fifth and sixth turns: Make 2 more turns, bringing the total to 6.

MAKES 1.2KG/2¾LB
PREPARATION TIME: 1 HOUR 10 MINUTES, PLUS 5 HOURS RESTING

INGREDIENTS

500g/1lb 2oz flour, plus extra for dusting

200ml/7fl oz water

12g/1¾ teaspoons salt

25ml/1fl oz white wine vinegar

50g/2oz butter, melted

400g/14oz butter, well chilled

(recipe continued overleaf)

STORING

Wrap the dough in polythene or greaseproof paper. It will keep in the fridge for up to 3 days, or can be frozen for several weeks. If you plan to keep it for any length of time, give the dough only 4 turns and complete the fifth and sixth turns when you use it. Chill for 30 minutes after these 2 final turns.

———— · ————

PÂTE À CHOUX

Choux paste

MAKES ABOUT 24 CHOUX BUNS
OR ÉCLAIRS

PREPARATION TIME:
20 MINUTES

COOKING TIME: 10–20 MINUTES,
DEPENDING ON THE SHAPE
AND SIZE OF THE BUNS

INGREDIENTS

125ml/4½fl oz water

125ml/4½fl oz milk

100g/4oz butter, finely diced,
plus extra for greasing

3g/½ teaspoon salt

5g/¾ teaspoon sugar

150g/5oz flour, sifted

4 eggs, total weight 240g/8½oz

THIS VERSATILE PASTE *was invented by the great Carême, and is used for making light puffs, both sweet and savoury.*

PREPARATION

Cooking the paste: Put the water, milk, butter, salt and sugar in a saucepan, set over high heat and boil for 1 minute, stirring continuously. Take the pan off the heat and quickly tip in the flour, stirring all the time.

Drying out: This stage is vitally important if you want to make good choux paste. When the mixture is very smooth, return the pan to the heat and stir with a wooden spatula for 1 minute. The paste will begin to poach and some of the water will evaporate. Take care not to let the paste dry out too much, or it will crack during cooking and the finished product will not be perfectly smooth. Transfer the paste to a bowl.

Adding the eggs: Immediately beat in the eggs one at a time, using a wooden spatula to beat well until the paste is very smooth. If you are not using it immediately, spread a little beaten egg over the surface to prevent a crust from forming.

Piping the paste: Using a piping bag fitted with an appropriate nozzle, pipe out your chosen shapes on to a greased or baking parchment-lined baking sheet.

BAKING

Preheat the oven to 220°C/425°F/gas 6.

Bake the choux in the oven for 4–5 minutes, then open the oven door and leave it slightly ajar while you finish cooking the choux. They will take 10–20 minutes, depending on the size and shape.

STORING

Place in an airtight container and keep in the fridge for up to 3 days, or freeze for up to 1 week.

———— · ————

BRIOCHE

Brioche dough

THIS IS A BUTTERY, *yeasty dough, which can be eaten on its own or used as a base for* savarins *and savoury dishes.*

PREPARATION
Put the yeast and milk in the bowl of your mixer and beat lightly with a whisk. Add the salt, then the flour and eggs. Switch the mixer on to medium speed and work the mixture with the dough hook for about 10 minutes, until the dough is smooth and elastic with plenty of body. If you are making it by hand, use a spatula and work the dough for about 20 minutes.

Mix together the butter and sugar, reduce the speed of the mixer to low and add the butter mixture to the dough, a little at a time, working the dough continuously. When all the butter is incorporated, increase the speed and mix for 8–10 minutes in the mixer or about 15 minutes by hand, until the dough is very smooth and glossy. It should be supple and fairly elastic and will be coming away from the sides of the bowl.

Cover the dough with a baking sheet or tea towel and leave it in a warm place (about 24°C/75°F) for 2 hours, until it has doubled in bulk.

Knock back the dough by punching it with your fist not more than 2 or 3 times. Cover it with a baking tray or tea towel and refrigerate for at least 4 hours, but not longer than 24 hours.

NOTES
The dough is ready to bake after a minimum of 4 hours in the fridge. It can be used to make either small or large brioches. Preheat the oven to 220°C/425°F/ gas 7 and cook a large brioche for 40–45 minutes or small ones for 8 minutes.

To freeze the dough, wrap it in polythene; it will keep well for several days. Before baking, leave the dough to thaw gradually in the fridge at 5°C/40°C for 2–3 hours.

MAKES 1.2KG/2¾ LB

PREPARATION TIME: 25 MINUTES IN AN ELECTRIC MIXER, 35 MINUTES BY HAND

RISING TIME: 2 HOURS, PLUS 4 HOURS RESTING

INGREDIENTS

15g/½oz fresh yeast

70ml/3fl oz milk, boiled and cooled to lukewarm

15g/½oz fine salt

500g/1lb 2oz flour

6 eggs

350g/12oz butter, at room temperature

30g/1oz sugar

LE PAIN

Bread

IF YOU KEEP A BATCH OF ROLLS *in the freezer, you can enjoy fresh bread every day without the chore of baking it daily.*

PREPARATION
The bread can be made by hand or in an electric mixer.
By hand: Put the flour, sugar and salt into a mixing bowl and make a well in the centre of the mixture.

In another bowl, mix the yeast and water and pour into the well. Mix the ingredients with your right hand until well blended, gradually drawing in the the flour with your left hand. Do not overwork the mixture.
Using an electric mixer: Put the water and yeast in the bowl of the mixer and beat lightly with a whisk. Fit the dough hook, add the flour, sugar and salt and beat on the lowest speed until thoroughly mixed.

MAKES 15–20 ROLLS

PREPARATION TIME: 35 MINUTES

RISING TIME: 2½ HOURS FOR ROLLS, ABOUT 3½ HOURS FOR A LOAF

BAKING TIME: ABOUT 12 MINUTES FOR ROLLS, 40–50 MINUTES FOR A LOAF

(recipe continued overleaf)

13

INGREDIENTS

450g/1lb strong bread flour

30g/1oz sugar

15g/½oz salt

15g/½oz live yeast

250ml/9fl oz water at 16°C/60°F

beaten egg, for glazing (optional)

RISING

Cover the dough with a damp cloth or baking sheet and leave to rise in a warm place (about 24°C/75°F) for about 2 hours, until doubled in bulk. Knock back the dough by flipping it over with your fingertips not more than 2 or 3 times.

SHAPING THE BREAD

Place the dough on a marble or wooden surface and, with a sharp knife, cut it into even pieces of the size you require. Shape these into balls or pull them into long rolls and place on a baking sheet. You can also make a single large loaf.

Using scissors or a razor blade set into a cork, make shallow slashes in the top of the long rolls and cut crosses in the top of the round rolls. Cover with clingfilm to prevent the dough from drying out and protect it from draughts. Leave to rise again at 24°C/75°F for about 30 minutes for the rolls and 1–1½ hours for a loaf. For a deep amber glaze, brush with beaten egg before baking.

BAKING THE ROLLS

Preheat the oven to 240°C/475°F/gas 9.

Stand small tins of water on the oven bottom; their steam will bake the bread perfectly. Bake the rolls for 12 minutes and the loaf for 40–50 minutes. For a shiny finish, brush the top with a lightly moistened pastry brush.

STORING

To freeze, cool on a wire rack, then immediately wrap in clingfilm and freeze. The bread will taste as good as if it were freshly baked if used within a few days.

Warm in a moderate oven (190°C/375°F/gas 5) for 5 minutes before serving.

Stocks and Sauces

~ FUMET DE POISSON ~

Fish stock

MAKES 4 LITRES/7PT

PREPARATION TIME: 15 MINUTES, PLUS 2–3 HOURS WASHING THE BONES

COOKING TIME: 30 MINUTES

INGREDIENTS

2kg/4½lb white fish bones and heads (turbot, brill, halibut or sole)

2 onions

white parts of 3 leeks

150g/5oz mushrooms, chopped

2 celery stalks

75g/3oz butter

500ml/18fl oz dry white wine

4 litres/7pt water

20 white peppercorns

1 bouquet garni

ALL STOCKS CAN BE MADE *in large quantities and frozen in small containers to use as you need them. Pour the stock into containers of the appropriate size, cool, label and freeze.*

PREPARATION

Roughly chop the fish bones. Remove the gills and any innards from the heads and wash the heads and bones under cold running water for 2–3 hours.

Wash and chop the vegetables, place in a saucepan with the butter and sweat until they are soft but have not taken on any colour. Add the fish bones and heads and simmer for 2–3 minutes. Pour in the wine, increase the heat and reduce by half. Add the water, heat until simmering and skim off any scum and grease from the surface. Add the peppercorns and bouquet garni and simmer gently for 20 minutes. Carefully strain the stock through a muslin-lined sieve into a bowl. Leave to cool, then store in the fridge.

STORAGE

The stock will keep for 1 week in the fridge, or can be frozen for several weeks.

FONDS BLANC DE VOLAILLE

Chicken stock

THIS DELICATE AND *classic stock forms the basis of innumerable soups and sauces. The addition of the veal knuckle gives more flavour and body to the stock.*

PREPARATION

Wash the chicken bones or boiling fowl and the veal knuckle under cold running water for 3–4 hours. Wash all the vegetables and tie the celery stalks and leeks together with string.

Put the chicken and veal knuckle in a large saucepan, cover with the water and bring to the boil. Lower the heat and simmer gently, skimming off the grease and scum from the surface. After 10 minutes, add all the vegetables, the peppercorns, bouquet garni and garlic. Simmer for 2½–3 hours, skimming the surface as necessary.

Strain the stock through a muslin-lined sieve into a bowl and leave in a cold place until completely cooled, then refrigerate.

STORING

The stock will keep for up to 1 week in the fridge, or can be packed into freezer bags or small containers and stored for several weeks in the freezer.

MAKES 3–4 LITRES/5½–7PT

PREPARATION TIME: 15 MINUTES, PLUS 3–4 HOURS WASHING THE CHICKEN AND VEAL KNUCKLE

COOKING TIME: 2½–3 HOURS

INGREDIENTS

2kg/4½lb chicken bones and trimmings or 1 boiling fowl

1 veal knuckle, split

200g/7oz carrots, peeled

2 onions, peeled and each stuck with 1 clove

2 celery stalks

white parts of 3 leeks

200g/7oz mushrooms

6 litres/10pt water

20 white peppercorns

1 large bouquet garni

2 unpeeled garlic cloves

FONDS DE VEAU

Veal stock

THIS INDISPENSABLE *stock can be reduced by half to give a* demi-glace, *or by three-quarters to give a rich meat glaze.*

PREPARATION

Preheat the oven to 220°C/425°F/gas 7.

Coarsely chop the veal bones and place in a roasting pan with the calf's foot. Place in the hot oven, turning the bones until lightly browned. Transfer them to a large saucepan and cover with water. Quickly bring to simmering point.

Pour off the fat from the roasting pan, then put in all the vegetables and garlic. Return it to the oven and cook, stirring occasionally, until the vegetables are pale golden. Deglaze the pan with the wine, scraping up all the crusty juices from the bottom. Pour the contents of the roasting pan into the saucepan and add the quartered tomatoes and bouquet garni. Bring the stock to a slow simmer and cook gently for 4–5 hours, skimming the scum and grease from the surface, particularly in the early stages. Top up the water if necessary.

Strain the stock through a sieve into a clean saucepan and reduce to 2–3 litres/3½–5¼pt, depending on the strength of stock you require, skimming the surface as necessary. Pass through a muslin-lined sieve into a bowl and leave in a cold place until completely cooled, then refrigerate.

STORING

The stock can be kept in the fridge for up to 10 days, or frozen in 100ml/3½fl oz or 200ml/7fl oz freezer bags or containers for up to 3 weeks.

MAKES 2 LITRES/3½PT

PREPARATION TIME: 15 MINUTES

COOKING TIME: 4–5 HOURS

INGREDIENTS

3kg/6lb 10oz veal bones

1 calf's foot, split lengthways

300g/11oz carrots, roughly chopped

150g/5oz onions, peeled and roughly chopped

2 celery stalks, roughly chopped

10 ripe tomatoes, quartered

200g/7oz mushrooms, chopped

4 unpeeled garlic cloves

700ml/1¼pt dry white wine

1 large bouquet garni tied with 8 tarragon stalks

⤙ SAUCE MAYONNAISE ⤚

Mayonnaise

MAKES 500ML/18FL OZ

PREPARATION TIME:
10 MINUTES

INGREDIENTS

3 egg yolks

1 tablespoon dijon mustard

7g/1 teaspoon salt

freshly ground white pepper

500ml/18fl oz vegetable oil, at room temperature

½ tablespoon white wine vinegar or lemon juice

1 tablespoon double cream

Mayonnaise is used as *a base for many sauces for meat and fish. It can be made with different flavoured oils. This is the version we use in our restaurants; at home, we personally prefer to use a mixture of two-thirds vegetable oil and one-third olive oil.*

PREPARATION

Combine the egg yolks, mustard, salt and pepper to taste in a bowl and mix with a balloon whisk. Gradually pour in the oil in a thin, steady stream, beating all the time. Stir in the vinegar or lemon juice, then add the cream and adjust the seasoning to taste.

STORING

Keep the mayonnaise at room temperature, not in the fridge. It will keep in the larder or a cool place for 2 or 3 days.

Desserts

⤙ CRÈME D'AMANDE ⤚

Almond cream

MAKES 1.15KG/2½LB

PREPARATION TIME:
20 MINUTES

INGREDIENTS

250g/9oz butter

250g/9oz icing sugar and 250g/9oz ground almonds, sifted together (*tant pour tant*)

50g/2oz flour

5 eggs

50ml/2fl oz rum (optional)

This cream *can be made even richer by adding 20–30 per cent* crème pâtissière *just before using it.*

PREPARATION

Cream the butter in a food processor or with a wooden spatula until very soft. Still beating, work in the *tant pour tant* and flour, then add the eggs one at a time, beating well between each addition, until the mixture is smooth and light. Stir in the rum if you are using it.

STORING

Put the almond cream in a bowl, cover tightly with clingfilm and refrigerate for up to 5 days. Remove from the fridge 30 minutes before using.

CRÈME PÂTISSIÈRE

Confectioner's custard

THIS IS THE BASIC *custard cream filling for innumerable pâtisseries, which is not difficult to make and is delicious when made correctly.*

PREPARATION
Put the egg yolks and about one-third of the sugar in a bowl and whisk until they are pale and leave a slight trail when you lift up the whisk. Sift in the flour and mix well.

COOKING
Put the milk, the remaining sugar and the split vanilla pod in a saucepan and bring to the boil. As soon as the milk begins to bubble, pour about one-third on to the egg mixture, stirring continuously. Pour the mixture back into the pan and cook very gently, stirring continuously. Boil for 2 minutes until the custard thickens, then pour it into a bowl. Flake a little butter or sprinkle some icing sugar over the surface to prevent a skin forming as the custard cools.

MAKES ABOUT 750G/1¾LB
PREPARATION TIME: 15 MINUTES

INGREDIENTS

6 egg yolks

125g/4oz sugar

40g/1½oz flour

500ml/18fl oz milk

1 vanilla pod, split

1 tablespoon butter or a little icing sugar

———— · ————

SIROP À SORBET

Sorbet syrup

THIS USEFUL SYRUP *is used in all sorbets and for moistening sponge cakes for pâtisserie.*

PREPARATION
Put all the ingredients in a saucepan and bring to the boil, stirring occasionally with a wooden spatula. Boil for 3 minutes, skimming the surface if it is necessary. If you have a sugar thermometer, the reading should be 30° Beaumé or 1.2624 density.

Pass the syrup through a conical sieve into a bowl and leave to cool completely before using.

STORING
Cover the syrup with clingfilm or place in an airtight container and keep in the fridge for up to 2 weeks.

MAKES ABOUT 1.4 LITRES/2½PT
PREPARATION TIME: 5 MINUTES
COOKING TIME: 20 MINUTES

INGREDIENTS

750g/1½lb sugar

650ml/1pt water

90g/3oz glucose

———— · ————

Normandy and Brittany

COASTS TEEMING WITH SEAFOOD, APPLE-LADEN ORCHARDS
AND LUSH DAIRY PASTURES

VERDANT NORMANDY, is the colour of hope; the woodlands and pastures, the wide meadows, the orchards are all green. It is a patchwork of small fields, enclosing many different landscapes. In parts, it resembles Brittany, with its heathland and heathers, gorges and escarpments. But rich meadows and pastures abound and the countryside is dotted with apple trees bending under the weight of the fruit. Tourists believe that the dovecotes and thatched houses are typical of Normandy, but in fact, they are only found in areas like the Auge valley. In other parts of the region, the houses are different; long farmhouses (called *courmasures*) in the pays de caux, solidly built houses of shale and granite in Contentin and sturdy stone dwellings.

Numerous rivers flow through the region; the Seine, the Eure, the Touques, the Dives, the Orne and the Vire. From Tréport to Mont-St-Michel, Normandy is united with the sea. In a vast sandy bay on the frontier with Brittany, there stands on its rocky base the amazing silhouette of Mont-St-Michel.

Those who love Normandy secretly enjoy the fine drizzle, the sudden capricious showers and the cloudbursts which sweep across the sky. The fine rain is rarely cold; it adds a lustre to the slate roofs and lashes the sea front whenever the wind rises.

We came to know Normandy through our mother, who comes from St-Julien-sur-Sarthe in the Orne. She gave us the taste for dishes drowning in cream and butter and, of course, cider, which we unashamedly adore. She told us about the *passés*, sweet-smelling strained

cheeses, marinated in cider for several months in pottery vats, which her family made. No other region can boast such a variety of cheeses.

It was our mother who took us, many years ago, to the Percheron stud at le Pin de Garenne to see the horses being reared. Since that time, we have often returned to this green region to select, among other good things, fine calvados with its unique, tempting bouquet. On one of these visits, in a little wayside bar, Albert tasted a bowlful of *moules poulette* with slightly soured cream. That simple dish was so delectable that he still savours it in his imagination!

Brittany is the prow of Europe, defiantly facing the immensity of the Atlantic ocean, its flanks attacked by the raging waves of the English Channel. Its tortured coastline exemplifies unity in diversity. This vast and multi-faceted region has a strong personality. Its people have always been fiercely independent and profoundly original; they have never completely melded into the national melting pot. They still proudly retain their special characteristics and their ancient celtic language, but there are as many different faces of Brittany as there are lace caps and calvaries!

The early Bretons were stone masons, who fashioned the rough local granite into a multitude of churches, chapels and calvaries which covered the whole area. St-Pol-de-Leon boasts two of the finest of such religious buildings in Brittany; the former cathedral, an elegant masterpiece in the Norman gothic style, and the magnificent Kreisker chapel belfry.

The numerous rivers which flow through the region – the Rance, the Vilaine, the Elorne, the Blavet, the Trieux, the Odet, the Aune and the Loc – all add to the area's natural beauty. The fertile soil is ideal for growing early vegetables. Lambs are pastured in the salt meadows of the bays of Mont-St-Michel and Frenaye; their special, salty flavour makes their meat highly prized. The coastal waters teem with fish and shellfish, which the Bretons cook very simply.

The tides in this area play a special part in the fascination of the sea. Twice a day, in a regular rhythm, they completely transform the coastline, as hundreds of islands are exposed and then hidden again. At high tide, the gulf is sparkling and alluring, wonderful for swimming; then, as the tide goes down, the coast takes on a melancholy aspect. It never loses its beauty, but the landscape becomes quite different. This is the time to go fishing on foot. The sea offers its edible produce – beds of oysters, pole-grown mussels and a hundred types of shellfish – to anyone who cares to take them.

Roscoff is the maritime port of this fertile coastal region. Its distribution centre exports shiploads of cauliflowers, artichokes and onions to England, while convoys of loaded lorries head towards Rungis market in Paris.

Brittany produces few wines. Three *appellation controlées* come from the region around Nantes; muscadet from the banks of the Loire, Sèvre et Maine and *gros plant*, all made from the white sauvignon grape. Once every two or three years, Michel treats himself to an orgy of wine tastings to assess the quality of the wine-making. This offers a good excuse to revitalise himself with a plateful of delicious shellfish.

The climate of Brittany is very changeable and cannot be precisely described. Finistère, for example, has a regular, abundant annual rainfall of 1.2–1.4m/4–4½ft. The Gulf of Morbihan and northern coasts are drier, with 70–90cm/27½–35½in of rain each year. There are very few days of extreme heat or cold. The winds are often strong, like the *noroit*, a fresh wind, which brings sudden showers over the Channel, or the humid, gentle *suroit* which sweeps over southern Brittany. The Bretons, like the Normans, say that these winds are no problem; you must just be well prepared!

An apple tree groaning under its harvest of cider apples, one of the countless thousands in this area.

HOMARD EN POT-AU-FEU

Pot-au-feu *of lobster*

SERVES 4

PREPARATION TIME:
1½ HOURS

COOKING TIME: 15 MINUTES
FOR THE LOBSTER, 5 MINUTES
FOR THE LANGOUSTINES

INGREDIENTS

4 small live lobsters, each weighing 400–500g/about 1lb

8 medium uncooked langoustines

150g/5oz tender young spinach

150g/5oz cauliflower

150g/5oz white part of leeks

80g/3oz butter

6 tablespoons olive oil

100ml/3½fl oz cider *eau-de-vie* or calvados

2 shallots, chopped

1 bouquet garni, with 2 branches of tarragon

150ml/5fl oz dry white wine (preferably muscadet)

300ml/11fl oz Fish stock (recipe page 14)

200ml/7fl oz double cream

500g/1lb 2oz mussels (preferably bouchot), scrubbed and debearded

4 scallops, with their corals

4 medium oysters

salt and freshly ground pepper

THIS IS A FINE DISH FOR *a special celebration! We often serve it at The Waterside Inn with plain boiled rice or a pilaff.*

PREPARING THE VEGETABLES

The spinach: Remove the stalks, wash the leaves and blanch in boiling water for 1 minute. Refresh, drain and set aside.

The cauliflower: Wash, separate into florets, blanch for 7 minutes, refresh, drain and set aside.

The leeks: Wash, slice finely, blanch for 2 minutes, refresh, drain and set aside.

COOKING THE LOBSTERS AND LANGOUSTINES

Plunge a darning needle deeply between the eyes of the lobsters to kill them instantaneously. Lay them on their backs on a chopping board, one at a time, and split them lengthways with a heavy knife. Discard the gritty sac. Scrape out all the creamy green and yellow parts, the coral and the eggs if there are any. Mix with 40g/1½oz butter and set aside.

Detach the claws from the body and crack them lightly with the flat of a knife. Prepare the langoustines in the same way and keep them separately.

Set a large sauté pan over high heat and heat 4 tablespoons olive oil. Put in the lobsters and claws and seal them all over. When they turn red, add the *eau-de-vie* or calvados and flame it. When the flames die down, add the shallots, bouquet garni and white wine, put on the lid and simmer for 8 minutes. Transfer the lobsters and their claws to a serving dish, cover with foil and keep warm.

Pour the fish stock into the pan and reduce by half. Meanwhile, in another sauté pan, heat the remaining olive oil, put in the langoustines and sauté them quickly for 3 minutes. Pour the contents of the first pan over the langoustines and simmer for 1 minute. Lift out the langoustines with a slotted spoon and put them with the lobsters.

THE SAUCE AND GARNISH

Add the cream to the stock in the pan, then increase the heat. Put in the mussels and, as soon as they open, pour everything into a colander set over a bowl. Remove the mussels from their shells and place them in a bowl. Pass the sauce through a conical sieve into a saucepan and reduce it to the consistency of a light juice.

Cut the scallops into 2 or 3 slices, depending on their thickness, and add them to the sauce. Simmer for 1 minute, then add the oysters with their juices, taking care that no grit goes into the sauce. Simmer for 1 minute, then add the mussels. Season to taste and lower the heat. Add the reserved lobster butter and swirl it into the sauce. Do not let it boil.

Heat the rest of the butter in a frying pan and sauté the vegetables for 2 minutes, without letting them colour.

SERVING

Arrange the vegetables around the shellfish in the serving dish and pour the boiling sauce and garnish over the lobsters and langoustines. Serve at once.

HOMARD EN POT-AU-FEU

OEUFS AU PLAT À LA CRÈME
ET AUX CREVETTES

Baked eggs with cream and shrimps

SERVES 4
PREPARATION TIME:
20 MINUTES
COOKING TIME: 5–6 MINUTES

INGREDIENTS

8 extra fresh farm eggs

2 slices of white bread, cut into small cubes

40g/1½oz clarified butter

160g/6oz large pink or grey shrimps, unpeeled

40g/1½oz butter

150ml/5fl oz double cream

a small pinch of nutmeg

salt and freshly ground pepper

EQUIPMENT

4 individual flameproof ramekins or small gratin dishes

THIS DISH MAKES A DIVINE *hors d'oeuvre – the contrast between the crunchy croûtons and the hot, soft-textured eggs and cream is an experience no gourmet should miss!*

PREPARATION

The croûtons: Heat the clarified butter in a frying pan and fry the bread cubes gently until golden. Drain in a conical sieve and spread on kitchen paper.
The shrimps: Peel them.
   Preheat the oven to 200°C/400°F/gas 6.

COOKING THE EGGS

Divide the butter between the 4 ramekins and melt it over very low heat. Season the bottom of every ramekin, then break 2 eggs into each and bake in the oven for 2 minutes. Meanwhile, put the cream and nutmeg in a saucepan and boil for 2–3 minutes. Take the eggs out of the oven; the whites should be half-set and the yolks not cooked, but just warm. Arrange the shrimps on top of the eggs and pour over the scalding cream. Return the ramekins to the oven for 2–3 minutes until the eggs are done to your liking.

SERVING

Put each ramekin on a doily-lined plate. Scatter over the croûtons and serve.

———— · ————

PALOURDES AU GRATIN

Gratin of clams

SERVES 4
PREPARATION TIME:
20 MINUTES
COOKING TIME: 4–5 MINUTES

INGREDIENTS

1kg/2lb 3oz clams

150ml/5fl oz sweet cider

1 small bouquet garni

80g/3oz butter, softened

1 shallot, finely chopped

1 garlic clove, finely chopped

2 tablespoons chopped parsley

30g/1oz fresh breadcrumbs

salt and freshly ground pepper

EQUIPMENT

1 large gratin dish

piping bag fitted with a plain 1cm/½in nozzle

BRITTANY HAS *an abundance of clams, whose fine flavour is brought out in this simple but delicious dish.*

PREPARATION

Wash the clams in plenty of cold water and drain. In a flameproof casserole, heat the cider with the bouquet garni. As soon as it comes to the boil, throw in the clams and cover the casserole. Stir the clams every minute until they have all opened, but are barely cooked (this will take about 2–3 minutes), then drain them and keep the cooking juice. Take off the top shells and arrange the clams on their half shells in a gratin dish.
The butter: Reduce the clam cooking juice to a *demi-glace*. With a spatula, work together the butter, shallot, garlic, parsley and reduced clam juice and season to taste. Fill a piping bag with the flavoured butter and pipe a little on to each clam. Sprinkle with breadcrumbs.
   Preheat the grill for 10 minutes.

SERVING

Place the gratin dish under the hot grill for about 2 minutes, until the clams are piping hot and begin to bubble. Serve them straight from the gratin dish.

PÂTÉ DE FOIE DE PORC

Pork liver pâté

W E LOVED THIS SIMPLE, *old-fashioned rustic pâté when we were children, and we enjoy it still.*

THE PÂTÉ MIXTURE

Pass the pork chine, liver, onion, tarragon and parsley twice through the mincer. Put the mixture into a bowl set on crushed ice and, using a spatula, mix in the eggs, one at a time. Beat in first the cream, then the calvados, working the mixture continuously. Add 20g/2 teaspoons salt and 5g/1 teaspoon pepper.

Preheat the oven to 180°C/350°F/gas 4.

ASSEMBLING THE TERRINE

Line the inside of the terrine with back fat, keeping a few slices to cover the pâté when the terrine is filled. Fill with the pâté, tapping the base of the terrine lightly to eliminate air bubbles. Cut the remaining back fat into thin strips and lay them in a lattice on top of the pâté. Lay the thyme and bay leaf on top and put on the lid.

Put the flour in a bowl, add a few drops of water and stir with a spoon to make a soft dough. Spread this between the terrine and the lid to form a seal.

COOKING

Line a deep baking dish with a sheet of greaseproof paper, put in the terrine and three-quarters fill the baking dish with cold water. Bring to a fast simmer over high heat, then immediately take the dish off the heat and place in the preheated oven for 2 hours. Add a little boiling water to the bain-marie every so often.

After 2 hours, plunge a darning needle into the pâté for 30 seconds to check the cooking; the tip of the needle should feel hot. Remove the terrine from the bain-marie, take off the lid and lay a small, foil-covered plank of wood over the pâté to press it down. Put a 500g/1lb 2oz weight on the plank and leave until the pâté is completely cold. Refrigerate for several days.

SERVING

Serve the pâté straight from the terrine, using a butcher's knife, and accompany it with toasted country bread.

SERVES 12–14

PREPARATION TIME:
35 MINUTES

COOKING TIME: 2 HOURS

INGREDIENTS

500g/1lb 2oz very fat pork chine, well chilled (almost frozen) and cut lengthways into thin strips

500g/1lb 2oz pig's liver, well chilled (almost frozen) and cut widthways into thin strips

2 medium onions, roughly chopped

1 tablespoon snipped tarragon

2 tablespoons chopped parsley

2 eggs

2 tablespoons double cream

50ml/2fl oz calvados

200g/7oz pork back fat, thinly sliced

1 sprig of thyme

1 bay leaf

3 tablespoons flour

salt and freshly ground pepper

EQUIPMENT

mincing machine with a fine blade

1 terrine with a lid, about 24 × 10 × 10cm/10 × 4 × 4in

a small wooden plank the size of the terrine, covered in foil

500g/1lb 2oz weight

MOULES AU CIDRE DU PAYS D'AUGE

Mussels in cider

SERVES 4
PREPARATION TIME:
20 MINUTES
COOKING TIME:
ABOUT 4 MINUTES

INGREDIENTS
1kg/2lb 3oz mussels (preferably bouchot), scrubbed, debearded and well washed

120g/4oz butter

3 shallots, finely chopped

400ml/14fl oz medium dry cider

1 sprig of thyme

1 bay leaf

200ml/7fl oz double cream

salt and freshly ground pepper

1 tablespoon snipped chives, to serve

ALBERT ADORES THIS SIMPLE *and delicious dish, especially when the sauce is made with slightly sour Normandy cream. For Michel, the great delight is to drink a medium dry cider with the mussels.*

COOKING THE MUSSELS

Melt 40g/1½oz butter in a large saucepan. Put in the shallots and sweat for 1–2 minutes, then add 300ml/11fl oz cider, the thyme and bay leaf. Reduce the cider by about one-third, then add the cream and mussels and cover the pan.

Raise the heat to very high and cook for 3–4 minutes, shaking the pan every minute, so that the mussels at the bottom rise to the top. When the mussels have opened, tip them and their juices into a colander set over a bowl.

Pour the juices into a saucepan and reduce to a light juice. Add the remaining cider, bring to the boil, then swirl in the rest of the butter by shaking the pan or using a wire whisk. Season with salt and pepper.

SERVING

Pour the mussels into a soup tureen or china salad bowl. Discard the thyme, bay leaf and any mussels which have not opened. Pour two-thirds of the sauce over the mussels, sprinkle with chives and serve the rest of the sauce separately. Do not delay before tucking into the mussels; they must be eaten piping hot.

NOTES

For a more attractive presentation, leave the mussels on the half shell. Place 25 or 30 mussels in individual deep plates and pour over the hot sauce.

SOLE À LA NORMANDE

Sole poached in cider with mussels, scallops and shrimps

SERVES 4
PREPARATION TIME:
50 MINUTES
COOKING TIME: 8 MINUTES

THIS CLASSIC DISH *has been served in restaurants in Deauville and Trouville for over twenty years; Michel always orders it when he spends holidays there. You can substitute lemon sole for the Dover sole and, if you prefer, use fillets. Personally, we prefer to leave the sole on the bone, as the flavour is better.*

PREPARATION

The sole: Take one sole and, with the point of a sharp knife, make a light incision through the skin on the tail to give your fingers a grip. Rub the skin lightly to loosen it, then pull it from the tail towards the head. Turn the fish over and repeat the process on the other side. Following the contours of the fish, cut off the 'skirt' with scissors, then cut off the head.

Using a knife, make a 5cm/2in incision in the middle of the backbone. With the point of the scissors, snip the backbone in two places through the opening. This will ensure that the sole cooks evenly if the fillets vary in thickness and prevent it from curling up during poaching. Prepare the other three sole in the

(*recipe ingredients overleaf*)

MOULES AU CIDRE DU PAYS D'AUGE

INGREDIENTS

4 Dover sole, each about 400g/14oz

120g/4oz butter

250g/9oz small button mushrooms

2 shallots, finely sliced

500g/1lb 2oz mussels (preferably bouchot), scrubbed, washed and debearded

200ml/7fl oz Fish stock (recipe page 14)

150ml/5fl oz medium dry cider

250g/9oz grey or pink shrimps

4 scallops, with their corals if possible

300ml/11fl oz double cream

1 egg yolk

salt and freshly ground pepper

same way. Freeze the heads and trimmings to use when you next make a fish stock. Wash the sole in very cold water for 1 minute, then pat dry. Grease the bottom of a gratin dish with 20g/¾oz butter.

The mushrooms: Peel them (just wipe the smallest ones), remove the stalks and reserve the caps. Finely slice the stalks and lay them in the bottom of the dish together with the shallots. Put the sole in the dish, season with salt and pepper and cover with a sheet of buttered greaseproof paper. Keep in a cool place.

The mussels: Put the mussels in a large saucepan with the fish stock and cider, cover and cook over high heat, shaking the pan every minute, until they have all opened. Discard any which do not. Transfer the mussels to a bowl, take them out of their shells and reserve the cooking liquor.

The shrimps: Peel, put in a bowl and keep in a cool place. In a food processor or pestle and mortar, grind the heads with the remaining butter, rub through a fine sieve and keep the shrimp butter at room temperature.

The mushroom caps and scallops: In a saucepan, heat about 150ml/5fl oz of the mussel liquor, put in the mushroom caps and simmer for 1 minute. Cut the scallops into 2 or 3 slices, depending on their thickness and add them to the pan. As soon as the mixture boils, transfer all the contents of the pan into a bowl.

Preheat the oven to 220°C/425°F/gas 7.

COOKING THE SOLE

Pour the remaining mussel liquor over the sole, cover with the buttered greaseproof paper and cook in the preheated oven for about 8 minutes. Carefully transfer the sole to a deep serving dish, cover with greaseproof paper and keep warm.

Reduce the oven temperature to 180°C/350°F/gas 4.

The sauce: Strain the cooking juices from the sole, mushrooms and scallops through a conical sieve into a saucepan, set over high heat and reduce to a rich juice. Add half the cream and simmer for 5 minutes. Whisk together the egg yolk and the rest of the cream and mix into the sauce. Before it begins to bubble, take the pan off the heat and beat in the shrimp butter, a small piece at a time. Season with salt and pepper, add the shrimps and keep warm.

SERVING

Arrange the mushrooms, scallops and mussels over the sole and heat in the oven for 2 minutes. Remove from the oven and immediately drain off any juices which have collected at the bottom of the dish. Pour the hot sauce over all the fish and shellfish and serve at once.

NOTES

If you wish, you can pass the dish under a salamander or very hot grill just before serving. This adds nothing to the flavour, but it does give it an attractive pale golden glaze.

If you have any spare puff pastry in the fridge or freezer, why not garnish the dish with some *fleurons?*

———— · ————

BLANQUETTE DE VEAU
⟶ DE NOTRE MÈRE ⟵

Our mother's blanquette *of veal*

THIS IS TRULY A DISH *'like granny used to make'. Our own mother prepares this family favourite to perfection. Her* blanquette *is divine and we adore it. To follow, she often serves a salad of cornsalad with fresh walnut halves.*

COOKING THE VEAL

Put the veal in a casserole, add enough chicken stock or water to cover the meat and season with a little salt. Bring to the boil over medium heat, then lower the temperature to 80°–90°C/175°–195°F, so that the liquid no longer boils, and skim the surface. Cook gently for 10 minutes, then add the carrots, large onion and bouquet garni and simmer for 30 minutes.

Add the small onions, simmer for 30 minutes, then add the mushrooms and cook for another hour. With a slotted spoon, carefully transfer the veal, small onions and mushrooms to a bowl, cover with a damp cloth and keep warm.

THE SAUCE

Remove the onion stuck with cloves and the bouquet garni. Pass the cooking broth through a conical sieve into a saucepan, set over high heat and reduce the liquid by half.

Put the cream, egg yolks and lemon juice in a bowl, beat lightly with a wire whisk, then pour on the cooking liquid, whisking all the time. Season with salt and pepper. Pour the sauce into a saucepan and cook gently for 30–45 seconds, stirring with a wooden spatula, as though you were making a custard. On no account let the sauce boil.

Take the pan off the heat and immediately stir in the veal and vegetables. Keep hot.

The croûtons: In a frying pan set over high heat, fry the bread in the clarified butter until golden on both sides. Drain on kitchen paper.

SERVING

Pour the *blanquette* into a soup tureen and arrange the croûtons on top.

NOTES

The best cut of veal to use for this dish is the *tendron* from the breast. This is available at all French butchers, but there is no exact English equivalent.

——— · ———

SERVES 4

PREPARATION TIME:
35 MINUTES

COOKING TIME: 2¼ HOURS

INGREDIENTS

800g/1¾lb *tendron* or flank or shoulder of veal, cut into 3cm/1¼in cubes

1 litre/1¾pt Chicken stock (recipe page 15) or water

2 medium carrots, peeled and washed

1 large onion, peeled and stuck with 2 cloves

1 bouquet garni

24 small white onions, peeled and washed

200g/7oz small button mushrooms, peeled and wiped or washed

300ml/½pt double cream

4 egg yolks

juice of ½ lemon

8 X 1cm/½in slices of bread cut diagonally from a *baguette*

80g/3oz clarified butter

salt and freshly ground white pepper

⤙ TRIPES À LA MODE DE CAEN ⤚

Tripe cooked with dry cider

SERVES 8
PREPARATION TIME: 1 HOUR
COOKING TIME: 12 HOURS

INGREDIENTS

3.2kg/7lb ox tripe (800g/1¾lb of each stomach [*panse, bonnet, caille, le feuillet*]), blanched

750g/1½lb carrots

500g/1lb 2oz onions

1 fresh pork rind, blanched

1 large bouquet garni

½ head of garlic, 2 cloves and 12 crushed peppercorns, tied up in muslin

1 ox trotter, split, blanched and cooked in vegetable stock for 2 hours in advance, reserve the stock

1 litre/1¾pt dry cider

2 tablespoons flour

50ml/2fl oz calvados

salt and freshly ground pepper

W E BOTH ADORE TRIPE, *especially when it is home-cooked. The commercial products which are now available are all too often tasteless and rubbery. Serve the tripe in deep dishes and give your guests soup spoons so that they can enjoy the heavenly cooking broth. Plain steamed potatoes make the best accompaniment to this dish.*

PREPARATION

The tripe: Cut each piece into 4–5cm/1½–2in squares.
The carrots and onions: Peel and wash. Cut the carrots into thick rings and slice the onions thinly.
  Preheat the oven to 160°C/300°F/gas 2.

COOKING THE TRIPE

Lay the pork rind fat-side down in the bottom of an ovenproof earthenware or cast-iron casserole.
  Make alternate layers of tripe, a few carrots and onions, the bouquet garni and muslin bag of spices and the ox trotter, finishing with a layer of tripe and vegetables. Salt lightly and pour in the cider. Add 1 litre/1¾pt stock from the ox trotter to come just to the top of the tripe and vegetables.
  Make a soft paste with the flour and a little water, put the lid on the casserole and seal it with the flour paste. Cook in the preheated oven for 12 hours.

SERVING

Break the seal between the casserole and lid, lift off the lid and spoon the fat off the surface of the tripe. Discard the bouquet garni, bag of spices and the bones from the ox trotter. Pour in the calvados, stir gently and adjust the seasoning if necessary. Serve the tripe piping hot straight from the casserole.

———— • ————

ROGNONS DE VEAU SAUTÉS
⤙ HAUT-BRETAGNE ⤚

Sauté veal kidneys

SERVES 4
PREPARATION TIME:
40 MINUTES
COOKING TIME: 6–8 MINUTES

S ERVE THIS BRETON DISH *with a cauliflower purée and a glass of good cider, and don't forget to provide a round country loaf.*

PREPARATION

The kidneys: Remove the membrane surrounding the kidneys. Finely dice the fat. Halve the kidneys lengthways and cut out the central white cores with the point of a knife. Cut the kidneys into 3cm/1¼in cubes.
The belly of pork: Place in a saucepan and cover with cold water. Bring to the boil and blanch for 10 minutes, refresh and drain. Cut off the rind with a knife, then cut the pork into large *lardons* and set aside.
The onions and peas: Peel, wash and drain the onions and set aside. Shell the peas, place in a saucepan, cover with water and blanch for 3 minutes. Refresh, drain and set aside.

(*recipe ingredients overleaf*)

ROGNONS DE VEAU SAUTÉS HAUT-BRETAGNE

SAUCE NORMANDE

COOKING THE KIDNEYS

Put 3 tablespoons kidney fat in a sauté pan and set over high heat, stirring with a spatula. Lightly season the kidneys and, when the fat is very hot, throw them into the pan and seal them on all sides. Reduce the heat and cook the kidneys gently for 3–4 minutes, so that they are still pink. Drain and set aside.

In the same pan, heat the rest of the kidney fat. Put in the *lardons* and brown lightly, then add the onions and unpeeled garlic cloves. Sprinkle with the *eau-de-vie* then the cider and put in the bouquet garni. Cover the pan and simmer for 8 minutes, then add the peas and cook for 2–3 minutes, until tender. Take the pan off the heat and beat in the butter, a little at a time. Season to taste and discard the bouquet garni. Add the kidneys, return the pan to a very low heat and warm the kidneys in the sauce for 2 minutes.

SERVING

Put the kidneys and vegetable garnish in a deep heatproof china dish and serve at once.

INGREDIENTS

3 veal kidneys, 350g/12oz each, trimmed weight, plus 100g/4oz of the fat

350g/12oz semi-salted belly of pork

250g/9oz baby onions

300g/11oz peas, preferably fresh

8 unpeeled garlic cloves

2 tablespoons cider *eau-de-vie* or calvados

300ml/½ pt medium dry cider

1 small bouquet garni

60g/2oz butter, cubed

salt and freshly ground pepper

SAUCE NORMANDE

A cream sauce for fish

THIS CLASSIC AND MUCH-LOVED SAUCE *from our national repertoire goes very well with almost any firm white fish.*

THE *VELOUTÉ*

Melt 30g/1oz butter in a saucepan, add the flour and cook for 2–3 minutes, whisking continuously with a wire whisk. Pour in the fish stock and bring to the boil, stirring occasionally. As soon as the mixture begins to boil, add the shallot, mushrooms and bouquet garni, lower the heat and simmer for 20 minutes, then pass the *veloute* through a fine conical sieve into another saucepan.

Cut the remaining butter into small pieces.

THE SAUCE

Add the liquor from the oysters and mushrooms to the *velouté* and reduce by one-third. In a bowl, beat together the cream and egg yolks and whisk into the *velouté*. As soon as it begins to boil, take the pan off the heat and whisk in the butter, a little at a time. Season to taste. Pass the sauce through the sieve again and keep it warm in a bain-marie until ready to serve.

NOTES

To obtain the oyster liquor, poach 6 oysters in their own juices. For the mushroom liquor, poach 100g/4oz mushrooms in 100ml/3½fl oz water. If you are serving a fish *à la normande* (recipe page 24), the oysters and mushrooms can then be used in the presentation, as they are part of the classical garnish which also includes shrimps, truffles, mussels, crayfish and croûtons.

SERVES 6

PREPARATION TIME: 15 MINUTES

COOKING TIME: ABOUT 45 MINUTES

INGREDIENTS

130g/4½oz butter

30g/1oz flour

500ml/18fl oz Fish stock (recipe page 14)

1 shallot, finely sliced

50g/2oz button mushrooms, sliced

1 small bouquet garni

50ml/2fl oz cooking liquor from poached oysters (see Notes)

100ml/3½fl oz mushroom cooking liquor (see Notes)

3 tablespoons double cream

3 egg yolks

salt and freshly ground white pepper

SALADE ROSCOVITE

Roscoff salad

SERVES 4
PREPARATION TIME:
35 MINUTES

INGREDIENTS

1 medium potato (about 150g/5oz)

1 small cauliflower

1 small cucumber

200ml/7fl oz Mayonnaise (recipe page 16)

100g/4oz grey or pink shrimps, cooked

4 hard-boiled eggs, each cut into 6 segments

2 tablespoons snipped tarragon

1 tablespoon snipped chervil

VINAIGRETTE

6 tablespoons groundnut oil

2 tablespoons cider vinegar

salt and freshly ground pepper

THIS DELICIOUS SALAD *makes a good summer main course. When artichokes are really tender at the beginning of the season, we like to add some lightly cooked, slightly crunchy quartered artichoke bottoms.*

PREPARATION

The vinaigrette: In a bowl, mix together the oil, vinegar, a pinch of salt and a little pepper.

The potato: Fill a small saucepan with salted water and cook the potato for about 20 minutes, until tender. Peel immediately, cut into small cubes and mix with half the vinaigrette. Keep at room temperature.

The cauliflower: Trim and separate into florets. Blanch in boiling water for 3 minutes. Refresh and drain, then mix with the remaining vinaigrette and keep at room temperature.

The cucumber: Peel, halve lengthways and remove the seeds with a teaspoon. Slice as finely as possible. Place in a bowl with a pinch of salt for 5 minutes (no longer, or it will lose its crunch) to draw out the bitter juices. Drain and gently squeeze out some of the water. Keep at room temperature.

SERVING

Carefully fold the potato, cauliflower and cucumber into the mayonnaise. Divide the mixture between 4 plates, arranging it in the centre, or place in a wooden salad bowl. Arrange the shrimps in a rosette on top with the eggs around the edge. Scatter over the snipped herbs.

NOTES

Do not refrigerate the cooked vegetables before assembling the salad, or they will lose some of their flavour and delicacy.

———— • ————

SALADE ROSCOVITE

BEIGNETS DE POMME
À LA NORMANDE

Apple fritters

SERVES 6

PREPARATION TIME:
20 MINUTES, PLUS 2–3 HOURS
RESTING

COOKING TIME: 2–3 MINUTES

INGREDIENTS

6 dessert apples, preferably cox
or reinette

juice of 1 lemon

100g/4oz sugar

3 tablespoons calvados

oil for deep-frying

2 egg whites

icing or caster sugar, for dredging

200ml/7fl oz lightly whipped
cream, for serving (optional)

BATTER

7g/1 teaspoon fresh yeast

75ml/3fl oz milk

130g/4½oz flour

60ml/2fl oz pale ale

1 egg yolk

a pinch of salt

2 tablespoons groundnut oil

W E ARE ALWAYS DELIGHTED *when our mother makes these homely fritters for us; they are delicious washed down with a bottle of sweet cider from the Auge valley.*

PREPARATION

The batter: In a bowl, mix the yeast with half the milk.

Put the flour into a mixing bowl and, beating continuously, add the rest of the milk, the ale, egg yolk and salt. Beat until smooth and homogenous. Add the milk and yeast mixture, then the oil and beat well. Cover the bowl and leave the batter to stand at room temperature for 2 or 3 hours.

The apples: Peel, core and cut into 5mm/¼in rings. Place in a bowl with the lemon juice, 50g/2oz sugar and the calvados and leave to macerate for about 30 minutes.

Heat the frying oil to 180°–200°C/350°–400°F.

COATING THE APPLES

Beat the 2 egg whites until just risen, then add the rest of the sugar and beat until firm. Carefully fold them into the batter, using a spatula. Dip several rounds of apple into the batter to coat them thickly.

COOKING THE FRITTERS

Use a fork to put the coated apples into the hot oil and fry for 2 or 3 minutes, until golden on both sides, turning them over with a fork as soon as they rise to the surface. Drain and place on absorbent paper. Keep the cooked fritters hot while you coat and fry the rest.

SERVING

Serve the fritters very hot, dredged with icing or caster sugar. Arrange them on a napkin-lined plate and serve some good Normandy cream separately.

———— · ————

BEIGNETS DE POMME À LA NORMANDE

↞ MIRLITONS ↠

Puff pastry tartlets with almonds

SERVES 8

PREPARATION TIME:
25 MINUTES, PLUS 20 MINUTES
CHILLING

COOKING TIME: 20 MINUTES

INGREDIENTS

300g/11oz Puff pastry (recipe page 11) or puff pastry trimmings

a pinch of flour

3 eggs

150g/5oz sugar

80g/3oz ground almonds

2 tablespoons cream

a few drops of orange flower water

16 whole blanched almonds

icing sugar, for dusting

EQUIPMENT

10cm/4in plain pastry cutter

8 tartlet tins, about 7cm/3in diameter, 3.5cm/1½in deep

THE RECIPE FOR THESE TARTLETS *originally comes from Rouen, where we have often had the good fortune to taste these famous pastries. You can occasionally find them in pâtisseries around Paris, but they do not have the fine flavour of the authentic* mirlitons *from Rouen.*

They are delicious served still slightly warm. When apricots are in season, serve the mirlitons *with an apricot* coulis, *which perfectly complements the almond flavour.*

PREPARATION

Lining the tartlet tins: On a lightly floured marble or wooden surface, roll out the pastry to a thickness of about 3mm/⅛in. Cut out 8 circles with the pastry cutter and line the tins with this pastry. Leave to rest in the fridge for about 20 minutes.

Preheat the oven to 220°C/425°F/gas 7.

The filling: Whisk the eggs and sugar in a bowl until the whisk leaves a trail when you lift it. Carefully fold in the ground almonds, cream and orange flower water.

BAKING THE *MIRLITONS*

Pinch up the edges of the pastry with your forefinger and thumb to make an even, straight border. Prick the bottom of the pastry cases with a fork, then fill with the almond mixture and bake immediately in the preheated oven for 10 minutes.

Quickly arrange 2 whole almonds end to end in the middle of each *mirliton* and immediately return them to the oven. Reduce the temperature to 200 °C/400°F/gas 6 and bake for another 10 minutes. Unmould the *mirlitons* as soon as they come out of the oven and leave to cool on a wire rack.

SERVING

Place a *mirliton* on each plate, sprinkle with icing sugar and serve at room temperature.

———— · ————

Normandy and Brittany

FRESHWATER FISH

Shad
Eel
Carp
Pike
Salmon
Tench
Trout
Salmon trout

SEA FISH

Anchovies
Brill
Monkfish
Dogfish
Conger eel
Sea bream
Smelts
Gurnard
Herrings
Coley
Lemon sole
Mackerel
Whiting
Hake
Cod
Plaice
Skate
John Dory
Sardines
Sole
Tuna
Turbot
Wrasse
Weever fish

CRUSTACEANS, SHELLFISH and BATRACHIANS

Spider crabs
Winkles
Prawns
Cockles
Scallops
Razor shells
Small crabs
Shrimps
Crayfish
Etrilles (small crabs)
Frogs
Lobster
Belon and Cancale oysters
Spiny lobster
Dublin bay prawns
Mussels
Ormers
Sea urchins
Palourdes (clams)
Pétoncles (queen scallops)
Praires (warty Venus)
Cuttlefish
Tourteaux (crabs)

POULTRY

Nantes duck
Rouen duck
Capon
Chicken
Poussin

GAME

Larks
Woodcock
Quail
Wild duck
Venison
Pheasant
Thrushes
Wild rabbit
Hare
Partridge
Wild boar
Teal

MEAT

Salt marsh lamb
Beef
Pork
Veal

CHARCUTERIE

Andouille
Smoked andouille from Vire
Andouille de Guéméné (large round sausage)
Andouillette from Caen, Pont-Audemer, Rouen
Boudin blanc
Boudin noir de montagne (for which there is an annual international competition)
Duck terrine
Cervelas
Fromage de tête (brawn)
Liver pâté
Pâté Nantais
Breadcrumbed sheep's and pig's trotters
Rillettes
Sausage in aspic
Tripes à la mode de Caen

VEGETABLES

Asparagus
Artichokes
Cardoons
Carrots
Celeriac
Mushrooms: field, boletus, chanterelles and morels
Cabbage
Cauliflower
Watercress
Samphire
Beans: broad, white and green
Navets and rave (turnips)
Onions
Barley
Sorrel
Peas
Leeks
Potatoes
Great variety of salads
Salsify
Buckwheat
Rye

CHEESE

Camembert
Coeur de Bray
Fromage de Monsieur
Gournay
Livarot
Neufchâtel
Pavé d'Auge
Petit gervais
Pont l'evèque
Rouy
Fresh fromage blanc

DAIRY PRODUCE

Renowned brands of cream
Butter from Isigny, Valognes, Saintes Mères de l'Eglise, Gournay etc.

FRUIT

Cherries
Strawberries
Chestnuts
Melons
Bilberries
Hazelnuts
Walnuts
Peaches
Pears
Eating and cider apples
Plums
Grapes

PÂTISSERIE

Beignets de mangos (sweet potato fritters)
Biscuits nantais
Quatre quart (pound cake)
Breton crêpes
Crêpes dentelles
Duchesses (large macaroons)
Far (prune flan)
Breton galette
Buckwheat galette
Nantais waffles
Gâteau de Pont-l'Abbé
Mirlitons (cream-filled puffs)
Grated apple with curd cheese
Roulette (brioche)
Shortbread
Apple sugar from Rouen
Cherry and fromage blanc flan

CONFECTIONERY

Candied angelica
Berlingots (boiled sweets)
Bigouden (almond paste)
Jams from Pornic
Crystallised strawberries
Apple jelly
Honey
Rigolettes (sweets from Nantes)

MISCELLANEOUS PRODUCTS

Benedictine
Calvados
Cider
Chouchen (mead from Rosporden)
Pickled samphire
Herb mustard
Tinned peas, sardines in oil, tuna in brine
Poirée (pear liqueur)

Anjou, Touraine and Maine

TEMPERATE AND TRANQUIL PLAINS AND WOODS THAT ARE JUSTLY CALLED THE 'THE GARDEN OF FRANCE'

THIS IS A REGION of astonishing architectural richness. Everywhere there are churches with handsome porches, abbeys, convents and ancient farms that are still untouched by progress. The famous châteaux, with their highly individual décor, induce a melancholy reverie and in summer, they offer fairy-like spectacles of *son et lumière*.

The beauty of the countryside and the gentle Angevin temperament make this a tranquil, untroubled region. Washed by the Loire and its tributaries, the Maine, the Mayenne, the Sarthe, the Huisne and the Loir, this area boasts more freshwater fish than any other. Its numerous canals play host to fine eels and delicious freshwater crayfish, although these, alas, are beginning to die out.

There are plains, too, like 'la Beauce', and woods and forests where a great variety of wildlife makes its home. Hunters tell of hares and wild boar; the foxes play hide-and-seek with the peasants and the buzzards vie with them for furred and winged game.

We are often lured to this region by its excellent food and wines. The cooking is homely, using only local produce; the food is delicious but simple. Angevin excels in many types of *charcuterie*. Its dairy products are among the best in France, especially the butter which ranks alongside Charentes butter as the very finest, and which makes the most delicious *beurre blanc* in the world. The rich soil also produces succulent button mushrooms, which are cultivated in great quantity.

As we drive through the countryside during our visits, we discover delightful orchards and fields carpeted with all manner of *primeurs*, the baby vegetables which can be found very early in the season at Rungis market in Paris. Anjou provides the very best fruit and vegetables both for home consumption and for export, with a range and quality which is equal even to that of Provence.

The climate is temperate, with plenty of sun and little wind, although in winter, the north-westerly *bise* blows and there is sometimes a light westerly wind (*la galerne*). The annual rainfall is variable, the figure quoted as 50–80cm/20–30 in. All this makes the area favourable for wine growing.

There are plenty of white wines, but few reds, one of the best being Saumur Champigny. The *grand cru* Coulée de Serrant is produced on the banks of the Loire at Savennières, and there are many other fine wines, such as Clos du Papillon, la Roche aux Moines and Château d'Epire. The banks of the Layon play host to such wines as Quart du Chaume, Clos de la Roche and Bonnezeaux. On the banks of the Saumur, there are Clos des Treilles, Clos des Murs, Clos des St Pères and numerous·others. Fine wines are also produced on the banks of the Loir and the Sarthe. Then there are the Anjou rosés, like Château de Chaintres, and Thoureil and the saumurs – Champigny, Dampierre and Parnay. Most of these are classified nationally and internationally as table wines, with a few exceptions, such as Coulée de Serrant. The grapes most commonly used in the wines of this region are chenin blanc, chardonnay, sauvignon blanc, melon, cabernet franc and cabernet sauvignon.

Chenonceaux Château on the banks of the Loire beckons you to look around and pass some time. These walls have witnessed great happenings in French history and hold many secrets. By night, their fairytale quality seems to lull you into a world of princely dreams.

SOUPE À LA TÊTE DE PORC

Pig's head soup

SERVES 12

PREPARATION TIME: 1 HOUR,
PLUS 24 HOURS SOAKING

COOKING TIME: 2 HOURS

INGREDIENTS

1 piglet's head, about 4.25kg/9½lb

1 large bouquet garni

2 medium onions, each stuck with 2 cloves

1 head of garlic

15g/½oz peppercorns, crushed

1kg/2lb 3oz medium carrots

1kg/2lb 3oz leeks

24 baby onions

2 medium spring cabbages

2kg/4½lb medium new potatoes, unpeeled

500g/1lb 2oz fresh white haricot beans, shelled

500g/1lb 2oz new turnips, unpeeled

500g/1lb 2oz fresh morels (optional)

salt

EQUIPMENT

Cooking thermometer (optional)

THIS DISH IS IDEAL *for large families and is still often made in the country areas of the region. It is best made in spring, especially in April or May when the vegetables are very young and fresh.*

PREPARATION

The pig's head: Trim and scrape with a very sharp boning knife. Leave to soak in very cold water for at least 24 hours.

COOKING THE PIG'S HEAD

Put the pig's head in a large flameproof casserole, cover with cold water and bring to the boil. Boil for 2 minutes, then refresh and drain. Cover with fresh cold water and bring to the boil. Lower the heat, add the bouquet garni, clove-studded onions, garlic and crushed peppercorns and cook gently at 90°C/195°F, skimming the surface if necessary. Meanwhile, prepare the vegetables.

The vegetables: Peel the carrots, leeks and baby onions, halve the cabbages, wash all the vegetables in plenty of cold water and drain.

When the pig's head has been cooking for 30 minutes, add the carrots, leeks and cabbage. Cook for another 30 minutes, then add the potatoes, haricot beans and baby onions. Cook for another 30 minutes, then add the turnips and morels and cook for a final 30 minutes, making 2 hours in all.

SERVING

Using a kitchen fork and large tongs, lift the pig's head out of the casserole and place it in a large deep dish. Arrange the vegetables around the head, keeping the different types separate if possible. Discard the bouquet garni and large onions and pour some of the cooking broth over the vegetables. Pour the rest into a sauceboat and serve separately.

NOTES

Let everyone help themselves and give them some country bread to mop up the broth. Any leftovers (if there are any!) will be delicious served at room temperature the next day, accompanied by a shallot vinaigrette or *sauce rémoulade.*

Soupe à la tête de porc

⤚ RILLETTES ⤙

Preserved pork and goose

RILLETTES MAKE A DELICIOUS *hors d'oeuvre and, since they keep for several months, they can be a great time-saver. In this region of France, sandwiches filled with* rillettes *are a popular mid-morning snack.*

PREPARATION

The kidney fat: Remove the thin membrane surrounding the fat. Mince the fat in a mincer with a coarse blade or dice it finely with a sharp knife.
The pork and goose meat: Cut into 4 × 2cm/1½ × ¾in strips in the direction of the grain.

COOKING THE *RILLETTES*

Put the kidney fat into a flameproof casserole, add 100ml/3½fl oz water and melt over very low heat. When the fat has completely melted, add the pork and goose, the bouquet garni, onion and carrot and bring to the boil. Immediately lower the heat and cook very gently at 70°–80°C/158°–175°F for 3 hours, stirring with a spatula every 20 minutes.

Take the casserole off the heat, remove the bouquet garni, onion and carrot and leave the meats to cool slightly in a cold place for 20 minutes.

POTTING THE *RILLETTES*

When the meat is lukewarm, spoon off a little of the fat floating on the surface and keep it in a bowl. With your fingertips, mash the meat slightly to break up any large pieces and especially any fibrous bits. With a spatula, stir the mixture thoroughly without overworking it, then season to taste.

Spoon the mixture into earthenware or china pots and put in a cold place until half-set. Pour over the reserved fat, sprinkle the top with crushed peppercorns and keep the *rillettes* in the fridge or a very cold place until you need them. When they are completely cold, cover with clingfilm.

SERVING

Put the pot of *rillettes* on the table with a butcher's knife and some toasted country bread and give your guests the pleasure of helping themselves.

NOTES

Vary the proportion of pork to goose according to your own taste. You can also make *rillettes* with duck or rabbit; in this case, add some green peppercorns or toasted, skinned hazelnuts to the cooked *rillettes* before potting them.

———— · ————

MAKES ABOUT 1.2kg/2¾lb (TO SERVE 12–14)

PREPARATION TIME: 25 MINUTES

COOKING TIME: 3 HOURS, PLUS 20 MINUTES COOLING

INGREDIENTS

300g/11oz very white veal kidney fat

800g/1¾lb chine of pork

400g/14oz goose meat, preferably from the leg

1 bouquet garni

1 medium onion, peeled and stuck with 2 cloves

1 medium carrot

10 peppercorns, crushed

salt and freshly ground pepper

EQUIPMENT

earthenware or china pots for the *rillettes*

mincing machine (optional)

cooking thermometer (optional)

MATELOTE D'ANGUILLE ET DE CARPE

MATELOTE D'ANGUILLE
ET DE CARPE

Eel and carp stew

THIS IS A REAL GOURMET'S *dish, which Michel has often enjoyed on his visits to the Loire valley. If you can persuade your fishmonger to prepare the eel and carp for you, the rest is child's play.*

PREPARATION

The mushrooms: Peel and wash. Finely slice the stalks and keep the caps whole.
The red wine: Pour into a saucepan, add the garlic, shallots, bouquet garni and sliced mushroom stalks. Bring to the boil over high heat and reduce by one-third. Add the fish stock, simmer for 30 minutes, pass through a conical sieve and keep hot.
The eel: Hold the tail in a cloth, lay the head on a stone or the corner of a table and kill it by hitting the head with a mallet. Using a very sharp knife, make an incision all round the head. Put a meat hook into the skin, hold the eel by the head and pull off the skin. Gut the eel and cut off the fins and head. Wash the eel in very cold water, then cut into 5–6cm/2–2½in chunks. Pat dry with a cloth and set aside.
The carp: Gut it and cut off the head. Wash the fish in very cold water and cut into eight 1.5cm/¾in chunks. Pat dry with a cloth and set aside.
The onions: Peel, wash, put in a shallow pan with 40g/1½oz butter and cook over low heat for 15 minutes, until pale golden and tender, but still firm. Keep warm.
The mushroom caps: If they are very large, quarter them. Heat 30g/1oz butter in a frying pan and sauté the mushrooms for 2 minutes. Keep warm.

COOKING THE FISH

Heat 80g/3oz butter in a shallow pan. Lightly salt the pieces of eel and carp and seal them in the butter without colouring for 2 minutes on each side. Pour in the cognac, flame it, then add the boiling poaching liquid. Lower the temperature of the liquid to just below boiling point (90°C/195°F) and cook for 15 minutes.
The croûtons: Heat the clarified butter in a frying pan and fry the bread until golden on both sides. Place on a wire rack.

SERVING

After 15 minutes cooking, check that the eel and carp are tender and cooked, then carefully lift them out of the liquid with a slotted spoon. Arrange the pieces of carp end to end in a shallow dish to reconstitute the shape of the whole fish. Lay the chunks of eel around the edge, cover the dish with foil and leave in a warm place for 5 minutes.

Over very high heat, reduce the poaching liquid by one-third. Using a wire whisk, whisk in the *beurre manié*, then add the cream. Reduce again by one-third, then add the onions and mushroom caps. Take the pan off the heat and whisk in the remaining butter. Season with salt and pepper and pour the sauce and garnish over the fish. Arrange the croûtons on top of the eel chunks, sprinkle the carp with parsley and serve at once.

NOTES

Serve this dish with plain, steamed, creamy white cauliflower and accompany it with a wine of the same type as you used for cooking the fish – but a touch older.

SERVES 8
PREPARATION TIME:
1¼ HOURS
COOKING TIME: 20 MINUTES

INGREDIENTS

1 live eel, 800g–1kg/1¾–2¼lb

1 carp, about 1.5kg/3lb 5oz

150g/5oz button mushrooms

4 shallots, peeled and finely sliced

1 bottle chinon rouge or bourgueil wine

2 garlic cloves, crushed

1 bouquet garni

300ml/½ pt Fish stock (recipe page 14)

24 baby onions

200g/7oz butter

4 tablespoons cognac

60g/2oz clarified butter

16 thin slices from a *baguette*

1 tablespoon *beurre manié* (20g/¾oz butter mashed with 10g/1 teaspoon flour)

150ml/5fl oz double cream

1 tablespoon chopped parsley

salt and freshly ground pepper

FRICASSÉE DE POULET DE VIHIERS
~ À L'ANCIENNE ~

Fricassée of farmhouse chicken with baby vegetables

SERVES 4

PREPARATION TIME:
30 MINUTES

COOKING TIME: 20–25 MINUTES

INGREDIENTS

1 farmhouse chicken, preferably from Anjou or le Mans, cut into 8 pieces; neck, feet, wing tips, carcass and gizzard chopped

12 small white onions

90g/3oz butter

150g/5oz small button mushrooms

½ lemon

300g/11oz fresh peas in the pod

300g/11oz small carrots with their tops or round *grelot* carrots

a pinch of sugar

30g/1oz clarified butter

3 shallots, thinly sliced

1 sprig of thyme

1 bay leaf

500ml/18fl oz dry white Anjou wine

300ml/½ pt Chicken stock (recipe page 15)

400ml/14fl oz double cream

1 tablespoon snipped chives

salt and freshly ground pepper

THIS DISH IS TYPICAL *of the Anjou region, which produces some of the best* primeurs *vegetables in France and is famous for its excellent poultry. It is prepared in much the same way as a* blanquette *of veal and has an extraordinarily delicate and fine flavour. We like to add sugarsnap peas or asparagus tips when they are in season.*

PREPARATION

The onions: Plunge into boiling water, refresh and peel. Heat 30g/1oz butter in a small saucepan, put in the onions, barely cover with water and cook gently for 10 minutes. Set aside.

The mushrooms: Peel and wash. Thinly slice the stalks and keep them for the sauce. Heat 30g/1oz butter in a small saucepan, put in the mushroom caps, 2 tablespoons water and a few drops of lemon juice. Bring to the boil, then set aside.

The peas: Shell them and cook in lightly salted boiling water for 2 minutes. Refresh, drain and set aside.

The carrots: Peel and wash. Place in a small saucepan with the remaining butter, a glass of water, a pinch each of sugar and salt and cook gently for 8 minutes, until cooked but still firm.

Preheat the oven to 220°C/425°F/gas 7.

COOKING THE CHICKEN

Heat the clarified butter in a shallow pan. Lightly season the chicken pieces with salt and pepper, put them in the pan and seal for 2 minutes on each side, without letting them colour. Cover the pan and cook the chicken in the preheated oven for 8 minutes. Take out the breasts and wings, cover them so that they do not dry out and keep warm. Replace the pan containing the rest of the chicken in the oven and cook for another 10 minutes. Remove the remaining chicken pieces and put them with the breasts and wings.

THE SAUCE

Set the shallow pan over medium heat, put in the chopped carcass and giblets, the mushroom stalks, shallots, thyme and bay leaf. Sweat without colouring for 2–3 minutes, then deglaze with the wine and reduce by half. Add the chicken stock, reduce by one-third, add the cream and cook until the sauce lightly coats the back of a spoon. Pass the sauce through a conical sieve and season to taste. Drain all the vegetables and add them to the sauce. Give it a bubble, take the pan off the heat and stir in the chives.

SERVING

Place the chicken pieces in a deep serving dish or deep plates, pour over the sauce and vegetables and serve at once.

———— · ————

FRICASSÉE DE POULET DE VIHIERS À L'ANCIENNE

CUL DE VEAU BRAISÉ ANGEVIN

CUL DE VEAU BRAISÉ ANGEVIN

Braised rump of veal in white white

SERVES 8

PREPARATION TIME:
30 MINUTES

COOKING TIME: 2 HOURS

THIS IS A SUCCULENT *dish, which makes the most of the tender young veal from this region. Any leftovers can be reheated or served cold; either way, they have an exquisite flavour, so do not be tempted to make the dish with a smaller piece of veal, or you will have none left!*

PREPARATION

Preheat the oven to 220°C/425°F/gas 7.

The onions: Peel and slice very thinly.

The carrots: Peel, wash and cut into very thin rounds.

The celery: Peel, wash and cut into very thin slices.

The belly of pork: Cut into large *lardons*, leaving on the rind. Blanch in a pan of boiling water for 2 minutes, refresh and drain.

COOKING THE VEAL

Line the bottom of a flameproof casserole with the pork rind, laying it fat-side down. Spread over the sliced vegetables.

Lightly season the veal all over with salt and pepper. Heat the clarified butter in a large frying pan, put in the veal and seal on all sides. Transfer it to the casserole. Put the *lardons* in the frying pan and seal lightly until very pale golden. Drain and put in the casserole with the veal. Deglaze the frying pan with the white wine, letting it bubble once only.

Leaving the casserole uncovered, cook the veal in the preheated oven for 30 minutes, turning it over after 15 minutes. Remove from the oven and reduce the temperature to 190°C/375°F/gas 5.

Pour over the *marc*, wine, veal stock and 200ml/7fl oz water. Add the bouquet garni and savory, set the casserole over high heat and bring to the boil. Put on the lid and return the veal to the oven for 1½ hours, turning it over after 1 hour.

When the veal is cooked, take it out of the casserole and keep warm. Discard the pork rind and bouquet garni, add the cream, bring to the boil and season to taste.

SERVING

Cut the veal into 5mm/¼in slices and arrange them in the centre of a serving dish. Pour over the sauce and arrange the vegetables and garnish around the edge. Serve very hot.

NOTES

Some local french beans cooked in water and added to the sauce at the last moment make an excellent vegetable accompaniment.

———— · ————

INGREDIENTS

1 rump of veal, about 1.8kg/4lb

300g/11oz medium onions

1kg/2lb 3oz medium carrots

½ head of celery

150g/5oz lightly smoked belly of pork

150g/5oz very fresh pork rind

60g/2oz clarified butter

500ml/18fl oz dry white Anjou wine

50ml/2oz *marc* from the region (optional)

300ml/½pt Veal stock (recipe page 15)

1 bouquet garni

a pinch of fresh savory

200ml/7fl oz double cream

salt and freshly ground pepper

L'ARC-EN-CIEL DE LÉGUMES
ANGEVIN

'Rainbow' of Anjou vegetables

SERVES 8
PREPARATION TIME:
2¼ HOURS

INGREDIENTS

THE BRAISED LETTUCES
(*LAITUES BRAISÉES*)

4 hearty lettuces

60g/2oz butter

200ml/7fl oz Chicken stock
(recipe page 15)

salt and freshly ground pepper

THE STUFFED ARTICHOKES
(*ARTICHAUTS FARCIS 'À
L'ANGEVINE'*)

8 artichokes, preferably Camus

juice of ½ lemon

2 tablespoons vinegar

150g/5oz button or local field
mushrooms

90g/3oz butter

2 garlic cloves, finely chopped

2 tablespoons fresh white
breadcrumbs

2 tablespoons chopped parsley

THE SPRING CABBAGE
(*CHOUX VERTS 'LA CHOUÉE'*)

2 hearty spring cabbages

100g/4oz butter

100ml/3½fl oz Chicken stock
(recipe page 15)

THE CHESTNUTS
(*CHÂTAIGNES 'NOUZILLARDS'*)

750g/1½lb chestnuts

1 litre/1¾pt milk

1 small bouquet garni

30g/1oz butter

THE ASPARAGUS (*ASPERGES AU
BEURRE À L'ÉCHALOTE*)

24 asparagus spears

1 tablespoon finely chopped
shallot

1 tablespoon white wine vinegar

60g/2oz butter

*(recipe ingredients continued
overleaf)*

THIS IS A DISH TO DELIGHT *the eyes and palate not only of vegetarians, but of carnivores too. All these vegetables are at their very best between April and June. Touraine, which lies next to this region, also offers a vast choice of delicious vegetables. Naturally, you can serve any one of these vegetable dishes alone. Vegetarians could substitute a good vegetable stock for the chicken stock.*

PREPARATION

The lettuces: Remove any withered outside leaves. Make an incision in the core with a sharp knife to ensure even cooking. Carefully wash the lettuces in cold water, leaving them whole. Bring a pan of lightly salted water to the boil, plunge in the lettuces and cook over medium heat for 5 minutes. Refresh, drain, then press lightly to extract as much water as possible.

Halve the lettuces, place in a shallow pan with the butter and cook until coloured on both sides, turning them carefully with a palette knife. Pour in the chicken stock, season lightly with salt and pepper and simmer gently until all the cooking liquid has evaporated. Keep warm.

The artichokes: Snap off the stalks and pare the bases with a sharp knife to remove all the leaves. Brush lightly with lemon juice. Bring a pan of lightly salted water to the boil, add the vinegar and plunge in the artichokes. Cook for 25–30 minutes, checking to see if the artichokes are tender with the point of a knife. Leave them in their cooking water.

Peel the mushrooms, wash or wipe with a damp cloth and chop finely. Heat 30g/1oz butter in a frying pan and sauté the mushrooms until all their water has evaporated. Add the garlic, breadcrumbs and parsley, then season to taste.

Using your thumb and forefinger, remove the chokes from the artichokes, rinse the bottoms in cold water and drain. Fill with the mushroom stuffing, heaping it into a dome. Grease a gratin dish with 30g/1oz butter and put in the stuffed artichokes. Cut the remaining butter into small pieces and dot them over the stuffing. Keep at room temperature and bake the artichokes in the oven at 220°C/425°F/gas 7 ten minutes before serving.

The spring cabbage: Remove any withered outside leaves, make an incision in the core with a sharp knife to ensure even cooking, then halve the cabbages lengthways. Bring a saucepan of lightly salted water to the boil, put in the cabbages and cook for about 20 minutes, until they are still quite firm but not crunchy. Drain, then press lightly to extract the cooking water.

Lightly butter a shallow pan, put in the cabbages, add the chicken stock and cook over medium heat until all the liquid has evaporated. Season lightly with salt and pepper, cut the remaining butter into small pieces and scatter them over the cabbages. Keep warm.

The chestnuts: Use a sharp knife to make a light incision in each, then place under a hot grill or in a very hot oven (250°C/500°F/gas 10) until they burst open slightly. Peel them and remove the skin with a sharp knife, taking care not to break the chestnuts. Place in a saucepan with the milk and bouquet garni and cook very gently for about 30 minutes. Leave the chestnuts in the milk in a warm place. Just before serving, half-melt the butter, remove the bouquet garni, drain the chestnuts and roll them in the butter.

The asparagus: Put the shallot and vinegar in a small saucepan and heat gently.

L'ARC-EN-CIEL DE LÉGUMES ANGEVIN

THE MOUSSERONS
(*MOUSSERONS SAUTÉS EN PERSILLADE*)

500g/1lb 2oz mousserons or button mushrooms

60g/2oz butter

1 tablespoon chopped shallot

1 tablespoon chopped parsley

THE CARROTS
(*CAROTTES À LA CRÈME*)

1kg/2lb 3oz young carrots with their tops or small round *grelot* carrots

a pinch of sugar

300ml/½pt double cream

1 tablespoon flat-leaved parsley leaves or chervil

THE POTATOES (*POMMES DE TERRE 'TROMPE BONHOMME'*)

1.25kg/2¾lb medium potatoes, about 80g/3oz each

300ml/½pt double cream

2 onions, finely chopped

2 tablespoons chopped parsley

3 tablespoons snipped chives

As soon as the liquid bubbles, add 2 tablespoons cold water. Take the pan off the heat and, using a small balloon whisk, beat in the butter, a little at a time. Reheat the pan for 30 seconds only in the middle of this operation. The finished sauce (a sort of *beurre blanc*) should be light and fluffy and barely warm.

Peel the asparagus stalks and snap them where they are tender. Just before serving, plunge the asparagus into a pan of lightly salted boiling water and cook for 7–8 minutes. At the last moment, drain them and pour the shallot butter over the tips.

The mousserons: Peel and wipe with a slightly damp cloth, then halve or quarter according to their size and your preference. Heat the butter in a frying pan and sauté the mousserons for 5 minutes, until all their water has evaporated. Add the shallot and cook for another 2 minutes. Sprinkle on the parsley just before serving.

The carrots: Peel and, if they are very young and tender, leave on some of the leaves. Place in a saucepan, pour in just enough water to cover the carrots, add a pinch of salt and sugar and cook over high heat until all the cooking water has evaporated and the carrots are cooked but firm. Add the cream, let it bubble for 3–4 minutes, season, sprinkle with parsley or chervil leaves and serve immediately.

The potatoes: Soak in cold water and brush the skins lightly to clean them. Prick them, place in a saucepan, cover with lightly salted cold water and cook for about 30 minutes. Use the point of a knife to check that the potatoes are tender. Just before serving, drain them, do not peel, but arrange them on the serving platter and leave everyone to peel them, help themselves to the cream (which should be served separately) and sprinkle on the chopped onions and herbs as they like.

SERVING THE 'RAINBOW'

Arrange all these beautiful and delicious vegetables on a large platter or individual plates and serve very hot.

———— · ————

CHAMPIGNONS ET PETITS POIS
~ À LA CRÈME ~

Mushrooms and peas in cream

SERVES 6

PREPARATION TIME: 40 MINUTES

COOKING TIME: ABOUT 10 MINUTES

INGREDIENTS

1 hearty lettuce

1kg/2lb 3oz peas in the pod

250g/9oz button mushrooms

60g/2oz butter

12 baby onions, peeled and quartered

1 bouquet garni

a pinch of sugar

200ml/7fl oz double cream

1 tablespoon chervil leaves

salt and freshly ground pepper

E VERYONE WILL ENJOY *these vegetables from 'the garden of France', which should be very tender to the bite and not at all crunchy. The dish makes an excellent accompaniment to* Cul de veau braisé angevin *(recipe page 47), but is also delicious served on its own.*

PREPARATION

The lettuce: Cut into quarters, cut off the hard part of the stalk, wash in cold water, drain and shred coarsely.

The peas: Shell, wash in cold water and drain.

The mushrooms: With a sharp knife, cut off the dirty part of the stalks, wipe the mushrooms with a damp cloth or wash quickly in cold water if necessary. Halve or quarter them, depending on their size, or leave them whole if they are small.

COOKING

Cook the mushrooms with half the butter in a frying pan over medium heat for 2 minutes, then drain off the cooking juices. In a flameproof casserole, melt the remaining butter over low heat, put in the onions and cook for 2 minutes. Add the lettuce and cook for another 2 minutes, stirring with a spatula, then add the peas, bouquet garni and a pinch of sugar, cover and cook for 3 minutes.

Add the cream, leave the casserole uncovered and bring to the boil, then lower the heat and simmer for another 3 minutes. Remove the bouquet garni and season the vegetables with salt and pepper.

SERVING

Tip the vegetables with their creamy sauce into a vegetable dish, scatter over the chervil and serve at once.

———— · ————

LE MANCEAU

Almond cream tart

THIS RICH AND CREAMY *tart from Le Mans should be eaten as soon as possible after cooking while it is still very fresh.*

PREPARATION

The pastry: On a lightly floured marble or wooden surface, roll out the pastry to a thickness of 2–3mm/⅛in. Butter the flan ring, place it on the baking sheet and line with the pastry. (You will be left with about 40g/1½oz trimmings.) Refrigerate for 30 minutes.

The crème pâtissiere: Follow the method on page 17. When it is nearly cold, stir in the rum.

The crème d'amande: Follow the method on page 16.

Preheat the oven to 180°C/350°F/gas 4.

The filling: Before the *crème pâtissière* becomes completely cold, beat in the almond cream with a wire whisk. Pour the mixture into the pastry case.

COOKING

Bake the tart in the preheated oven for 50 minutes, taking care not to let it brown too much. Leave in the flan ring on the baking sheet for 10 minutes, then remove the ring and slide the tart on to a cooling rack.

Increase the oven temperature to 250°C/500°F/gas 10.

Glazing the tart: When the tart is completely cold, heat the apricot jam in a saucepan, brush it thinly and evenly over the tart and leave to set. Meanwhile, mix the rum and icing sugar to make a transparent, slightly syrupy glaze. Brush this over the apricot glaze and place the tart in the very hot oven for 30 seconds to harden the glaze.

NOTES

It is very important to get the cooking just right to produce a soft, creamy tart, which must be eaten within 48 hours.

———— · ————

SERVES 6

PREPARATION TIME: 1 HOUR

COOKING TIME: 50 MINUTES

INGREDIENTS

350g/12oz *Pâte sucrée* (recipe page 11)

a pinch of flour

30g/1oz butter, for greasing

CREME PÂTISSIÈRE

2 eggs

50g/2oz sugar

75g/2½oz sifted flour

250ml/9fl oz milk

65ml/2½fl oz rum

CRÈME D'AMANDE

125g/4½oz butter

250g/9oz *tant pour tant* (equal quantities of icing sugar and ground almonds sifted together)

2 eggs

GLAZE

75g/2½oz sieved apricot jam

2 tablespoons rum

4 tablespoons icing sugar

EQUIPMENT

1 flan ring, about 22cm/9in diameter, 4cm/1½in deep

PITHIVIERS FONDANT

Pithiviers with fondant icing

SERVES 6
PREPARATION TIME:
20 MINUTES
COOKING TIME: 20 MINUTES

INGREDIENTS

100g/4oz whole unskinned almonds

130g/5oz sugar

75g/3oz softened butter

3 eggs

40g/1½oz sifted cornflour

30g/1oz melted butter, for the tin

a pinch of flour

75g/3oz sieved apricot jam

30g/1oz fondant icing

2 drops of pink food colouring

100g/4oz mixed glacé fruits and angelica, for decoration

12 flaked almonds for decoration

EQUIPMENT

1 cake tin, about 18cm/7in diameter, 4cm/1½in deep

THE FORERUNNER OF A MODERN *pithiviers, this version has nothing in common with the rich pastry cake we know today, since the base is not made with almond cream wrapped in puff pastry, but simply from almond paste glazed with a light fondant icing. It is rustic, but nonetheless delicious.*

PREPARATION

Preheat the oven to 180°C/350°F/gas 4.

The almond paste: In a saucepan, bring about 300ml/½ pt water to the boil, plunge in the almonds and boil for 2–3 minutes. Drain on a tea towel and press the almonds between your thumb and index finger so that they pop out of their skins.

Grind the almonds in a food processor, adding 100g/4 oz sugar a little at a time, until you have a raw almond paste. Put the paste in a bowl and, in the given order, using a spatula, work in the remaining sugar, softened butter, then the eggs, one at a time. Finally, add the cornflour, working the mixture continuously until the paste is very smooth.

Generously brush the inside of the tin with melted butter. Put in a pinch of flour and rotate the tin so that the flour coats the entire surface. Turn the tin over and tap the base to tip out the excess flour. Pour in the almond paste.

COOKING

Bake the pithiviers in the preheated oven for 20 minutes. Leave in the tin for 10 minutes, then unmould and place on a wire rack to cool.

Raise the oven temperature to 250°C/500°F/gas 10.

The glaze: Warm the apricot jam in a saucepan and brush it lightly over the top of the cooled pithiviers. Leave to set for about 10 minutes.

The icing: Put the fondant icing in a saucepan with a few drops of water and the pink colouring. Set over very low heat and work to a heavy syrupy consistency. Using a pastry brush, spread the tepid icing evenly over the apricot glaze, then place the pithiviers in the very hot oven for 30 seconds to give it a beautiful shine.

SERVING

Decorate with glacé fruits, angelica and flaked almonds.

LE MANCEAU AND PITHIVIERS FONDANT

TARTE DE TOURS AU NOUGAT

Nougat tart from Tours

SERVES 8

PREPARATION TIME:
30 MINUTES

COOKING TIME: 30 MINUTES,
PLUS 15 MINUTES BAKING
BLIND

INGREDIENTS

a pinch of flour

150g/5oz *Pâte brisée* (recipe
page 10)

butter for greasing

40g/1½oz glacé cherries

40g/1½oz candied orange peel

40g/1½oz candied angelica

200ml/7fl oz rum

75g/3oz sieved apricot jam

4 egg whites

50g/2oz sugar

100g/4oz ground almonds, mixed
with 50g/2oz icing sugar

30g/1oz icing sugar, for dusting

EQUIPMENT

1 flan ring, about 22cm/9in
diameter, 2cm/¾in deep

baking or dried beans

THIS DELICIOUSLY SWEET *and rich tart is a smooth combination of candied fruits, jam and ground almonds.*

PREPARATION

The pastry case: On a lightly floured marble or wooden surface, roll out the pastry as thinly as possible.

Grease the flan ring, stand it on a baking sheet and line with the pastry. You will be left with about 20g/¾oz trimmings. Pinch up the edges of the pastry to make an attractive, even frill. Refrigerate for 30 minutes.

15 minutes before you take the pastry case out of the fridge, preheat the oven to 200°C/400°F/gas 6.

BAKING THE PASTRY CASE BLIND

Prick the bottom of the pastry case with the point of a knife or a fork, line it with greaseproof paper or foil, fill with baking beans and bake blind in the preheated oven for about 15 minutes. Leave to cool slightly, then remove the beans with a spoon and lift out the paper or foil.

Reduce the oven temperature to 180°C/350°F/gas 4.

The candied fruits: Cut into small dice and place in a saucepan with the rum. Warm slightly to speed up the maceration and leave to macerate.

The apricot glaze: Put the jam in a saucepan and heat until reduced by one-quarter. Immediately brush the glaze over the bottom of the pastry case. Spread the candied fruits as evenly as possible on top of the glaze.

The almond mixture: With an electric mixer, beat the egg whites until firm, then beat in the 50g/2oz sugar. Using a slotted or metal spoon, gently fold in the ground almond and icing sugar mixture, taking care not to overwork. Pour the mixture into the pastry case and smooth the surface with a palette knife. It should be very smooth.

COOKING

Bake in the preheated oven for 30 minutes. Leave in the tin for 10 minutes, then unmould the tart and place on a wire rack to cool.

SERVING

Sprinkle lightly with icing sugar and serve this dessert still just warm.

Anjou, Touraine and Maine

FRESHWATER FISH

Shad
Eel
Barbel
Bream
Pike
Carp
Gudgeon
Perch
Salmon
Tench

CRUSTACEANS

Crayfish

POULTRY

Barbary duck
Capon
Turkey
Goose
Poularde (roasting chicken)
Chicken
Guinea fowl

GAME

Lark
Quail
Wild rabbit
Thrushes
Hare
Partridge
Teal

MEAT

Lamb
Choletais beef from Craon
Pork
Veal

CHARCUTERIE

Andouille de Garron
Andouillette de St Hilaire
Boudin blanc
Boudin noir
Rabbit pâté
Rillauds d'Angers (fried diced belly of pork)
Rillons d'Authon (diced pork preserved in fat)
Tripes à la mode d'Anthon
Rillettes from Angers, Mamers, Le Mans and Saumur

VEGETABLES

Artichokes
Asparagus
Carrots
Mushrooms: cultivated, morels, mousserons
Cauliflower and calabrese
Pumpkin
Shallots
Beans: white and green
Turnips
Sorrel
Peas
Potatoes
Various salads

CHEESE

Caillebotte d'Anjou (curd cheese)
Chèvre de Montreuil-Bellay (goat)
Fromage de Chouze
Port-Salut

FRUIT

Apricots
Nectarines
Cherries
Chestnuts
Strawberries
Cantaloupe melons
Hazelnuts
Peaches
Pears (beurre hardi, belle Angevine, Duchesse, bon chrétien, William and others)
Apples (Reinette de Mans and others)
Plums
Grapes

PÂTISSERIE

Aniseed biscuits
Almond and hazelnut boulettes
Fouée (peasant tart)
Prune jellies from Anjou
Shortbread from Sarthe

CONFECTIONERY

Candied apple from Chantrigne

MISCELLANEOUS PRODUCTS

Cider eau-de-vie
Pear eau-de-vie
Sweet cider from Sarthe
Cointreau (Angers)
Local fruit liqueurs
Poirée d'Anjou

Vendée, Poitou and Charentes

SANDY COASTS, SALT MARSHES AND A LUSH INTERIOR
RICH IN FISH AND FOWL

F OR US THE VENDÉE conjures up memories of boyhood holidays: the sun, the salt marshes, shrimping, trawling for sardines in a little fishing boat, scrabbling in the sand at low tide for cockles and razor shells, gathering blackberries for our mother to make delicious jam. We shall never forget the little village of St Gilles, opposite the Île d'Yeu, where we spent our holidays year after year.

The region enjoys a very pleasant climate, sunny in summer and mild in winter. Annual rainfall is never more than 70–80cm/27½–31½in and the gentle, humid *suroit* wind is infrequent and not unpleasant.

This is still an area of poultry, fishing, hunting and good eating. The food of the region is simple, very rustic and exceedingly tasty. Here, the women leave the pots to simmer for as long as it takes to make a good dish! Traditional soups made with salt pork, vegetables, fish or sorrel are still served at almost every meal. There is a huge variety of both sea and freshwater fish, for the Vendée is on the Atlantic coast, while Poitou and Charentes are criss-crossed by many rivers and tributaries: the Sèvre Niortaise, the Sèvre Nantaise, the Vienne, the Creuse, the Gartempe and the Charente. The marshes of all these regions play host to many unusual waterfowl. Market gardeners still bring produce from their own gardens to the markets along the coast: two or three bunches of herbs, a few onions and a dozen frogs' legs, caught the day before. Long may they prosper!

The area produces few wines; these include Thouars, Loudun, Foye Monjault and Mareuil (the rosé is particularly pleasant). They do not travel well and should be drunk the year they are produced.

Albert bought a small house in St-Jean-de-Mont for our mother, who now spends several months a year there. Whenever possible, Albert joins her; he takes advantage of these visits to search around for new food producers. On one of these expeditions, he discovered M. Couthouis' farm, 5 kilometres from Challans. Here, chickens and ducks live happily in vast acres of pastureland and roam freely about the surrounding marshes. For several years now, M. Couthouis has been supplying our London restaurants with excellent *canards croisés* and barbary ducklings.

It is enormously satisfying to find such a sympathetic farmer. Just as a wine producer will present us with a bottle of wine when we visit him, M. Couthouis always gives Albert a duckling which he cooks that day for mother. Sometimes, though, he leaves that task to the real expert, our mother, especially when tiny turnips with blue tops are in season!

Fishing nets swing over the shimmering silver Atlantic before being lowered to the ocean bed to do their work. The fishermen pass hours dreaming of the size of the catch, hoping for nets filled with spoils.

SOUPE À L'OSEILLE

Sorrel soup

SERVES 4

PREPARATION TIME:
25 MINUTES

COOKING TIME: ABOUT
30 MINUTES

INGREDIENTS

125g/4oz sorrel

200g/7oz small potatoes or
50g/2oz tapioca

30g/1oz butter

750ml/1¼ pints Chicken stock
(recipe page 15) or water

2 egg yolks

150ml/5fl oz double cream

salt and freshly ground pepper

ORIGINALLY, THIS SOUP FROM POITOU *was thickened not with tapioca or potatoes, but with stale bread, which made it rather heavy and indigestible. Admittedly soups in those days constituted a whole meal, but times have changed and this modern version is a robust but not heavy soup, which leaves your guests plenty of room to enjoy the courses that follow it.*

PREPARATION

The sorrel: Remove the stalks, wash the leaves in cold water and drain. Pile up 5 or 6 leaves, roll them into a sausage shape and shred finely. Shred all the sorrel in this way.

The potatoes: Peel, wash in cold water and cut into 0.5cm/¼in slices.

COOKING THE SOUP

Heat the butter gently in a saucepan and sweat the sorrel over low heat for 3 minutes. Add the chicken stock or water and a little salt and bring to the boil. Cook for 5 minutes, then add the potatoes or shower in the tapioca, reduce the heat and simmer gently for 15 minutes if you are using tapioca, or 20 minutes for the potatoes.

   Put the egg yolks and cream in a bowl and pour in a little of the liquid from the soup, whisking continuously. With the pan off the heat, pour the egg mixture back into the soup, stirring with a ladle. Season to taste and keep hot, but do not let the soup boil.

SERVING

Pour the soup into a tureen and serve very hot.

When you can get marvellous small new potatoes like these, use them in preference to tapioca to thicken your Soupe à l'oseille.

MOUCLADE D'AUNIS

Mussels in a lightly curried cream sauce

THIS IS MICHEL'S PERSONAL *interpretation of a popular dish from the Vendée and one which he often prepared when he was chef to the Rothschild family. Be discreet in your use of the curry powder; the flavour must be very subtle. A rice pilaff perfectly complements the sauce.*

PREPARATION

The mussels: Scrub and debeard them and rub them vigorously together in a little cold water. Wash in several changes of water and drain.

Put the mussels in a saucepan with the wine, cover and cook over high heat for 3–4 minutes, stirring every minute, until all the mussels have opened. They are cooked as soon as they open; discard any which do not. Drain them in a colander set over a bowl to catch all the cooking liquor. Cover the mussels with a cloth soaked in cold water so that they do not dry out. Strain the liquor into a measuring jug; there should be about 400ml/14 fl oz.

THE SAUCE

Gently melt the butter in a shallow pan. Add the onions, cook for 1 minute, then stir in the curry powder and flour and cook gently for 4 minutes. Pour in the mussel liquor and bring to the boil, stirring continuously to prevent lumps from forming. Add the bouquet garni and simmer the sauce very gently for 20 minutes.

Meanwhile, take the mussels out of their shells and remove any remaining beards. Place the mussels in a bowl, cover with a damp cloth and leave in a warm place.

When the sauce is cooked, remove the bouquet garni, add the cream and bubble briskly for 5 minutes. Season to taste and keep hot.

SERVING

Put the mussels into the hot sauce and heat for 2 minutes, until the sauce comes to the boil. Immediately, spoon the mussels and sauce into 4 deep bowls and serve. Be sure to give your guests spoons to eat this dish – it is the only way!

———— · ————

SERVES 4

PREPARATION TIME:
30 MINUTES

COOKING TIME: 25 MINUTES
FOR THE SAUCE

INGREDIENTS

2kg/4½lb mussels, preferably bouchot or Welsh

300ml/½pt dry white wine

60g/2oz butter

100g/4oz onions, finely chopped

1 tablespoon madras curry powder

40g/1½oz flour

1 bouquet garni

300ml/½pt double cream

salt and freshly ground pepper

PÂTÉ VENDÉEN

Rabbit pâté

SERVES 12

PREPARATION TIME: 1½ HOURS

COOKING TIME: ABOUT 2 HOURS, PLUS 26 OR 27 HOURS CHILLING

INGREDIENTS

2 wild rabbits, each about 1kg/ 2lb 3oz, skinned and drawn (keep the liver, heart and kidneys)

200g/7oz pork back fat, cut into long strips

2 garlic cloves, finely chopped

2 tablespoons chopped parsley

10g/1 teaspoon mixed spice

3 tablespoons cognac

1 bottle dry white wine

400g/14oz pork chine

1 tablespoon groundnut oil

1 calf's foot, split lengthways, blanched, poached for 2 hours and boned (keep the bones and 500ml/18fl oz of the poaching liquid)

2 carrots, peeled and sliced

1 large onion, peeled and thinly sliced

1 bouquet garni, with plenty of thyme

2 cloves

1 large pig's caul, well washed

3 tablespoons flour

salt and freshly ground pepper

EQUIPMENT

1 oval or round terrine with a lid, about 26cm/10in diameter, 7cm/ 3in deep

mincing machine

DURING THE SCHOOL HOLIDAYS, *when all her children were at home together, our mother would prepare a huge selection of pâtés for us, each one better than the last. This terrine from the Vendée was always one of our favourites. It is very cheap to make, since wild rabbit is not much in demand and is therefore inexpensive, and will keep well in the fridge. Farmed rabbit can be used instead.*

PREPARATION

The rabbits: Bone them with a sharp knife, then put the small pieces of flesh, the liver, heart and kidneys in a dish. Cut the fillets from the saddle and the best pieces of meat into 12 neat escalopes about 1cm/½in thick and refrigerate.

Fit a mincing machine with a medium blade and mince the remaining rabbit meat, offal and pork back fat. Put this mixture into a bowl and, using a wooden spatula, work in the garlic, parsley, spice, cognac and one-third of a bottle of white wine. Season, cover with clingfilm and refrigerate for 2 or 3 hours.

The pork chine and calf's foot: Cut the pork into 1.5cm/1in cubes. Heat the oil in a flameproof casserole, put in the cubes of pork, the meat and bones from the calf's foot, the rabbit bones, carrot and onion. Pour in the remaining wine and the reserved poaching liquid, add 2 glasses of water, the bouquet garni and cloves. Simmer gently for 45 minutes, then lift out the meat from the calf's foot and the pork cubes with a slotted spoon and keep at room temperature. Simmer the poaching liquid and bones for another 45 minutes, then strain through a conical sieve and leave to cool. This will be the jelly for binding the pâté.

Preheat the oven to 220°C/425°F/gas 7.

ASSEMBLING THE PÂTÉ

Line the terrine with the pig's caul, leaving an overhang. Cut the meat from the calf's foot into very small dice and mix into the minced meats. Add the cooled cubes of pork and spread a 2cm/¾in layer of this mixture over the bottom of the terrine. Arrange some of the rabbit fillets on top, then spread over another layer of minced meats. Make more layers in this way, ending with a layer of minced meats. Bring the ends of the caul over the top to enclose the contents of the terrine completely. Mix the flour with a little cold water to make a soft dough. Put the lid on the top of the terrine to seal it and spread the dough between the edge of the lid and the terrine.

COOKING

Lay a sheet of greaseproof paper in the bottom of a roasting pan, put in the terrine and fill the pan with enough cold water to come halfway up the sides of the terrine. Cook in the preheated oven for 2 hours, topping up the water after 1½ hours if necessary.

Take the cooked pâté out of the bain-marie, break the dough seal and remove the lid. Using a soup spoon or syringe, remove the excess fat and replace it with the jelly you made earlier. Lay a wooden board over the surface and place a 500g/1lb 2oz weight on top. Leave to cool for about 3 hours, then remove the weight and wood and refrigerate the pâté for at least 24 hours.

SERVING

Serve the pâté straight from the terrine, with a well-sharpened knife to cut it, accompanied by a loaf of good country bread.

PÂTÉ VENDÉEN

MAQUEREAU AU RIZ

Baked mackerel with rice

SERVES 4

PREPARATION TIME:
20 MINUTES

COOKING TIME: 20 MINUTES,
PLUS 10 MINUTES RESTING

INGREDIENTS

4 mackerel, about 350g/12oz each

60g/2oz butter

1 medium onion, cut into thin rings

250g/9oz rice

750ml/1¼pt boiling Chicken stock (recipe page 15) or boiling water

1 large bouquet garni

1 tablespoon chopped parsley

salt and freshly ground pepper

EQUIPMENT

1 flameproof earthenware or cast-iron dish with a lid, large enough to hold all the mackerel

T HIS IS A SIMPLE, ECONOMICAL *dish, in which the rice takes on the deliciously rich flavour of the fish. In summer, you can add a handful of the broad beans or peas which abound in this region to the rice after the dish is cooked; this adds a touch of colour and a fresh taste of green vegetables.*

PREPARATION

Preheat the oven to 220°C/425°F/gas 7.

The mackerel: Cut off the heads and gut the fish through the resulting opening, without slitting the bellies. Cut off the fins and the end of the tails with scissors. Rinse the fish in cold water and pat dry with kitchen paper. With a sharp knife, make 3 slashes in the fleshiest part on each side of the mackerel so that they cook more evenly.

COOKING

Gently heat the butter in the flameproof dish, add the onions, cook over low heat for 1 minute, then add the rice. Stir with a spatula and cook gently for 2 minutes, stirring continuously. Pour in the boiling chicken stock or water, add the bouquet garni and put in the mackerel, pushing them down so that they are half covered by the liquid. Season with salt and pepper, cover and bake in the preheated oven for 20 minutes. Remove the dish from the oven and leave in a warm place, still covered, for at least 10 minutes before serving.

SERVING

Remove the bouquet garni, check the seasoning of the rice and add salt and pepper if necessary. Scatter over the parsley and serve the mackerel straight from the dish.

FOIE DE PORC RÔTI AUX HERBES

Roast pig's liver with herbs

THIS RUSTIC DISH *was traditionally served by farmers at family get-togethers after the killing of the pig. You can, of course, use calf's liver instead; it is much more delicate but also far more expensive. Serve this savoury, herby dish with braised green cabbage or puréed potatoes.*

SERVES 6

PREPARATION TIME: 15 MINUTES

COOKING TIME: 30–35 MINUTES, PLUS 15–20 MINUTES RESTING

PREPARATION

Preheat the oven to 240°C/475°F/gas 9.

Spread a double thickness of caul on a work surface and sprinkle over the shallots and all the herbs. Dry the liver with absorbent paper, season all over with salt and pepper and lay it on the caul. Fold the caul over the liver to enclose it completely.

COOKING

Heat the clarified butter in the pan over medium heat. Put in the liver and seal for 2 minutes on each side, then roast in the preheated oven for 25–30 minutes, basting it with the cooking butter every 10 minutes. Transfer the cooked liver to a wire rack set over a plate, cover with foil and keep warm for 15–20 minutes before serving. It should still be slightly pink in the middle, but not rare.

SERVING

Place the whole liver on a serving plate. Lightly sprinkle the watercress with lemon juice and arrange it around the edge. Take the liver to the table and use a ham knife to carve it thinly in front of your guests.

INGREDIENTS

1 pig's liver, 1.2–1.4kg/2¾–3lb

250g/9oz pig's caul, soaked

4 shallots, finely chopped

4 tablespoons chopped parsley

2 tablespoons shredded tarragon

1 tablespoon chopped thyme

60g/2oz clarified butter

salt and freshly ground pepper

1 large bunch of watercress, for serving

juice of ½ lemon

EQUIPMENT

1 cast-iron pan large enough to take the whole liver

We use shallots constantly in our cooking. At the market you can select those in the best condition.

CANETTE DE CHALLANS AUX NAVETS BLEUS

CANETTE DE CHALLANS
AUX NAVETS BLEUS

Challans duckling with baby turnips

THE VENDÉE IS FAMOUS *for its fine-flavoured Challans ducks. Our mother often treats us to this simple, honest dish when we visit her at St. Jean de Mont.*

SERVES 2

PREPARATION TIME:
25 MINUTES

COOKING TIME: 35 MINUTES

INGREDIENTS

1 duckling, preferably Challans, about 1.25kg/2lb 12 oz

1 fine strip of barding fat large enough to cover the breast

300g/11oz baby new turnips, preferably blue-topped

12 baby onions

200g/7oz young broad beans

30g/1oz clarified butter

20g/¾oz sugar

2 sprigs of thyme

1 tablespoon flour

1 tablespoon vinegar

200ml/7fl oz Chicken stock (recipe page 15)

30g/1oz butter

salt and freshly ground pepper

a small bouquet of watercress, for serving

PREPARATION

The duckling: Singe over a flame for 30 seconds and pull out the feather stumps with the point of a knife if necessary. Clean the duckling, pull out the breastbone, sprinkle the cavity with salt and pepper and truss the bird. Cover the breast with barding fat and secure it loosely with kitchen string. Chop the neck and wingtips and keep the giblets for the sauce.

The turnips: Wash in cold water. You need not peel them, especially if they are young and tender, but cut off the tops and the beard-like root.

The onions: Peel, wash and pat dry.

The broad beans: Shell them and, unless they are very young and tender, remove the outer skin. Cook for a few minutes in boiling salted water; they should still be slightly crunchy. Refresh and drain.

COOKING THE DUCKLING

Put the clarified butter in a flameproof casserole and set over medium heat. Seal the duckling until golden on all sides. Add the turnips and onions and brown them for 2 minutes. Add the sugar and thyme, cover and cook over low heat for 25 minutes, turning the duck halfway through cooking. The breast should still be slightly pink.

Remove the barding fat and string and place the duck breast-side down on a plate. Transfer the turnips and onions to another plate and cover with foil.

THE SAUCE

Pour off half the fat from the casserole, put in the chopped duck neck, wings and giblets and brown lightly. Sprinkle with flour and stir with a wooden spatula. Deglaze with the vinegar and chicken stock and reduce the liquid by one-third. Strain the sauce through a conical sieve into a saucepan, whisk in the butter and season to taste. Stir in the broad beans and keep hot.

SERVING

Carve off the duck legs, then the breast fillets. Arrange the duck pieces in the centre of a deep dish with the turnips and onions around them, then pour the hot sauce and broad beans over the duck. Garnish with watercress and serve immediately.

NOTES

Freeze the carcass to use in the sauce when you next cook a duckling.

———— · ————

PIGEONNEAUX AUX PETITS POIS
~ ET HERBILLETTES ~

Pigeon with peas and fresh herbs

SERVES 4
PREPARATION TIME:
25 MINUTES
COOKING TIME: 17 MINUTES

INGREDIENTS

4 young pigeons, preferably from the Vendée or Bresse, trussed and barded with a fine layer of pork back fat (reserve the neck, wing tips and giblets)

1 firm-hearted lettuce

1kg/2lb 3oz fresh peas in the pod

30g/1oz butter

a pinch of sugar

100g/4oz raw ham, cut into large julienne

4 tablespoons snipped fresh herbs (equal quantities of basil, flat-leaved parsley, chives, hyssop and chervil)

1 tablespoon groundnut oil

8 garlic cloves, unpeeled

2 shallots, peeled and finely diced

1 carrot, peeled and finely diced

1 sprig of thyme, chopped

150ml/5fl oz Chicken stock (recipe page 15)

salt and freshly ground pepper

a bouquet of watercress, for serving

THE VENDÉE IS NOTED FOR *its excellent salads, marvellous peas and succulent pigeons. The smell and flavour of these birds scented with the delicate herbs of the region are quite delicious.*

PREPARATION

Quarter the lettuce, wash in cold water, drain and shred. Shell the peas and rinse in cold water. Put the butter and lettuce in a casserole and sweat for 1 minute. Add the peas and sugar, cover the casserole and simmer for 2–3 minutes until the peas are cooked. Add the ham and keep warm.

Preheat the oven to 240°C/475°F/gas 9.

COOKING THE PIGEONS

Season the cavities with salt and pepper and put a spoonful of fresh herbs into each one. Heat the oil and garlic cloves in a roasting pan, add the pigeon trimmings and giblets, put in the pigeons and brown quickly on all sides. Scatter the shallots, carrot and thyme around the edge and cook in the preheated oven for 14 minutes.

Remove the trussing string and barding fat from the cooked pigeons and lay the birds breast-side down on a dish. Cover with foil and keep warm. Put the garlic cloves in the casserole with the peas.

THE SAUCE

Pour off half the cooking fat, deglaze the roasting pan with the chicken stock, strain the sauce through a conical sieve, then season with salt and pepper and keep warm.

SERVING

Either split the pigeons or leave them whole and lay them on the bed of peas, lettuce and garlic. Garnish with watercress and serve the light sauce separately in a sauceboat.

——— · ———

PIGEONNEAUX AUX PETITS POIS ET HERBILLETTES

SAUTÉ DE CABRI À L'AIL
~ ET AUX PRIMEURS ~

Kid sauté with garlic and vegetables

SERVES 6
PREPARATION TIME: 1 HOUR
COOKING TIME: 25–30 MINUTES

KID TASTES RATHER LIKE BABY LAMB, *but its flesh is more watery, hence the need to flavour it with herbs. Ask your butcher to cut up the kid for you; it will take him only a few minutes. If he gives you the liver, sauté it in butter, slice it and serve with the kid for a delectable treat.*

This is a springtime dish, to be made between March and May when the kids are young and tender.

INGREDIENTS

1 young kid, 30–40 days old

24 baby onions

1.5kg/3lb 5oz small new potatoes

1kg/2lb 3oz fresh peas in the pod

60g/2oz clarified butter

24 fresh garlic cloves, unpeeled

60g/2oz butter

75g/2½oz fresh white breadcrumbs

2 tablespoons chopped parsley

1 tablespoon fresh thyme leaves

1 teaspoon finely chopped rosemary

salt and freshly ground pepper

1 bunch of watercress and 1 lemon, for serving

PREPARATION

The kid: Using a boning knife, cut off the shoulders and hind legs. With the point of a knife, make light incisions in 2 or 3 places in the flesh to ensure even cooking. Cut the saddle into 2 pieces and the ribs into 3 pieces.

The onions: Peel and set aside.

The potatoes: Scrape them, blanch in boiling water for 2 minutes, drain and set aside.

The peas: Shell them, cook for 2 or 3 minutes in salted boiling water, refresh, drain and set aside. `

Preheat the oven to 240°C/475°F/gas 9.

COOKING THE KID

Put the clarified butter in a roasting pan and set over high heat. Lightly season the pieces of kid with salt and pepper and sauté them quickly in the butter until golden on all sides. Add the onions, cook for 2 minutes, then add the potatoes. Cook in the preheated oven for 10 minutes, then add the unpeeled garlic cloves, turn over the pieces of kid one at a time, and cook for a further 10 minutes. The kid pieces should still be soft in the centre; do not overcook them. Leave the legs in the roasting pan and transfer the other pieces to a plate, cover with foil and keep warm.

Return the roasting pan containing the legs and vegetables to the oven for 4 minutes, then add the peas and gently stir the vegetables with a wooden spatula. Return the pan to the oven for 1 more minute.

SERVING

Put the vegetables on a china platter and arrange the pieces of kid on top.

Quickly heat the butter in a frying pan and throw in the breadcrumbs, parsley, thyme and rosemary. Leave the butter to foam for 1 minute, then spoon a little of this scented mixture over each piece of kid. Decorate the platter with watercress, squeeze over some lemon juice and serve at once.

———— · ————

SAUTÉ DE CABRI À L'AIL ET AUX PRIMEURS

⟜ FLAN AUX PRUNES ⟝

Plum tart

SERVES 8
PREPARATION TIME:
35 MINUTES, PLUS 20 MINUTES
RESTING
COOKING TIME: 50 MINUTES

INGREDIENTS

800g/1¾lb plums, preferably
quetsches

40g/1½oz granulated sugar

260g/9oz *Pâte brisée* (recipe
page 10)

2 pinches of flour

20g/¾oz butter

120ml/4fl oz milk

120ml/4 fl oz double cream

½ vanilla pod, split lengthways

4 eggs

200g/7oz sugar

EQUIPMENT

24cm/10in loose-bottomed flan
tin, about 2.5cm/1in deep

baking or dried beans

THIS DESSERT IS A LITTLE LIKE *a cherry or pear* clafoutis. *The region is famous for its plums, so generations of housewives have enjoyed the gastronomic treat of making delicious plum tarts.*

PREPARATION

Preheat the oven to 220°C/425°F/gas 7.

The plums: Wash, halve lengthways and remove the stones. Lay them skin-side down in a roasting pan and sprinkle over half the granulated sugar. Place in the preheated oven for 5 minutes to precook them a little and to make the juice run out. Carefully transfer them to a wire rack or colander.

The pastry case: On a lightly floured marble or wooden surface, roll out the pastry into a circle 2–3mm/about ⅛in thick. Grease the flan tin with the butter and line it with the pastry. Pinch up the edges, then roll the rolling pin over the top of the flan tin to trim off the excess pastry. Leave to rest in the fridge for 20 minutes.

Line the pastry case with a circle of greaseproof paper and fill with baking or dried beans.

BAKING THE PASTRY CASE BLIND

Bake in the preheated oven for 15 minutes. Carefully remove the beans and greaseproof paper and keep the pastry case at room temperature. Lower the oven temperature to 200°C/400°F/gas 6.

THE CUSTARD FILLING

In a saucepan, boil the milk, cream and vanilla pod for 1 minute. In a bowl, lightly whisk the eggs with the caster sugar, then add a pinch of flour. Pour the boiling milk on to the eggs, stirring continuously. Leave the custard to cool in a cold place and stir it from time to time to prevent a skin from forming.

FILLING AND COOKING THE TART

Lay the plums skin-side up in the pastry case. When the custard is lukewarm, remove the vanilla pod, then pour the custard over the plums. Immediately, bake in the oven for 30 minutes. As soon as the tart is cooked, slip off the side of the flan tin, leaving the base in place.

SERVING

Just before serving, sprinkle the top of the tart with the remaining granulated sugar and place it on a serving plate. It is at its best when served just warm.

TOURTEAU FROMAGÉ

Cheesecake

THIS POPULAR CHEESECAKE *is unique to the Vendée and Poitou region. It is best eaten when very fresh, within 24 hours of baking. Commercially produced* tourteaux *are made with extra flour or cornflour to give them a rounded top; this looks nicer, but what the cakes gain in presentation, they lose in taste.*

THE PASTRY CASE
On a lightly floured marble or wooden board, roll out the pastry to a thickness of 2–3mm/about ⅛in. Generously grease the cake tin with butter and line it with the pastry. Pinch up the edges with your fingertips to make a small frill and refrigerate for 20 minutes.

Preheat the oven to 180°C/350°F/gas 4.

THE FILLING
In a mixing bowl, work together the soft cheese, milk and sugar until very smooth. Separate the eggs and work in the yolks one by one, beating all the time. Scrape the black seeds out of the vanilla pod with the point of a knife and beat them into the mixture. Finally, add the flour.

Beat the egg whites until well risen, then add a pinch of sugar and beat until firm. Use a balloon whisk to fold one-third of the whites into the mixture, then carefully fold in the rest with a spatula. Gently pour this smooth, rich mixture into the cake tin.

COOKING
Immediately bake the cheesecake in the preheated oven for 45 minutes; the top should look almost burnt. Leave to cool completely before unmoulding.

SERVING
Serve the cheesecake whole with a fresh fruit compôte – cherries in summer or pears in winter.

SERVES 8

PREPARATION TIME:
20 MINUTES, PLUS 20 MINUTES
CHILLING

COOKING TIME: 45 MINUTES

INGREDIENTS

350g/12oz *Pâte brisée* (recipe page 10)

a pinch of flour for dusting

30g/1oz butter

300g/11oz fresh soft white goat's cheese

75ml/3fl oz milk

200g/7oz sugar, plus a pinch

6 eggs

1 vanilla pod, split lengthways

85g/3oz flour

EQUIPMENT

24cm/10in cake tin, about 4cm/1½in deep

FLAN MARAÎCHIN

Custard tart

SERVES 8

PREPARATION TIME:
20 MINUTES, PLUS 20 MINUTES
CHILLING

COOKING TIME: 65 MINUTES

INGREDIENTS

a pinch of flour

450g/1lb *Pâte sucrée* (recipe page 11)

30g/1oz butter, for greasing

eggwash (1 egg yolk mixed with 1 coffee spoon milk)

FILLING

6 eggs

300g/11oz sugar

1 litre/1¾ pt milk

1 vanilla pod, split lengthways

1 cinnamon stick

EQUIPMENT

22cm/9in flan ring, about 4cm/1½in deep

baking or dried beans

THIS RICH TART *from the Marais area of Vendée is usually served at the end of a festive Easter meal.*

PREPARATION

The pastry case: On a lightly floured marble or wooden surface, roll out the pastry to a thickness of about 2–3mm/⅛in. Grease the flan ring and line it with the pastry, pulling the edges up gently with your fingertips to make a frill. Slide the ring on to a baking sheet and refrigerate for 20 minutes.

Meanwhile, preheat the oven to 220°C/425°F/gas 7.

BAKING THE PASTRY CASE BLIND

Prick the bottom of the pastry case with the point of a sharp knife or a fork, line it with greaseproof paper or foil, fill with baking beans and bake blind in the preheated oven for 15–20 minutes. Leave to cool slightly, then lift out the beans with a spoon and remove the paper or foil.

With a pastry brush, brush all over the inside with eggwash, then return the case to the oven for about 5 minutes, until the glaze is lightly coloured. Leave in the flan ring and keep at room temperature.

Reduce the oven temperature to 150°C/300°F/gas 2.

The filling: Put the eggs in a mixing bowl with about half the sugar and beat with a whisk until pale and of a ribbon consistency.

In a saucepan, bring the milk to the boil with the split vanilla pod, cinnamon stick and the rest of the sugar. As soon as it boils, pour it on to the egg mixture in the bowl, whisking continuously. Scrape the seeds out of the vanilla pod into the mixture, then discard the pod and cinnamon stick. Pass the custard through a conical sieve, pour into the pastry case and cook immediately in the oven for about 45 minutes, until the filling is just set; the top should be an attractive nutty brown.

SERVING

When the flan is almost cold, lift off the ring, carefully slide the flan on to a serving plate and serve immediately at room temperature.

FLAN MARAÎCHIN AND TOURTEAU FROMAGÉ

GALETTE DE MÉNAGE

Flat 'household' cake

SERVES 8–10

PREPARATION TIME:
40 MINUTES, PLUS 1 HOUR
RESTING

COOKING TIME: 30 MINUTES

INGREDIENTS

2 eggs

250g/9oz sugar

a pinch of salt

300g/11oz softened butter, at
room temperature

2 tablespoons cognac (optional)

500g/18oz flour, plus a pinch for
dusting

eggwash (1 egg yolk mixed with
1 tablespoon milk)

THIS IS A VERY ANCIENT RECIPE *from Poitou, which is also known as* le broyé de Poitou. *It is still very popular in country areas and is often served on Sundays.*

PREPARATION

The dough: Put the eggs, sugar and a pinch of salt in a bowl and beat with a whisk until the mixture leaves a faint trail when you lift it. Whisk in the softened butter, a little at a time, then the cognac if you are using it. Finally, work in the flour with a spatula, then mix with your hands to make the dough completely smooth. Tear it into small pieces, then roll it lightly back into a ball without overworking the dough. Cover it with a cloth and leave to rest in the fridge for at least 1 hour.

Preheat the oven to 200°C/400°F/gas 6.

ROLLING OUT THE DOUGH

On a lightly floured marble or wooden surface, roll out the dough into a circle about 38cm/15in diameter and 7mm/¼in thick. Roll it on to the rolling pin, then unroll it on to a baking sheet. Brush the top with eggwash and draw decorative lines with the prongs of a fork, or leave it undecorated if you prefer.

COOKING

Bake the cake in the preheated oven for 30 minutes. If you want it to be golden brown, raise the oven temperature to 220°C/425°F/gas 7 a few minutes before taking it out of the oven. Use a palette knife to slide the cake on to a wire rack.

SERVING

Serve the cake on a large strong plate. Place it in front of the head of the household, who should smash it with his fist, then leave everyone to help themselves to the pieces.

Vendée and Poitou

FRESHWATER FISH

Eel
Pike
Carp
Gudgeon
Roach
Tench
Trout

SEA FISH

Hake
Lamprey
Mackerel
Mullet
Skate
Sardines
Sole
Turbot
Tuna

SHELLFISH, CRUSTACEANS, MOLLUSCS
and
BATRACHIANS

Grey and pink shrimps
Cockles
Razor shells
Crabs
Frogs
Crayfish
Petits gris snails
Oysters
Lobster
Spiny crayfish
Lumas (small snails)
Mussels
Palourdes (clams)
Pétoncles
(queen scallops)
Tourteaux (crabs)

POULTRY

Challans duck
Turkey
Rabbit
Goose
Pigeon
Chicken

GAME

Lark
Woodcock
Quail
Wild duck
Wild rabbit
Hare
Partridge

MEAT

Beef
Lamb
Goat and kid
Pork
Veal

CHARCUTERIE

Grillons de porc
(small pieces of
preserved pork)
Smoked ham
from Montaigu
Rabbit pâté
Rillettes
Saucisse à la boudine
(made with bacon,
chard, sorrel)
Chicken flan
Tripes à la poitevine

VEGETABLES

Garlic
Artichokes
Asparagus
Chard
Cauliflower and
calabrese
Marrows
Broad beans
White beans
Onions
Peas
Dandelions
Leeks
Potatoes
Radishes
Innumerable salads
Tomatoes

CHEESE

Caillebotte de
Parthenay
Chabichou
Goat cheese from
Civray, la Motte
St Heraye etc.
Fresh fromage blanc
in crocks
Fromage de St.Lou

FRUIT

Angelica
Cantaloupe melons
Cherries
Chestnuts
Melons
Walnuts
William pears
Apples
Grapes

PÂTISSERIE

Bottreaux de Vendée
(large doughnuts)
Fouace
(peasant cake from
Poitou)
Frangipane from
Thouars
Flameaux
(apple cake)
Angelica galette
Gâteau Poitevin
(with angelica and
meringue)
Lusignan macaroons
from Poitiers
Pruné (plum tart)
Tourteau fromagé
(goat cheese tart)

CONFECTIONERY

Candied angelica
from Niort
Berlingolette de
Chatellerault
(boiled sweets)
Angelica sweets
Délice Thoursais
(sweets from Thouars)
Nougatine from Poitiers
Honey

MISCELLANEOUS PRODUCTS

Tinned sardines
and tuna
Walnut oil
Angelica liqueur
from Niort
Sea salt

Guyenne

THE VAST PROVINCE of Guyenne embraces the former provinces of Bordeaux (birthplace of the famous chef Adolphe Dugléré), Périgord, Agen, Quercy and Rouergue, all famous for their excellent cuisine and produce. We are particularly fond of the rustic, peasant cooking of this region. Rich, opulent and robust ingredients are simmered and brewed into many fine dishes. Goose fat is often used for cooking instead of oil and verjuice (the acid juice of unripe grapes) is commonly substituted for vinegar. From here comes the custom of pouring a little red wine into your soup to make a *chabrot*.

We visit the region quite often to buy foie gras in the markets and to meet our wine suppliers. These markets, like St Michel in Bordeaux, offer a profusion of produce and every kind of food. The 'grey' geese from the Landes and the cross-bred *mulard* ducks are force-fed from October to November to produce unctuous, pink-tinged foie gras – the ultimate treat, especially for Christmas and New Year feasts. Our visits to this area always provide an excuse for memorable tastings, which leave us feeling stuffed but not satiated.

This is the land of the celebrated Périgord truffle, the 'black diamond', nature's alchemy – without doubt one of the jewels of the region. More modest, but undeniably delicious, are the ceps, not to mention the lamb from Pauillac and the black- and yellow-legged chickens for which this area is famous.

The rivers and streams are also wonderful sources of food; the Isle, the Vézère, the Dordogne, the Lot, the Aveyron, the Tarn and

the Garonne offer lampreys and shad, while the Atlantic washing the shores of the Gironde is full of sea fish. Finally, there is the famous Arcachon basin, where more than twenty years ago, Michel tasted the very finest shellfish including Portuguese oysters. Alas, they were wiped out by a recent epidemic, but they have been replaced with Japanese and Pacific oysters, which are equally good.

Not surprisingly, when you consider the span of this region, the climate varies from area to area. The Lot and Garonne and the Gironde have an annual rainfall of only 60–95cm/ 23½–37½in. Summer days are very sunny and often extremely hot in the Gironde. By contrast, the Aveyron has an annual rainfall of 1–1.2m/3–4ft, sometimes as high as 1.4m/ 5ft, while in Cantal, near the Massif Central, the rainfall also reaches 1.3m/over 4ft. There are no winds of any consequence in the region.

As for the wines of this region, they are esteemed, adored and envied; they are spoken of throughout the world. Dealers follow the price of the *grands crus* clarets like a kind of stock market; it guides the price of wines even in other countries and continents. Every wine producer wants to emulate the success of Bordeaux; some fools even believe they can achieve the impossible and surpass it one day.

Every year, the vintage varies slightly in quality; the world awaits the verdict with bated breath. Yet Bordeaux almost never fails in its duty to offer the finest and greatest wines.

The best-known wine producing areas are Graves, Haut-Médoc, Médoc, Margaux, Pauillac, Pomerol, St Emilion, St Estèphe and St Julien. Since the Paris Exhibition in 1855, the great wines of this region have been classified into five groups, from *premier* to *cinquième*

cru; since that time, only one wine in the top league has been reclassified – in 1973, Château Mouton-Rothschild was promoted from *deuxième* to the pinnacle of *premier cru*.

The most commonly used grapes for red wine are cabernet franc and cabernet sauvignon; smaller quantities of malbec, petit verdot and merlot are also used. However, in the case of St Emilion and Pomerol, the merlot grape is king. The sauvignon blanc dominates the dry white wines, while the semillon is used for sauternes, with an additional small percentage of the muscadelle.

All the other vineyards of this region produce less renowned wines – sometimes VDQS or very inexpensive *vins du pays*. The following grape varieties are used for these wines: petit manseng, negrette, tannat, ruffiac, fer-savadou and du baroque.

In the early 1960s, Michel was fortunate enough to cook for the Rothschild family at Château Lafite during the grape harvest. In the early mornings, the town of Pauillac, on the banks of the Gironde, would be shrouded in mist as he set out to buy the ingredients for lunch or dinner. Back at the château, over the grate heated by wood from the vines, he cooked yellow-legged cockerels and gigots, best ends or saddles of Pauillac lamb. He can still smell the wood smoke and the roasting meat, which scented the air like some ineffable incense. Other favourite dishes were lampreys *à la bordelaise*, fricassee of ceps and various local specialities. His ultimate delight was to taste the end of a bottle of Château Lafite-Rothschild and to share a meal with the grape-pickers: a *daube de boeuf*, marinated before cooking in local wine, then simmered for several hours to make a feast for sixty people.

The famous grey geese from La Lande are not only found on larger farms but also in almost every family's back garden. During the months of October and November the force-feeding process begins, preparing the foie gras *for Christmas and New Year festivities around the world.*

77

TOURTIÈRE AUX MORILLES

TOURTIÈRE AUX MORILLES

Morel tart

GUYENNE OFFERS A HUGE RANGE *of wild mushrooms. The morels give this delectable tart its subtle aroma, but if they are not available in your area, chanterelles can be successfully used instead.*

PREPARATION

The morels: If necessary, cut off the ends of the stalks to get rid of any hard, woody or gritty parts. Keep the small morels whole, halve the medium ones lengthways and quarter the large ones. Soak in cold water with the vinegar for 5 minutes, then rinse in several changes of cold water to eliminate all the grit. Drain and dry as thoroughly as possible with a cloth.

In a deep frying pan, heat the oil and 30g/1oz butter until very hot, add the morels and cook over medium heat for 5 minutes, stirring every minute with a wooden spatula. Add the shallots and cook for 1 minute, then pour in the cream and cook over low heat for 10 minutes. Meanwhile, prepare the garnish.

The garnish: Cut the ham into julienne, put in a pan with 30g/1oz butter and sweat gently for 1 minute, then add the diced truffles and cook for 1 minute. Pour in the port, reduce for 3 minutes, then pour the mixture into the pan with the morels. Season and leave in a cold place for 3–4 hours.

ASSEMBLING THE TART

Preheat the oven to 220°C/425°F/gas 7.

On a lightly floured marble or wooden surface, roll out two-thirds of the puff pastry to a thickness of 3mm/⅛in. Lightly butter the cake or flan tin and line it with the pastry. Pinch up the edges and refrigerate for 30 minutes.

Brush the edges of the chilled pastry case with eggwash and pour in the morel mixture. Roll out the rest of the pastry to a thickness of about 5mm/¼in and lay it over the morels to make a lid. With your thumb and forefinger, pinch together the edges of the 2 pastry layers to seal them well. If necessary, cut off any excess pastry with a sharp knife. Brush the pastry lid with eggwash and decorate with the back of a fork. Make a small hole in the centre of the tart with the point of a knife so that the steam can escape.

COOKING

Bake in the preheated oven for 50 minutes.

SERVING

Carefully unmould the tart on to a round old-fashioned china plate, taking care not to damage it, and serve it whole, leaving your guests to help themselves.

———— · ————

SERVES 6

PREPARATION TIME: 40 MINUTES, PLUS SEVERAL HOURS RESTING

COOKING TIME: 50 MINUTES

INGREDIENTS

FILLING

600g/1lb 6oz fresh morels, or 150g/5oz dried morels, soaked in cold water for 6 hours

1 tablespoon vinegar

1 tablespoon olive oil

80g/3oz butter

2 shallots, finely chopped

200ml/7fl oz double cream

150g/5oz raw country ham, thinly sliced

2 fresh truffles, about 50g/2oz each, peeled and cut into large dice

100ml/3½fl oz ruby port

salt and freshly ground pepper

PASTRY CASE

a pinch of flour

600g/1lb 6oz Puff pastry (recipe page 11)

eggwash (1 egg yolk mixed with 1 tablespoon milk)

EQUIPMENT

1 loose-based cake or flan tin, 20cm/8in diameter, 3–4cm/1¼–1½in deep

∼ SARDINES GRILLÉES AUX FÈVES ∼

Sardines barbecued over vine shoots with baby broad beans

SERVES 4

PREPARATION TIME:
30 MINUTES

COOKING TIME: 3 MINUTES

INGREDIENTS

24 very fresh sardines, about 70g/3oz each

1kg/2lb 3oz young, tender broad beans in the pod

75g/3oz sorrel

60g/2oz butter

4 tablespoons olive oil

1 bundle well-dried vine shoots

1 large sprig of thyme

salt and freshly ground pepper

EQUIPMENT

barbecue

Sardines are best cooked on a barbecue.

MICHEL ADORES THIS SIMPLE DISH, *which he occasionally cooked in the kitchen hearth at Château Lafitte-Rothschild during the 1960s. Nowadays, he often prepares it at his house in Gassin.*

PREPARATION

The broad beans: Shell and skin them. Plunge into boiling salted water for 2 minutes, then drain. Remove the sorrel stalks and wash and drain the leaves. Roll them into a fat cigar shape and finely shred the sorrel.

In a saucepan, sweat the broad beans with half the butter for 2–3 minutes, then add the shredded sorrel. Bring to the boil and immediately take the pan off the heat. Add 1 tablespoon cold water and swirl in the remaining butter by shaking the pan from side to side. Keep warm, but not hot.

The sardines: Carefully scale them with the back of a knife. Cut a small opening in the bellies with scissors and clean out the guts with your index finger. Pat dry with a cloth and arrange the sardines in a deep dish. Pour over half the olive oil and turn the sardines in the oil taking care not to damage them.

COOKING THE SARDINES

Arrange the vine shoots on the barbecue and ignite them 15 minutes before you plan to serve the sardines. Vine shoots burn extremely quickly and you will very soon have hot embers to cook on.

Lay the sardines on the barbecue grill, which should by now be red hot, and cook for 1½ minutes. Brush the sardines with the thyme dipped in olive oil and carefully turn them over. Cook for only 1½ more minutes, then transfer the sardines to a dish.

If all 24 sardines will not fit on the barbecue at once, grill them in batches.

SERVING

Lightly season the sardines. Arrange 6 on each plate and divide the broad beans between the plates. Serve at once.

NOTES

The delicacy of this dish depends upon the vine shoots, which give the sardines a distinctive flavour and the short cooking time (only 3 minutes per sardine). They must be moist and tender at the backbone, just warm, but barely cooked.

———— · ————

SARDINES GRILLÉES AUX FÈVES

ESTOUFFAT DE LIÈVRE
~ QUERCINOIS ~

Hare stew

SERVES 6

PREPARATION TIME:
40 MINUTES, PLUS 12 HOURS
MARINATING

COOKING TIME:
1 HOUR 20 MINUTES

INGREDIENTS

1 young hare, about
3.5–4kg/7¾–9lb, not skinned or
drawn

300g/11oz carrots, peeled and cut
into 5mm/¼in rings

12 medium shallots, peeled

1 bouquet garni

3 garlic cloves, peeled and
chopped

10 black peppercorns, crushed

2 tablespoons olive oil

1 tablespooon wine vinegar

2 tablespoons *marc* or armagnac

1½ bottles red bordeaux
(preferably Graves)

300g/11oz Agen prunes

150g/5oz sugar

zest of 1 orange

300ml/½pt Veal stock (recipe
page 15)

30g/1oz butter

salt and freshly ground pepper

THIS SIMPLE WINTER DISH *is easy to prepare; ask your butcher to cut the hare into portions if you don't want to do it yourself. We like to serve the hare with salsify* meunière *and thick slices of warm country bread for our guests to dip into the sauce. Serve a mature bordeaux with this dish (perhaps an older vintage of the wine you use for cooking the hare).*

PREPARATION

The hare: Skin and draw it, keeping the blood from the throat and around the lungs. Cut away the gall from the liver and put the liver in a bowl with the blood, cover with clingfilm and keep in a cool place.

With a boning knife, cut off the front legs and the haunches. With a cleaver, divide the haunches in 2 and cut the saddle into 3 equal pieces. Use the cleaver to cut off the larger part of the rib cage and cut the upper part of the back into 3 equal pieces.

Put the hare portions into a bowl with the carrots and whole shallots. Add the bouquet garni, garlic, crushed peppercorns, 1 tablespoon olive oil, the vinegar, *marc* or armagnac and a bottle of red wine, cover with a plate and leave in a cold place to marinate for 12 hours.

The prunes: Meanwhile, rinse the prunes in cold water and soak them in the rest of the wine for 2 or 3 hours. Put the soaked prunes and wine in a saucepan with the sugar and orange zest. If necessary, add a little water; the prunes must be completely submerged in liquid so that they will swell properly during cooking. Poach them for about 1 hour, until swollen and soft, then keep warm.

COOKING THE HARE

Drain all the contents of the bowl in which you marinated the hare. Heat 1 tablespoon olive oil in a large casserole and sweat all the vegetables, including the bouquet garni for 3 minutes. Add all the hare except the back, the marinade and the veal stock, bring to the boil, then reduce the heat, cover the casserole and cook very gently for 1 hour 20 minutes, skimming the surface when necessary. Add the back after 20 minutes cooking.

SERVING

Carefully tip the contents of the casserole into a colander set over a bowl and discard the bouquet garni. Arrange the hare and vegetables in a deep earthenware or rustic china dish, or serve in individual deep plates.

Reduce the sauce for 15 minutes, pass through a conical sieve, then, off the heat, add the blood and liver from the hare. Swirl in the butter, season with salt and pepper and pour the hot sauce into the dish or plates. At the last moment, drain the prunes, taking care to discard the orange zest and serve them separately in a bowl or glass dish. Serve immediately.

———— · ————

ESTOUFFAT DE LIÈVRE QUERCINOIS

ENTRECÔTE À LA BORDELAISE

ENTRECÔTE À LA BORDELAISE

Entrecôte steak with red wine, bone marrow and shallots

A FEW CEPS OR ALTERNATIVELY *some puréed potatoes make a marvellous accompaniment to this delicious dish.*

PREPARATION

The sauce: Melt half the butter in a saucepan, add the shallots and sweat for 2 minutes. Add the red wine, bouquet garni and crushed peppercorns and bring to the boil. Reduce the liquid by one-third, then add the veal stock. Cook over low heat for 20 minutes, then remove the bouquet garni. Using a whisk, beat in the remaining butter, season with salt and pepper and keep hot.
The bone marrow: Using the back of a meat cleaver, crack open the bone encasing the marrow (or ask the butcher to do it for you). Put the marrow in a saucepan with a little cold water, bring to the boil, remove from the heat and set aside.

COOKING

Brush the steak with groundnut oil, lightly salt both sides and cook to your taste in a frying pan or under a very hot grill. Allow 2 minutes per side for rare steak, longer if you like your meat better done. Leave the steak to rest on a rack for 3 minutes so that the blood does not run out when you serve it.

SERVING

Cut the steak into 4 diagonal slices and arrange on a heated serving dish. Drain the marrow and cut it into large cubes or rounds. Add it to the hot sauce and immediately pour the sauce over the meat. Sprinkle with parsley and garnish with a bunch of watercress. Serve at once.

SERVES 2

PREPARATION TIME: 20 MINUTES

COOKING TIME: 30 MINUTES

INGREDIENTS

1 entrecôte steak weighing about 450g/1lb

60g/2oz butter

60g/2oz shallots, finely chopped

150ml/5fl oz red bordeaux

1 small bouquet garni

10g/¾ oz white peppercorns, crushed

100ml/3½fl oz Veal stock (recipe page 15)

1 marrow bone (to give about 200g/7oz marrow)

1 tablespoon groundnut oil

1 tablespoon chopped parsley

1 small bouquet of watercress, to garnish

salt and freshly ground pepper

These herbs will make a most glorious bouquet garni, and their flavour is the secret of our Sauce bordelaise.

GIGOT D'AGNEAU DE PAUILLAC À NOTRE FAÇON

Leg of Pauillac lamb cooked our way

SERVES 6

PREPARATION TIME:
45 MINUTES, PLUS 10 MINUTES
RESTING

COOKING TIME: 55 MINUTES

INGREDIENTS

1 leg of Pauillac or salt marsh (*pré salé*) lamb, about 2kg/3½lb, chump bone removed

12 medium asparagus spears

2 raw truffles, about 50g/2oz each

1 sprig of thyme, finely chopped

2 tablespoons chopped parsley

3 tablespoons fine fresh breadcrumbs

6 garlic cloves, peeled and finely chopped

50ml/2fl oz olive oil

1.5kg/3lb 5oz small new potatoes

60g/2oz clarified butter

6 unpeeled garlic cloves

salt and freshly ground pepper

THIS SIMPLE BUT FESTIVE DISH *is one of our family favourites. It needs no accompanying sauce or gravy and is particularly delicious in the months from March to June, when the lamb is young and tender.*

PREPARATION

The asparagus: Peel the stalks with a potato peeler and cut off the ends to leave the tips and only 5–6cm/2–2½in stalk. Cook in boiling salted water for 7 minutes, until just cooked, tender but still firm. Refresh in cold water, drain, place on a plate and cover with a damp cloth.

Preheat the oven to 220°C/425°F/gas 7.

The truffles: Place in a bowl of cold water and brush gently. Pare them thinly with a potato peeler only if the skin seems a little tough. Slice them as thinly as possible, place in a bowl and cover with clingfilm.

COOKING THE LAMB

Mix together the thyme, parsley, breadcrumbs and chopped garlic. Make sure that the lamb leg bone is short and has been sawn off neatly. Set an empty roasting pan over high heat for 2 minutes. Brush the lamb with olive oil, season with salt and pepper and put it in the hot roasting pan. Place immediately in the preheated oven. Turn the lamb over after 10 minutes' cooking.

The potatoes: As soon as the lamb is in the oven, peel the potatoes, halve or quarter them lengthways, depending on their size, rinse in cold water and pat dry. Heat the clarified butter in a frying pan, put in the potatoes and cook over high heat for 10 minutes, until pale golden. Arrange them around the lamb in the roasting pan.

By this time, the lamb will have been cooking for about 25 minutes. Arrange the unpeeled garlic cloves amongst the potatoes and season lightly. Sprinkle the lamb with half the seasoned breadcrumb mixture and leave to cook for a further 10 minutes, making 35 minutes in all. Turn the lamb over and sprinkle with the rest of the breadcrumbs. Stir the truffle slices into the potatoes with a wooden spatula and add 3 tablespoons cold water. Cook for another 10 minutes (making 45 minutes in all), then remove the lamb from the roasting pan, wrap it in foil and leave to rest for 10 minutes.

Reduce the oven temperature to 180°C/350°F/gas 4, add the asparagus to the potatoes, truffles and garlic and return the pan to the oven for 10 minutes.

SERVING

Arrange the mixture of vegetables around the edge of a serving platter, slice the leg of lamb and reassemble it on the platter. Serve at once.

NOTES

If fresh truffles are not in season, use top quality preserved truffles and add them to the potatoes only 5 minutes before you finish cooking them.

—————— · ——————

GIGOT D'AGNEAU DE PAUILLAC À NOTRE FAÇON

LA JEUNE DINDE
'IVRE D'ARMAGNAC'

Young turkey 'drunk on armagnac'

SERVES 8

PREPARATION TIME:
30 MINUTES, PLUS 24 HOURS
MARINATING

COOKING TIME: ABOUT 2 HOURS

INGREDIENTS

1 young turkey, about 2.8kg/
6¼lb

250g/9oz smoked belly of pork,
cut into 16 thin slices

400g/14oz carrots, finely diced

200g/7oz large onions, finely
diced

1 large bouquet garni

6 garlic cloves, peeled

strips of peel from 2 large oranges

1 bottle madiran red wine

4 tablespoons olive oil

100g/4oz butter

2 tablespoons sugar

50g/2oz flour

2 large pig's trotters, cooked and
each cut into 4 pieces

300ml/½pt armagnac

1 litre/1¾pt Chicken stock
(recipe page 15)

32 baby onions

32 button mushrooms

salt and freshly ground pepper

4 tablespoons chopped parsley

16 balls of pumpkin, cooked in
boiling salted water until tender,
to decorate

THIS RECIPE *was given to us the* chef-patron *of a restaurant in Landes, where the cooking is exquisitely refined and imaginative – a joy to those who taste it.*

PREPARING AND MARINATING THE TURKEY

The day before you cook the turkey, cut it into 16 pieces, using a large heavy knife. Lay the pieces on a flat surface and season with a few turns of pepper; you will not need salt, as the pork belly is already salty.

Roll each piece of turkey in a slice of pork belly and secure the ends with a wooden cocktail stick. Put the prepared turkey in a large bowl and cover with the diced carrots and onions, bouquet garni, garlic cloves, orange peel and the bottle of red wine.

COOKING THE TURKEY

The next day, drain the turkey pieces and pat dry with a cloth. Heat the olive oil in a frying pan until it begins to smoke, then put in the turkey and seal for 5 minutes on each side until golden.

Melt 50g/2oz butter in a cast-iron casserole and transfer the turkey from the frying pan to the casserole with a slotted spoon. Drain the diced carrots and onion and add them to the turkey. Sprinkle on the sugar and cook, stirring, until the vegetables are golden. Sprinkle on the flour and cook uncovered for 5 minutes, stirring with a wooden spatula.

Lay the pieces of pig's trotter on top of the turkey and vegetables, then pour over the armagnac and flame it briefly. Add the wine from the marinade, the bouquet garni, garlic and chicken stock. Bring to the boil, cover and simmer gently for 1¾ hours.

Thirty minutes before the end of cooking, sauté the baby onions and mushrooms in the remaining butter until golden and add them to the casserole. When the turkey is cooked, lift out the turkey pieces, pig's trotters, baby onions and mushrooms with a slotted spoon. Remove the cocktail sticks and keep everything warm. Discard the bouquet garni, pour the cooking liquid into a food processor or blender, with half the diced onions, carrots and orange peel and process to a smooth sauce.

SERVING

Put the turkey, pig's trotters and the remaining diced vegetables back into the casserole (or use a more sophisticated serving dish if you prefer). Pass the sauce through a muslin-lined conical sieve over the contents of the casserole and scatter on the baby onions and mushrooms. Sprinkle with chopped parsley, decorate with the pumpkin balls and serve.

SAUCE PÉRIGUEUX

Truffle and madeira sauce

THIS SAUCE WILL ADD A NOTE *of great festivity and richness to beef and lamb. You can use a fine dry white wine instead of madeira, but you will lose that special flavour which marries so well with the truffles.*

PREPARATION

Heat half the butter in a saucepan, then add the shallots and mushrooms and sweat for 2 minutes. Add the veal stock and reduce by half over a gentle heat. Pour in the madeira and cook gently for 5 minutes, then pass the sauce through a conical sieve and keep hot.

Peel the truffles and cut into small dice or thin rings. Heat the rest of the butter in a small saucepan, put in the truffles and sweat for 2 or 3 minutes.

Tip the truffles into the sauce, stir with a spatula and season to taste. Cover the pan and leave to infuse for several minutes.

SERVING

Coat the meat you are serving with the hot sauce, or serve it separately in a sauceboat.

NOTES

If truffles are not available, morels will do equally well.

SERVES 6

PREPARATION TIME:
10 MINUTES

COOKING TIME: ABOUT 1 HOUR

INGREDIENTS

50g/2oz butter

2 medium shallots, thinly sliced

125g/4oz button mushrooms, peeled or washed and thinly sliced

600ml/1pt Veal stock (recipe page 15)

100ml/3½fl oz top quality madeira

100g/4oz truffles, preferably fresh and raw

salt and freshly ground pepper

Morels are an acceptable substitute for truffles (and not so expensive!) in Sauce périgueux.

89

CÈPES À LA BORDELAISE

Ceps in olive oil, garlic and parsley

SERVES 6

PREPARATION TIME:
15 MINUTES

COOKING TIME: 30 MINUTES

INGREDIENTS

1kg/2lb 3oz ceps

50g/2oz butter

juice of 1 lemon

100ml/3½fl oz olive oil

2 garlic cloves, finely chopped

3 tablespoons chopped parsley

salt and freshly ground pepper

HAVING EATEN CEPS WITH ALL *manner of sauces, we firmly believe that this bordelaise method of cooking them is the best. Some people substitute shallots for the garlic or add fresh white breadcrumbs, but do try our simple recipe.*

PREPARATION

Peel and trim the ceps with a small sharp knife, then wipe with a damp cloth or wash quickly in cold water if necessary.

COOKING

Heat the butter and half the lemon juice in a shallow pan, add the ceps, cover and sweat gently for 5 minutes. Drain the ceps and carefully pat each one dry with kitchen paper. Slice them diagonally or leave whole, depending on their size.

Heat the olive oil in a frying pan or flameproof earthenware dish, put in the ceps and cook over high heat for 3 minutes. Lower the heat and simmer gently for 20 minutes. Season to taste.

SERVING

Just before serving, add the garlic and cook gently for 1 minute, then stir in the parsley and the remaining lemon juice. Tip this glorious panful of ceps into a vegetable dish and serve at once.

Ceps abound in this region, and during their season you should spoil yourself by making Cèpes à la bordelaise.

FICHAISES ou MERVEILLES ou OREILLETTES

Sweet fritters

THESE SWEET FRITTERS, *also known as 'marvels' or 'pillows' are rather like the famous Lyonnais* bugnes. *They are generally served at country festivals and are much enjoyed by young and old. They are extremely simple to make and are best eaten the day they are cooked.*

PREPARATION

The dough: Put the flour in a mixing bowl, make a well in the centre and put in all the other dough ingredients. Using a spatula, mix together very rapidly; the dough should not have too much body, but be fairly malleable. Wrap in greaseproof paper and refrigerate for about 1 hour.

On a lightly floured marble or wooden surface, roll out the dough as thinly as possible. Cut out shapes with pastry cutters.

COOKING

Heat the oil until very hot but not smoking (if it is too hot, it will dry out or discolour the fritters) and, using a fork, plunge in a few of the fritters and fry until puffy and golden. They will cook very quickly; the precise time will depend on the size and shape. Drain and place on kitchen paper or a cloth. Keep warm while you fry the remaining fritters in batches. Roll the cooked fritters in icing or caster sugar.

SERVING

Serve on a large dish lined with a doily or, better still, a linen napkin.

———— · ————

SERVES 6

PREPARATION TIME: 15–20 MINUTES, PLUS 1 HOUR CHILLING

COOKING TIME: 2–3 MINUTES

INGREDIENTS

DOUGH

500g/1lb 2oz flour

4 eggs

100g/4oz sugar

75g/3oz softened butter

5g/¾ teaspoon salt

250ml/9fl oz milk

a pinch of powdered vanilla

5g/1 teaspoon baking powder

1 teaspoon orange flower water

1 tablespoon armagnac

grated zest of ½ lemon

a pinch of flour, for dusting

oil for deep-frying

75g/3oz icing or caster sugar

TARTELETTES À L'ENCALAT

Rich curd tartlets from Encalat

SERVES 4

PREPARATION TIME:
35 MINUTES, PLUS 1½ HOURS
CURDLING

COOKING TIME: 20 MINUTES

INGREDIENTS

850ml/1½pt milk

½ coffee spoon rennet

½ coffee spoon white wine vinegar

1 egg

65g/2½oz sugar

15g/½oz flour, plus a pinch for dusting

25ml/1fl oz double cream

100g/4oz Brioche dough (recipe page 14)

30g/1oz butter, for greasing

EQUIPMENT

conical sieve lined with muslin

4 tartlet tins, 8cm/3½in diameter, 2cm/¾in deep

THIS DELICIOUS RECIPE IS FUN *to prepare and will keep for a day or two. It also freezes well, so we suggest that you make a batch of several tartlets, or perhaps one large tart. Strictly speaking, this dessert comes from a few kilometres away from Guyenne, but we like it so much that we decided to include it in this region.*

PREPARATION

The filling: In a saucepan, heat the milk to 37°C/98.6°F. Take off the heat, add the rennet and vinegar and immediately beat well with a whisk. Cover with a plate and leave at room temperature for 1½ hours until the milk has curdled.

Drain in a muslin-lined conical sieve to remove all the whey. Put the curds in a bowl and beat by hand or with an electric whisk at medium speed until smooth and creamy. Gradually beat in the egg, sugar, flour and finally the cream, beating the mixture until smooth between each ingredient.

Preheat the oven to 240°C/475°F/gas 10.

The brioche dough: Butter the tartlet tins and place on a baking sheet.

Divide the dough into 4. On a lightly floured marble or wooden surface, roll out one half of the dough as thinly as possible (about 3–4mm/⅛in) into a circle. Use it to line one of the tins, cutting off the excess dough with a sharp knife. Carefully pinch up the edges to make a frill above the edge of the tin. Repeat with the other pieces of dough. Place the tins in the fridge for a few minutes to firm up the dough.

COOKING

Pour the filling into the moulds, dividing it equally between them. Place immediately in the preheated oven and cook for 20 minutes. Carefully unmould the tartlets before they have cooled completely.

SERVING

Serve the tartlets at room temperature.

NOTES

When you take the tartlets out of the oven, they will have risen like soufflés. They will then collapse, but do not worry; this is normal and the taste is quite delicious.

Depending on the milk, you may find small granules, like grains of rice, in the curds. Do not worry if they will not dissolve; they have quite a pleasant texture.

———— · ————

TARTELETTES À L'ENCALAT

MILLAS LANDAIS

Maize cake

SERVES 8–10

PREPARATION TIME:
15 MINUTES

COOKING TIME: 1 HOUR 25
MINUTES

INGREDIENTS

350ml/12fl oz milk

90g/3oz maize or cornflour, sifted

160g/5½oz sugar, plus 20g/¾oz
for the egg whites

grated zest of 1 lemon

2 tablespoons rum

4 eggs, separated

20g/¾oz butter and a large pinch
of flour, for the tin

EQUIPMENT

1 cake tin, about 22cm/9in
diameter, 4cm/1½in deep

THIS CAKE FROM THE LANDES *is very easy to make, but its delightful, velvety smooth texture will please all your friends.*

PREPARATION

Preheat the oven to 180°C/350°F/gas 4.

The mould: Generously brush the cake tin with butter. Put in a pinch of flour and rotate the tin so that the flour covers the whole surface. Turn the tin upside down and tap the bottom to remove the excess flour.

The cake mixture: Warm the milk in a saucepan and beat in the maize or cornflour with a whisk. Add the sugar, lemon zest and most of the rum and cook very gently until the mixture is thick; do not let it boil.

Take the pan off the heat and add the egg yolks one at a time, beating well between each one to prevent them from cooking too quickly.

Beat the egg whites in an electric mixer until stiff, then whisk in the 20g/¾oz sugar until they hold firm peaks. Using a slotted or metal spoon, carefully fold the whites into the cake mixture; do not overwork. Pour the mixture into the tin.

COOKING

Put the tin in a bain-marie and cook in the preheated oven for 80–85 minutes. Remove from the oven and leave for a few minutes before unmoulding the cake. Place it the right way up on a cooling rack and sprinkle with the remaining rum.

SERVING

Place on a china cake stand and serve just warm.

NOTES

If the mixture should accidentally boil, take the pan off the heat and whisk vigorously. Leave to cool slightly, whisking all the time – but gently, so as not to destroy the texture. The mixture will become smooth and homogenous.

Guyenne

FRESHWATER FISH

Shad
Eel
Barbel
Pike
Carp
Sturgeon
Gudgeon
Lamprey
Perch
Salmon
Tench
Trout
Salmon trout

SHELLFISH, CRUSTACEANS, MOLLUSCS *and* BATRACHIANS

Scallops
Pink shrimps
Crayfish
Snails
Frogs
Arcachon oysters
Spiny lobsters
Mussels

SEA FISH

Cod
Whiting
Mullet
Skate
Sole
Tuna
Turbot

POULTRY

Duck
Capon
Turkey
Goose
Pigeon
Guinea fowl
Chicken

GAME

Woodcock
Quail
Vineyard thrushes
Wild rabbit
Hare
Larks
Ortolans
Wood pigeon
Partridge
Wild boar

MEAT

Lamb: salt marsh,
and from Rouergue
and Pauillac
Mutton: salt marsh,
and from Rouergue
and Pauillac
Beef from la Réole
and Medoc
Pork
Veal from la Réole
and Medoc

CHARCUTERIE

Confits of goose,
duck and pork
Stuffed goose neck
Foie gras:
terrines, tinned and
bottled, whole, mousse,
truffled or plain

Grattons de la Réole
(pork crackling)
Hams from Rouergue
Chicken pâté
with salsify
Pâté de grillon
from Perigord
Sausage from St Afrique
Tripe with saffron
from Cahors

VEGETABLES

Garlic
Artichokes
Asparagus
Aubergines
Mushrooms: boletus,
ceps, cultivated,
courcoules,chanterelles,
morels, oronges
Cabbage
Cucumber
Shallots
Gesse
(a type of chick pea)
Beans: white and green
Onions
Peas
Sorrel
Potatoes
Primeurs
(very young vegetables)
from Pessac
Black radish
Salsify
Scorzonera
Marmande tomatoes
Truffles from Bazas,
Périgord, Quercy
and Sarladais

CHEESE

Cabecou from
Rocamadour and
Rouergue
Cajassou from Cubjac

Fresh fromage blanc
from Rouergue
Ewe's and goat's cheese
from Rouergue and
Entraygues-sur-
Truyères
Goat cheeses
Languiole-Aubrac
Roquefort from
Rouergue

FRUIT

Apricots
Bigarreau cherries
Chestnuts
Strawberries from
Pessac
Melons from Rouergue
Hazelnuts
Walnuts
Vineyard peaches
William pears
Pink apples from
Bénauge
Plums from Agen
and Cahors
Prunes from Agen
and Cahors
Chasselas grapes
Grapes from Bas Quercy

PÂTISSERIE

Cajasse (sweet flan)
Agen crêpes
Fougasse
Agen prune tart
Jacques (crêpes with
bread and apples)
Macaroons from
St Emilion and
Bordeaux
Millas à la cudéry
from St Emilion
Néné
(aniseed cake from
St Afrique)

Tortillon de l'Agenois
Tourte Bazadaise
Tourteaux
(cornmeal crêpes)

CONFECTIONERY

Bouchons
(chestnut flour sweets)
Watermelon jam
Chocolate-stuffed dates
Fanchonnettes
bordelaises
(filled sweets)
Marrons glacés
Honey from la Réole,
Rouergue, the
Sauternais
Niniches
(soft caramel sweets)
Stuffed walnuts

MISCELLANEOUS PRODUCTS

Sturgeon caviar from
the Gironde
Walnut kernels
Tinned or bottled ceps,
foie gras, sardines
Plum eau-de-vie
Quince liqueur
Walnut oil

Pays Basque and Béarn

ANCIENT CULINARY TRADITIONS IN A LANDSCAPE
OF BREATHTAKING BEAUTY

I N OUR OPINION, this province, where the Basques wear red berets and the Béarnais black ones, is one of the most beautiful in France. On the Atlantic coast lies the Pays Basque, with its coastal scenery, the gulf of Gascony, the seemingly endless beach at Hendaye, the almost unreal port of St-Jean-de-Luz and the seductive elegance of Biarritz.

On the other side, stand the majestic Pyrenées, towering over the countryside of Béarn, a patchwork of delightful small plains, through which flow tributaries of the Adour, the Gave de Pau, the Gave d'Oloron, the Saison and the Nive. This is truly an idyllic area for nature-lovers.

The people are as proud of their tradition of hunting, fishing and vine growing as they are of their province. The villages have a curious, old-fashioned charm; nothing has changed here for hundreds of years. The mentality and attitudes of the locals is as unchanged as their architecture. In this part of France, friendship is not an empty word. Its genuine warmth makes one forget the damp climate, where an annual rainfall of up to 2m/6½ft has been recorded. Fortunately, the sudden downpours and storms do not last long and they keep the magnificent countryside green, while the sun does not confine itself to Biarritz – which is renowned as one of the sunniest cities in France.

We both love this part of France and have often visited it not only for professional reasons, but also for all too short summer holidays. It is a region of good eating. We have eaten more foie gras here than anywhere else, prepared in numerous delectable ways. But the region has other gastronomic delights to offer. Michel, who has a passion for honey, particularly remembers St-Pé-sur-Nivelle, where he stayed several years ago and sampled what he regards as the finest honey in France. And what could be more delicious than a *pipérade* or a fine local melon? There are wonderful red peppers which are laid out to dry in the sun before being stored for the winter. These are rubbed over hams, which are then rolled in local rock salt to produce that heavenly bayonne ham. You must also leave room for a piece of the famous Basque custard tart, advertised in every village. It is simple, but always very good.

In the autumn, when the hunting season begins, all other activities cease while the locals engage in the traditional sport of pigeon shooting. We like to eat pigeon and other local dishes washed down with a mellow red or white Jurançon wine. These wines can be dry or sweet; the grapes used are petit manseng and gros manseng. We also enjoy a Madiran, made from tannat, fer or cabernet grapes or a simple red Irouléguy, which is what the locals drink.

This picture-postcard village, nestling in its green valley, is just one of so many in the region. It makes us recall another age – a time of serenity, sincerity, friendship and all that is good in the world.

CHIPIRONS À LA GUIPUZCOANE

Baby squid with pimentos and white wine

SERVES 4

PREPARATION TIME:
30 MINUTES

COOKING TIME: ABOUT 1 HOUR

INGREDIENTS

1.25kg/2¾lb baby squid

4 tablespoons olive oil

200g/7oz onions, chopped

200ml/7fl oz dry white wine

1 bouquet garni

2 small dried chillies, crushed, or 1 teaspoon powdered pimento

4 garlic cloves, chopped

salt and freshly ground pepper

THE BASQUE PEOPLE *adore* chipirons *(baby squid) and cook them in all manner of ways, including stuffing the larger ones. They fish for squid mostly in the summer months, when they are young and tender. For this recipe, the squid should not be longer than about 10cm/4in, or they will have a firmer texture and will need longer cooking.*

PREPARATION

The squid: Pull out the quills from the body and keep every last drop of ink which runs out of the sacs. Wash the white parts very thoroughly in cold water and remove the thin membrane which covers the body and tentacles. Drain well and pat dry with kitchen paper. Cut the tentacles, fins and body into medium-sized pieces.

Cooking the onions: In a flameproof casserole, heat the oil and sweat the onions very gently for 15 minutes, stirring frequently with a wooden spatula, until very pale golden.

COOKING THE SQUID

Add the squid pieces to the onions and seal over medium heat for 2 minutes, stirring with a spatula. Add the wine, bouquet garni, chillies or pimentos, squid ink, garlic and 50ml/2fl oz water. Salt lightly, cover and cook gently for 1 hour, stirring every 20 minutes, until the squid are tender. Discard the bouquet garni and season the squid to taste. If the bouillon seems too liquid, strain and keep the squid warm to one side, reduce for several minutes and then thicken with 5g/1 teaspoon cornflour mixed with 1 teaspoon water. Take off the heat as soon as the bouillon boils.

SERVING

Place the squid in a deep dish and serve as hot as possible.

NOTES

Serve a separate dish of buttered broad beans with the squid; the contrast of colours and textures is delightful.

New season garlic in this part of the world will be flavoursome but not overpowering in Chipirons à la guipuzcoane.

～ PIPÉRADE ～

Scrambled eggs with tomatoes, peppers and onions

Mᴵᴄʜᴇʟ ᴏꜰᴛᴇɴ sᴇʀᴠᴇᴅ ᴛʜɪs ᴅɪsʜ *to Mlle Cécile de Rothschild in Paris; it was a great favourite of hers. It makes a good hors d'oeuvre or light summer lunch dish and is also delicious cold.*

SERVES 4

PREPARATION TIME:
35 MINUTES

COOKING TIME: 45 MINUTES

INGREDIENTS

4 thin slices of bayonne ham

250g/9oz onions, peeled and chopped

300g/11oz red or green peppers

4 tablespoons olive oil

2 garlic cloves, peeled and crushed

750g/1½lb very ripe tomatoes, peeled, deseeded and chopped

8 eggs

salt and freshly ground pepper

COOKING THE VEGETABLES

Trim off the fat from the edges of the ham and cut the fat into small dice. Put into a heavy pan with 3 tablespoons olive oil and heat gently. Immediately add the onions, cover the pan and sweat for 15 minutes.

Remove the stalks from the peppers, halve them lengthways and discard the white membrane and seeds. Finely dice the peppers and add them to the onions, together with the crushed garlic. Cover the pan and cook over low heat for 10 minutes, stirring every 5 minutes. Add the chopped tomatoes and cook, uncovered, for about 15 minutes, until their juices have evaporated. The vegetable mixture should be melting and soft but not liquid. Season to taste, transfer two-thirds of the vegetables to a saucepan and keep warm.

COOKING THE *PIPÉRADE*

Break the eggs into a bowl, season with salt and pepper, beat lightly with a fork and tip into the pan containing one-third of the vegetable mixture. Cook over low heat, stirring with a wooden spatula as though you were making scrambled eggs. As soon as the eggs start to set, add a tablespoon of olive oil. Stop cooking when the *pipérade* has the consistency of a creamy purée.

SERVING

Divide the *pipérade* between 4 deep plates and spoon the reserved vegetable mixture into the centre. Place the plates in a warm oven for 1 minute while you warm the ham for 30 seconds on a griddle or under the grill. Place a slice of ham in the middle of each plate and serve immediately.

NOTES

The vegetable mixture can be prepared and cooked a day or two in advance and reheated when you add the eggs; this can be very convenient when you are entertaining guests.

If you prefer, the peppers can be skinned before cooking.

——— · ———

FOIES DE VOLAILLES AUX RAISINS

FOIES DE VOLAILLES AUX RAISINS

Chicken or duck livers with grapes

THIS RICH, GENEROUS HORS D'OEUVRE *can also be served as a main course. Foie gras, of course, makes a mellower, more delicate dish (see note below). Either way, this dish is quite delectable.*

SERVES 4

PREPARATION TIME:
35 MINUTES, PLUS 1 HOUR
SOAKING THE LIVERS

COOKING TIME: 1½–2 MINUTES

PREPARATION

The livers: With a sharp knife, cut away all traces of greenish gall. Soak the livers in the milk for 1 hour.

The mushrooms: Peel, wipe with a damp cloth or wash in cold water if necessary. If they are large, cut into 2 or 3 pieces. Heat 30g/1oz butter in a frying pan and fry the mushrooms for 2 minutes. Drain in a colander set over a bowl to catch the cooking juices. Keep the juices.

The croûtons: Heat 80g/2½oz clarified butter in a frying pan and fry the bread until pale golden on both sides. Place on a wire rack.

COOKING THE LIVERS

Drain the livers well and pat dry. Heat the remaining clarified butter in a frying pan and sauté the livers for about 1½ minutes, until lightly coloured on all sides, but still very pink in the middle. Pour over the armagnac and flame it. Lift out the livers with a slotted spoon and place on a plate. Keep warm.

THE SAUCE

Pour off most of the fat from the pan. Pour in the veal stock and cooking juices from the mushrooms, reduce gently until syrupy, then add the cream and mushrooms. Cook for 3 minutes, then add the grapes and swirl in the remaining butter by shaking the pan gently. Season to taste with salt, pepper and nutmeg.

SERVING

Heat the oven to 160°C/310°F/gas 2–3.

Place 3 slices of fried bread on each plate, spoon the chicken livers over the bread and heat in the oven for 2 minutes. Pour over the sauce, mushrooms and grapes and serve at once.

NOTES

If you are using foie gras, do not soak it in milk. Prepare the sauce and garnish, then cut the raw foie gras into 1cm/¾in slices and, at the last minute, fry over high heat for 1 minute on each side. Serve as above.

——— · ———

INGREDIENTS

400g/14oz fine, large, pale pink chicken or duck livers, or 1 fresh duck foie gras, about 350g/12oz

500ml/18fl oz milk

150g/5oz button mushrooms

90g/3oz butter

120g/4½oz clarified butter

12 thin diagonal slices from a *baguette*

2 tablespoons armagnac or cognac

100ml/3½fl oz Veal stock (recipe page 15)

3 tablespoons double cream

150g/5oz grapes, preferably white, peeled and deseeded

a small pinch of nutmeg

salt and freshly ground pepper

TTORO

A rich fish stew

INGREDIENTS

SERVES 6
PREPARATION TIME: 1 HOUR
COOKING TIME: ABOUT 1 HOUR
10 MINUTES

INGREDIENTS
FUMET

2 heads of cod, hake or conger eel, split lengthways and soaked to remove all the blood

white part of 1 leek, finely sliced

2 medium onions, finely sliced

3 tablespoons olive oil

2 red peppers, deseeded and finely chopped

1 red chilli, deseeded and shredded, or a pinch of cayenne pepper

4 large tomatoes, peeled, deseeded and chopped

4 garlic cloves, peeled and crushed

1 large bouquet garni

a pinch of saffron

200ml/7fl oz dry white wine

12 thin slices of country bread

1 garlic clove

1.6kg/3½lb of mixed fish (use at least 2 of the following: gurnard, hake, monkfish, scorpion fish), cut into thick slices or chunks

60g/2oz flour

4 tablespoons olive oil

12 live or raw langoustines or large prawns

1kg/2lb 3oz mussels, scrubbed, debearded and washed

3 tablespoons chopped parsley

salt and freshly ground pepper

THIS FAMOUS BASQUE DISH *is a particular speciality of the area around Saint-Jean-de-Luz. Originally a simple, fishermen's staple dish of cod and vegetables, it has now become more sophisticated with the addition of langoustines and sometimes crayfish. This rich stew somewhat resembles a* bouillabaisse *from the Côte d'Azur. It is a complete meal in itself, being both hors d'oeuvre and main course. Everyone will enjoy it, but do beware of the bones.*

PREPARATION

The fumet: In a flameproof casserole or dutch oven, sweat the fish heads, leek and onions in the oil for 5 minutes, stirring occasionally. Add the red peppers, chilli or cayenne, tomatoes, garlic, bouquet garni and saffron. Pour in the wine and simmer for 5 minutes, stirring with a spatula, then add 1.75 litres/3pt water. Bring to the boil, skimming the surface from time to time, then lower the heat and simmer gently for 45 minutes. Remove the bouquet garni and pass the *fumet* through a conical sieve into a saucepan, rubbing the fish and vegetables with the back of a ladle to extract as much flavour as possible. Keep hot.
The croûtons: Toast the bread in the oven until dry and golden, then rub with the garlic dipped in a little salt. Place in a serving dish.

COOKING THE FISH AND SHELLFISH AND SERVING

Pat the fish dry and dip in seasoned flour. In a frying pan, heat the olive oil and fry the fish for 1½ minutes on each side until lightly coloured, but still only half-cooked. Arrange the fish in a deep serving dish and lay the langoustines or prawns on top, then the mussels. Pour over the hot *fumet*, place the dish in a medium oven or over high heat and bring to the boil. As soon as the mussels have fully opened (this will take about 5–7 minutes), sprinkle the *ttoro* with parsley and serve it straight from the dish. Serve the croûtons separately.

Red peppers are everywhere here, both growing in gardens and on the market stalls. We adore them, especially in Ttoro.

TTORO

THON AUX OIGNONS

THON AUX OIGNONS

Fresh tuna with onions

TRY TO FIND WHITE-FLESHED *tuna, as the red-fleshed variety is a little too dry for this recipe. Baby broad beans, skinned and sweated in butter for 2 minutes with a julienne of sorrel make a heavenly accompaniment to this dish.*

COOKING

The onions: Warm the olive oil in a flameproof casserole, add the onions, cover tightly and sweat over very low heat for 40 minutes, without lifting the lid, so that the onions cook in their own juices. Add the vinegar, thyme and garlic and season with salt and pepper.

The tuna: Remove any scales, wipe the skin and bury the tuna in the onions. Replace the casserole lid and cook for 15–20 minutes over very gentle heat. Sprinkle with parsley.

SERVING

Serve the tuna and onions straight from the casserole, carefully removing the skin from the fish as you serve it.

SERVES 6

PREPARATION TIME: 15 MINUTES

COOKING TIME: 60–65 MINUTES

INGREDIENTS

1 thick slice of tuna, preferably white-fleshed, weighing about 1kg/2lb 3oz

2 tablespoons olive oil

1kg/2lb 3oz onions, thinly sliced

1 tablespoon aged wine vinegar

1 sprig of lemon thyme, chopped

2 garlic cloves, crushed

1 tablespoon flat-leaved parsley

salt and freshly ground pepper

You may have to visit more than one fish shop to find the perfect tuna for Thon aux oignons, *but believe us, it will be worth it!*

105

⟶ LOTTE À LA BASQUAISE ⟵

Monkfish with peppers, onions and tomatoes

SERVES 4

PREPARATION TIME:
40 MINUTES

COOKING TIME: 18 MINUTES

INGREDIENTS

8 monkfish cutlets,
1.5cm/½–¾in thick (about 120g/
4oz each)

300g/11oz onions, finely sliced

100ml/3½fl oz olive oil

800g/1¾lb beef tomatoes, e.g.
Marmande peeled, deseeded and
chopped

300g/11oz mixed green, red and
yellow peppers

1 sprig of lemon thyme

4 garlic cloves, peeled and cut
into slivers

salt and freshly ground pepper

THIS SIMPLE DISH IS EASY TO PREPARE *and tastes delicious. Try to find large monkfish cutlets (about 10cm/4in diameter) cut from the middle of the tail. Swiss chard cooked* à la meunière *goes well with this dish.*

PREPARATION

The onions and tomatoes: Put the onions and half the oil in a cassserole, cover and sweat over very low heat for 40 minutes. Add the tomatoes, season, stir gently with a wooden spatula and cook gently for a further 20 minutes.

The peppers: Remove the stalks, halve the peppers lengthways and discard the white membrane and seeds. Cut the peppers into large julienne. Sauté quickly in a frying pan with a little olive oil until half-cooked. Add the thyme and drain immediately.

COOKING THE MONKFISH

Heat the oven to 220°C/425°F/gas 7.

Season the monkfish. Pour the remaining olive oil into a frying pan and cook the monkfish slices for 3 minutes on each side, until pale golden. Arrange the monkfish in a serving dish, toss the garlic into the hot oil from the fish and cook until pale golden. Lift out the garlic with a slotted spoon and sprinkle it over the fish. Scatter over the strips of pepper and place in the preheated oven for 10 minutes.

SERVING

Spread the softened onions and tomatoes (which should be piping hot) over the bottom of the serving dish, put in the monkfish and arrange the three different coloured peppers on top.

*These young, tender swiss chard
are the ideal accompaniment for
the* Lotte à la Basquaise.

CONFIT DE CANARD

Duck preserved in its own fat

OTHER MEATS CAN BE PRESERVED *in exactly the same way – goose, rabbit, pork, turkey and boiling fowl. Indeed, fifty years ago, it was the custom for country people to make assorted* confits *and swap the pots, just as some people do today with jams.*

PREPARATION

Cut off the duck breasts and legs from the carcass. Freeze the carcass for stock or to use in another recipe.

Salting the duck meat: Using your fingertips, rub each piece of duck with coarse salt for about 15 seconds. Do not use more salt than you need. Gently shake off the excess. Put the duck pieces in a bowl, cover with a dry cloth and leave in a dry place for 36 hours.

COOKING THE *CONFIT*

In a copper casserole, gently melt the lard and duck fat with 100ml/3½fl oz water. As soon as they have melted, add the muslin bag of aromatics.

Rinse the duck pieces in lukewarm running water, then pat dry very thoroughly. Put them into the melted fat and cook at a steady 80°–90°C/175°–195°F for 1 hour 20 minutes, turning the duck with a spatula at least twice and skimming the surface whenever necessary.

To check if the duck is cooked, insert a trussing needle into the flesh; the juices should run out clear. If they are pink, cook the duck for a little longer. The precise cooking time will depend on the thickness of the duck pieces.

POTTING THE *CONFIT*

Rub the inside of a stoneware pot with the garlic clove. Put a good pinch of coarse salt in the bottom of the pot. Arrange the pieces of hot cooked duck on the salt, then pour the fat through a conical sieve over the duck. Leave to cool in a dry place.

As soon as the fat has started to set, sprinkle on the crushed peppercorns and lay a piece of greaseproof paper directly on the fat. Leave the *confit* in the cellar or refrigerate it at 10°–12°C/50°–54°F for at least 2 months before eating it.

NOTES

The *confit* is delicious reheated in its fat. Serve it with sautéed potatoes and a well-seasoned salad.

———— • ————

SERVES 4

PREPARATION TIME:
20 MINUTES, PLUS 36 HOURS
SALTING

COOKING TIME: ABOUT 1 HOUR
20 MINUTES

INGREDIENTS

1 duck, about 2kg/4½lb

50g/2oz coarse salt

500g/1lb 2oz lard

1kg/2lb 3oz duck fat

1 garlic clove, peeled, for the stoneware pot

10 peppercorns, crushed, for topping the cooked *confit*

AROMATICS

all tied together in a muslin bag,
3 cloves; 10 peppercorns, crushed;
2 unpeeled garlic cloves; ½
cinnamon stick, broken into
pieces; a pinch of nutmeg

EQUIPMENT

1 copper casserole

1 stoneware pot

cooking thermometer (optional)

SALMIS DE PALOMBES

Wood pigeon in red wine with bayonne ham

SERVES 4

PREPARATION TIME:
50 MINUTES

COOKING TIME: 20–25 MINUTES

INGREDIENTS

4 wood pigeons,
300–350g/11–12oz each

6 tablespoons olive oil

2 tablespoons armagnac

500ml/18fl oz red bordeaux

500ml/18fl oz Veal stock (recipe page 15)

1 bouquet garni

40 baby onions

300g/11oz ceps, preferably fresh, or bottled

150g/5oz bayonne ham, or top quality raw ham, cut into small sticks

80g/3oz clarified butter

8 thin slices cut from a *baguette*

salt and freshly ground pepper

BOTH ALBERT AND MICHEL *are crazy about this delectable dish. Serve it with a few French beans or some spinach – 'c'est tout . . . et c'est suffisant' ('that's all and that's enough').*

THE PIGEONS

Preheat the oven to 240°C/475°F/gas 9.

Draw the pigeons, remove the wishbones and truss the birds. Heat 2 tablespoons olive oil in a roasting pan, put in the pigeons and seal on all sides until pale golden. Cook in the preheated oven for 15 minutes; the breasts should still be slightly pink.

Place the pigeons on a plate, breast-side down and leave to rest for 10 minutes. Remove the legs, then the breasts. Divide the legs into thighs and drumsticks, keep the thighs and breasts warm and roughly chop the carcasses and drumsticks.

THE SAUCE

Put the carcasses and drumsticks into the roasting pan and place in the oven for about 10 minutes, until lightly browned. Immediately pour in the armagnac, then the red wine. Set over high heat, bring to the boil, then tip into a saucepan and reduce by one-third. Add the veal stock and bouquet garni, simmer for 45 minutes, then pass through a conical sieve. Reduce the sauce until half syrupy, season with a little salt and plenty of pepper, cover and keep warm.

THE GARNISH

The onions: Peel and wipe. Heat 1 tablespoon olive oil in a sauté pan and cook the onions until soft and pale golden.

The ceps: Peel, wipe and cut into small pieces. Heat 2 tablespoons olive oil in a frying pan and sauté the ceps for 3 minutes, then drain.

The ham: In the pan in which you cooked the ceps, heat 1 tablespoon olive oil and sauté the ham over high heat for 1 minute. Drain and put with the ceps.

The croûtons: In a frying pan heat the clarified butter over medium heat, and fry the bread until golden on both sides, then place on a wire rack.

SERVING

Preheat the oven to 180°C/350°F/gas 4.

Arrange the pigeon breasts in a serving dish and place in the oven for 5–7 minutes. Meanwhile, simmer the thighs in the sauce for 5 minutes. 2 minutes before serving, add the ceps, onions and ham to the sauce. As soon as it begins to bubble, pour everything over the pigeon breasts and scatter on the croûtons.

Serve very hot.

SALMIS DE PALOMBES

GARBURE BÉARNAISE

Vegetable soup with preserved goose and haricot beans

SERVES 6
PREPARATION TIME:
45 MINUTES
COOKING TIME:
ABOUT 2½ HOURS

INGREDIENTS

250g/9oz raw ham on the bone, or, failing that, 150g/5oz boned raw ham

400g/14oz semi-salted shoulder of pork

300g/11oz fresh shelled white haricot beans, or dried white haricot beans, pre-soaked for 6 hours

1 large bouquet garni, including a stick of celery

2 medium onions, each stuck with 2 cloves

400g/14oz potatoes

200g/7oz carrots

200g/7oz leeks

1 small white or green cabbage

100g/4oz turnips

1 red or green pepper

3 garlic cloves, crushed and chopped

12 chestnuts

500g/1lb 2oz preserved goose (*Confit de canard* page 107)

100g/4oz goose or duck fat

6 slices of country bread

salt and freshly ground pepper

IT IS THE CUSTOM OF THE REGION *to serve the broth poured over toasted bread. The locals like to start with a little red wine in their bowls as well. This is known as making a* goudale. *You can use any seasonal vegetables for the* garbure. *Some people like to grate gruyère over the vegetables and brown the top under the grill, but we prefer to serve the vegetables plain, enriched with a little goose fat.*

PREPARATION
The raw ham and shoulder of pork: Place in a saucepan, cover with cold water, bring to the boil and blanch for 5 minutes. Refresh in cold water, then put into a pot large enough to take all the meats and vegetables.

COOKING
Generously cover the ham and pork with cold water. Add the haricot beans and bring to the boil over high heat. Reduce to a simmer, skim, then add the bouquet garni and onions and cook for 30 minutes.
The potatoes, carrots and leeks: Peel, wash and cut into large cubes. Add to the beans after 30 minutes' cooking and cook for a further 20 minutes.
The cabbage, turnips and red or green pepper: Quarter the cabbage, cut off the rounded edges and cut the rest into thick strips. Peel the turnips and cut into quarters. Cut off the stalk end of the pepper, halve it horizontally and discard the white membrane and seeds. Slice the pepper and add it to the *garbure*, together with the cabbage, turnips and the chopped garlic.
The chestnuts: Make a slight incision in the skin with a knife and grill lightly, then peel and add them to the soup. Continue to cook the soup gently until all the vegetables are almost overcooked. Bury the preserved goose in the vegetables and simmer for 5 or 10 minutes.

SERVING
Using a slotted spoon, remove the bouquet garni and onions. Drain the vegetables, reserving the cooking broth, and pile them pell-mell into a deep heatproof dish. Spread the goose fat over the top and heat in the oven at 180°C/350°F/gas 4 for about 20 minutes, until you are ready to serve the soup.

Slice or cut up the meats, arrange them in another dish and keep warm. Lightly toast the bread in the oven and place on a plate. Season the broth with salt and pepper and serve it separately.

Set out on the table the dishes of soup, meats, vegetables and bread and leave everyone to help themselves. Remember that you will need soup plates deep enough to hold this great bounty of ingredients.

———— · ————

POIS CHICHES AU LARD ET
AUX PIMENTS DOUX

Chick peas with bacon and peppers

C HICK PEAS ARE A POPULAR VEGETABLE *in this region and are often served as an hors d'oeuvre. You can add some Toulouse sausages at the end of the cooking time to transform this dish into a main course.*

SERVES 8

PREPARATION TIME:
30 MINUTES, PLUS 6–8 HOURS
SOAKING

COOKING TIME: 2½ HOURS

PREPARATION

The chick peas: Soak in cold water for 6–8 hours, unless they are new crop, in which case 2 hours will be enough. Rinse and drain, then place in a flameproof casserole with the pork rind, bouquet garni, carrots, onion, garlic and bicarbonate of soda and cover with cold water. Bring to the boil over medium heat, then simmer gently for 1 hour, skimming the surface whenever necessary and adding a little more hot water if required.

The peppers: Brush with a tablespoon of oil, then place under a hot grill, turning occasionally, until they blacken and blister all over. Hold under cold running water and rub off the skin with your fingers, then carefully rinse the peppers. Halve lengthways, remove the white membrane and seeds, cut the flesh into large lozenge shapes and place in a bowl.

The bacon: When the chick peas have been cooking for 1 hour, add the *lardons*, cover the casserole and simmer for another 30 minutes. Add the peppers, cover and simmer for 1 hour more. Check that the chick peas are now tender.

SERVING

Discard the bouquet garni, carrots, onion and pork rind and stir in the remaining olive oil. Season to taste and serve the chick peas straight from the casserole or in a pottery dish.

INGREDIENTS

250g/9oz chick peas

150g/5oz fresh pork rind, rolled into a sausage shape and tied with string

1 bouquet garni

2 carrots, peeled

1 medium onion, peeled and stuck with 2 cloves

2 garlic cloves, peeled and crushed

a small pinch of bicarbonate of soda

2 red or green peppers

3 tablespoons olive oil

200g/7oz semi-salted streaky bacon, blanched and cut into *lardons*

salt and freshly ground pepper

New blue turnips can almost be eaten raw, but their flavour and colour are best when cooked in Garbure béarnaise.

GÂTEAU BASQUE

A custard tart from the Pays Basque

SERVES 8

PREPARATION TIME:
20 MINUTES

COOKING TIME: 45 MINUTES

INGREDIENTS

160g/5½oz butter, at room temperature

160g/5½oz sugar

2 eggs

240g/9oz flour

5g/1 teaspoon baking powder

1 coffee spoon orange flower water

200ml/7fl oz *Crème Pâtissière*, well flavoured with vanilla or 3 tablespoons rum (recipe page 17)

eggwash (1 egg yolk mixed with 1 tablespoon milk), to glaze

20g/¾oz softened butter and 20g/¾oz flour, for the tin

EQUIPMENT

1 cake tin, about 18cm/7in diameter, 5cm/2in deep

piping bag with a plain 6mm/⅝in nozzle

THIS TART IS BEST EATEN *within 24 hours. It makes a most delicious summer dessert, which can be enjoyed at any time of day.*

THE MIXTURE

Using a bowl and whisk or an electric mixer, beat 160g/5½oz of the butter until smooth. Add the sugar and beat for 3 minutes. Still beating, add first one egg, then the other and finally beat in the flour, baking powder and orange flower water. The mixture should be very smooth.

Preheat the oven to 200°C/400°F/gas 6.

MOULDING AND COOKING

Butter the inside of the cake tin and sprinkle with flour. Turn over the tin and tap out the excess flour.

Fill the piping bag with some of the mixture. Starting from the outside and working inwards, pipe the mixture into a spiral so that the bottom of the tin is entirely covered, with no gaps between the spirals.

Carefully spoon the *crème pâtissière* into the centre of the tin. Spread it out slightly, but leave at least 2cm/¾in uncovered all round the edge of the tin. Continue to pipe spirals from the outside inwards, piping one on top of the other so that the *crème pâtissière* is completely enclosed on all sides by the mixture.

Brush the top of the tart with eggwash and cook in the preheated oven for 45 minutes. Leave to cool, then unmould on to a wire rack.

SERVING

Serve the tart on a dish, accompanied if you wish by some home-made jam or, better still, redcurrant jelly.

NOTES

If you like, you can decorate the top of the tart just before cooking. Glaze with eggwash, then score a lattice pattern with a fork.

———— · ————

GÂTEAU BASQUE

CROUSTADE AUX POMMES

Flaky apple tart

SERVES 6

PREPARATION TIME:
45 MINUTES, PLUS 1½ HOURS
RESTING

COOKING TIME: 20–25 MINUTES

INGREDIENTS

THE PASTRY

250g/9oz superfine pastry flour,
plus a pinch for dusting

1 egg

100ml/3½fl oz lukewarm water

2 tablespoons groundnut oil

a pinch of salt

butter, for greasing

FILLING

100g/4oz melted butter

150g/5oz sugar

3 medium dessert apples
(preferably coxes), peeled,
quartered and very thinly sliced

2 tablespoons armagnac

EQUIPMENT

1 cast-iron frying pan or a
22cm/9in flan tin

THIS WONDERFUL, FEATHERLIGHT *apple tart actually originates from Gascony or, more precisely, the Gers, but since that region is not included in this book, we decided to slip it into the Pays Basque area, which is very close by.*

PREPARATION

The pastry: Put the flour in a bowl and make a well in the centre. Put in the rest of the pastry ingredients and, using the fingertips of one hand, gradually draw the flour into the centre, working the mixture with the fingertips of your other hand until you have a smooth, fairly soft dough. Hit the dough in the bowl for 1–2 minutes with your fist to make it smooth and give it a bit of body. Roll it into a ball, cover with a damp cloth and leave in a cold place for 1½ hours.

ROLLING OUT THE PASTRY BASE

Using a heavy knife, cut the dough into 2 equal pieces. Lay a smooth, dry cloth on your work surface and flour it very lightly. Put one piece of dough on the cloth and start to stretch it outwards with your fingertips, taking care not to tear the dough. (It is easier to do this operation with two people – four hands are better than two!) The dough should be stretched so thin that you can see through it. Leave it in a dry place on an immaculately clean surface while you repeat the operation with the second piece of dough. Leave both pieces to dry out slightly for 5–10 minutes

Dip a pastry brush into the melted butter and sprinkle droplets of butter over the surface of the pastry. Scatter over 120g/4oz sugar, then cut out three 22cm/9in circles from each piece of pastry. Keep the trimmings.

ASSEMBLING THE *CROUSTADE*

Preheat the oven to 230°C/450°F/gas 8.

Grease the frying pan or flan tin with butter and loosely lay 3 pastry circles one on top of the other in the bottom, without pressing them down. Arrange the sliced apples on the pastry and moisten with armagnac, then sprinkle with the remaining sugar. Layer the 3 remaining pastry circles on top of the apples and scatter the pastry trimmings randomly over the surface.

COOKING

Bake the *croustade* in the preheated oven for 20–25 minutes, until it is a delicate nutty brown, then use a palette knife to slide it on to a wire rack.

SERVING

Serve the *croustade* just warm; it will be wonderfully succulent. Give your guests a serrated knife and let them help themselves.

————— • —————

Pays Basque and Béarn

FRESHWATER FISH

Shad
Eel
Chevine
Lamprey
Minnows
Pike
Salmon
Trout

SEA FISH

Anchovies
Brill
Cod
Hake
Bream
Loubine and mulet
(grey mullet)
Red mullet
Whiting
Sardines
Sole
Tuna

SHELLFISH
and
CRUSTACEANS

Spider crab
Squid
Shrimps
Crayfish
Lobster
Oysters
Spiny crayfish
Dublin Bay prawns
Cuttlefish
Tourteaux (large crabs)

POULTRY

Duck
Goose
Chicken

GAME

Quail
Wild duck
Gélinotte des Pyrénées
(hazel grouse; very rare)
Thrushes
Hare
Marcassin and sanglier
(wild boar)
Pigeon and wood pigeon
Partridge
Venison

MEAT

Beef
Mutton
Pork
Veal

CHARCUTERIE

Andouille
Cherimous
(residue from pig's livers
and confits)
Confits
(preserved goose,
duck and pork)
Confit of sausage
from Béarn
Bayonne ham
(Orthez is the
best known)
Smoked tongue
from Bayonne
Pepper sausage
Basque sausage
Tripotcha
(herb-flavoured
tripe sausage)

VEGETABLES

Aubergines
Artichokes
Chard
Cabbage
Beans: broad, red or
white kidney, green
Sweetcorn
Mushrooms: morels,
oronges, ceps
Onions
Sorrel
Peppers: green, red
and yellow
Pimentoes
Chick peas
Salsify
Tomatoes

CHEESE

Sheep's cheese
from Bayonne
Fromage d'Urt
(a type of Port Salut)

FRUIT

Apples
Apricots
Almonds
Cherries
Chestnuts
Figs
Melons
Hazelnuts
Walnuts
Peaches
Pears

PÂTISSERIE

Cream choux buns
from Pau
Crespets
(fritters from Béarn)
Basque flan
Chocolate galettes
from Béarn
Macaroons from Orthez
and St Jean de Luz
Milhassou
(sweet maize flan
with orgeat syrup)
Pastiza (Basque cake)
Rousquille d'Oloron
(dry cake)

CONFECTIONERY

Chocolate from
Bayonne
Stuffed walnuts
from Ciboure
Pastis from Béarn
Touron (almond paste)
Honey from St-Pée-
sur-Nivelle

MISCELLANEOUS PRODUCTS

Eau-de-vie from
the Pyrenées
Basque cider
(the oldest in Europe)
Izarra
(Basque liqueur)

115

Île de France

THE GASTRONOMIC CENTRE OF FRANCE, ENJOYING
A VARIETY OF GLITTERING AND SOPHISTICATED DISHES

THE ÎLE DE FRANCE represents and pays homage to all the provinces and tastes of France, for many people have left their native provinces and gathered in this cosmopolitan city, lured by its glittering lights. All too often, unfortunately, the pure characteristics of their region have been diffused and, where cooking is concerned, the regional character has been lost to accommodate a wider market. Thus in our view, the delicate artifice of luxurious Parisian restaurants has become a shade too contrived and over-elaborate and the experience of sophisticated eating now depends much more upon presentation than upon the taste of the food.

Paris is the economic and intellectual centre of France. It is also the centre of philosophical, literary, scientific and artistic life and of so-called classic *cuisine*.

Over the years, the countryside and gardens around Paris and the suburbs, which were its most charming features, have been eroded and pushed further and further out. Tractors, excavators and concrete mixers have transformed these open spaces into little boxy towns. Many smallholdings have disappeared, too, and with them, a large number of market gardens. Only thirty years ago, the markets were full of asparagus from Argenteuil, peas from Clamart, carrots from Crécy, beans from Soisson, flageolets from Arpajon, peaches from Montreuil and cherries from Montmorency, but, alas! over half these products have now disappeared although fortunately, in this area of rich soil, a few market gardens do still continue to flourish today.

Although the towns still nibble away at the countryside, the climate favours all sorts of cultivation. The annual rainfall is only 60cm/23½in, but it does rain often, in short showers. There are snow flurries every winter, but the snow vanishes as quickly as it appears and, on the whole, the region around Paris does not suffer extremes of temperature.

At the age of seven, Michel arrived in St-Mandé, where he spent the rest of his childhood. Thursday and Saturday were market days, full of excitement. Michel adored meandering through the market and hearing the traders loudly hawking their wares, especially at the end of the day; he loved the whole atmosphere of a market town.

At fourteen, Albert began his apprenticeship in pâtisserie at St-Mandé and Michel followed in his footsteps five years later, at Belleville. Thus we learnt to rise at dawn, for in France, bakers and pâtissiers start work at 4 o'clock each morning to prepare the dozens of different kinds of breads and pastries which are unique to our country.

At the weekend, our classmates would dress in all their finery and head for the famous suburban cafés to drink and dance. These cafés were scattered all along the Seine, the Dise and the Marne, the favourites being at Joinville le Pont and Meudon. They served delicious fried fish, which the patron or his wife had caught in the river that very morning. We bitterly resented working at weekends, because we could hardly ever join our friends as they danced to tunes played on the accordion.

In 1961, Michel went to work for Mlle Cécile de Rothschild at in Paris. His years of service with her were the most rewarding and interesting of his life. When she was not entertaining guests, she liked to treat herself to 'caretaker's food' – her name for simple but delicious home cooking. Whether it was vegetable soup or stew, the smells which wafted out of her caretaker's lodge at mealtimes were certainly delectable. Michel had to re-create these good smells in the dishes he prepared – which, of course, is easier said than done!

In spring and summer, he would set off in his 2CV to cook for his employer at her country estate at Noisy-sur-Oise, about 20 kilometres from Paris. From this estate, perched high on a hill, Michel could admire the calm, serene river Oise, dotted with fishermen and the occasional passing barge. He could shop for food in the markets at either Chantilly or Senlis; here he found, among much else, superb boxes of watercress from Villers Coteret. In those days, most of the produce he bought for his employer came from local farms – turnips, carrots, asparagus and cauliflowers.

Albert loves buying the fruit, vegetables and fish for our restaurants. He recaptures a little of the past, on a huge scale, whenever he visits the market at Rungis, the 'stomach of France'. Here, one finds without doubt the greatest and finest variety of produce in the world. The market is served and linked by a motorway, an airport and a railway.

So often, our memories lead us inexorably back to Paris, where Albert spent ten years of his life and Michel twice that. That is why the Île de France will always be magical to us.

Even the humble loaf plays a spectacular role in this baker's window – in such shapes it is pure fantasy.

⤙ POTAGE SAINT-GERMAIN ⤚

Pea soup

SERVES 4
PREPARATION TIME:
15 MINUTES
COOKING TIME: 20 MINUTES

INGREDIENTS

500g/1lb 2oz fresh peas in the pod

30g/1oz butter

100g/4oz potatoes

1 litre/1¾pt Chicken stock
(recipe page 15) or water

2 slices of white bread

60g/2oz clarified butter

3 tablespoons double cream,
lightly whipped

salt and freshly ground pepper

Tᴴɪꜱ ᴘᴏᴘᴜʟᴀʀ ꜱᴏᴜᴘ *comes originally from the Paris area. It is particularly delicious when fresh peas are in season. Like a fine watercress soup, its strength lies in its simplicity and delicacy; this is one of our favourite soups.*

PREPARATION

The peas: Shell them and blanch in boiling water. Refresh, drain and reserve about 30 of the smallest peas for the garnish. Keep these in a separate bowl.

COOKING

Put the peas for the soup in a saucepan and sweat with the butter for 2 minutes. Peel and quarter the potatoes, wash and add them to the peas together with the chicken stock or water. Cook briskly for 20 minutes.

Pour the contents of the pan into a food processor or blender and purée the mixture for 2 minutes, then pass the soup through a conical sieve. Season to taste and keep hot.

The croûtons: Cut the crusts off the bread and cut the bread into small cubes. Heat the clarified butter in a frying pan over medium heat and fry the croûtons until golden. Drain and place on kitchen paper.

SERVING

Divide the blanched peas for the garnish between 4 soup plates, then pour over the hot soup. Spoon some lightly whipped cream into the centre of each plate and scatter over the croûtons. Serve at once.

———— · ————

COQUILLES SAINT JACQUES ⤙ À LA PARISIENNE ⤚

Scallops with mushrooms and cream

SERVES 4
PREPARATION TIME:
55 MINUTES
COOKING TIME: 7–10 MINUTES

Tᴴɪꜱ ᴅɪꜱʜ ʀᴇᴍɪɴᴅꜱ ᴍɪᴄʜᴇʟ *of his days as an apprentice pâtissier at the Pâtisserie Loyal in Paris. Every week, he would make a regular trip on the métro to les Halles to buy 20 kilo sacks of scallops and baskets of mushrooms to make the immensely popular* coquilles St Jacques.

PREPARATION

The scallops: Scrub the shells with a brush under cold running water. Lay the scallops on a hotplate or place in a hot oven for 1–2 minutes, until they begin to open slightly. Slide the blade of a filleting knife between the flat shell and the scallop and lift off the shell. Slide the knife blade between the scallop and the concave shell to detach the scallop and coral. Keep the 4 best concave shells for serving, brush them under cold water and dry them out in a very slow oven.

Peel off the membrane surrounding the scallops, then separate the whites and corals and wash them gently in cold water to eliminate any grains of sand. Drain and keep in a bowl.

The mushrooms: Scrape the stalks with a small knife and wash the mushrooms or wipe them with a damp cloth. Slice thinly, leaving the caps and tails attached.

(recipe ingredients overleaf)

COQUILLES SAINT JACQUES À LA PARISIENNE

INGREDIENTS

12 scallops in the shell

200g/7oz button mushrooms

300g/11oz medium baking potatoes

4 egg yolks

130g/5oz butter

juice of ½ lemon

500ml/18fl oz Fish stock (recipe page 14)

30g/1oz flour

200ml/7fl oz double cream

15g/½oz finely grated gruyère

15g/½oz fine breadcrumbs

salt and freshly ground white pepper

EQUIPMENT

piping bag with a large ridged nozzle

Preheat the oven to 220°C/425°F/gas 7.

The duchesse potatoes: Brush under cold running water and prick in 2 or 3 places with the point of a knife. Place on a baking sheet and bake in their jackets for 35–40 minutes, or until soft.

Slide the point of a knife into the centre of the potatoes to check they are cooked, then halve them, scoop out the pulp with a spoon and rub it through a hard sieve into a bowl. Add 2 egg yolks and 30g/1oz butter and work with a wooden spatula until smooth. Season lightly with salt and pepper. Fill a piping bag with this mixture and pipe an attractive ribbon of potato around the edge of each concave scallop shell.

COOKING THE SCALLOPS AND MUSHROOMS

Put the scallops, corals, mushrooms and lemon juice in a saucepan with the fish stock, set over low heat and slowly bring to the boil. Lower the heat and simmer very gently at about 90°C/195°F for another minute. Keep the scallops and mushrooms in the stock at room temperature.

THE SAUCE

Melt 50g/2oz butter in a saucepan, stir in the flour and cook for 2 minutes to make a roux. Take the pan off the heat and strain in the stock from the scallops and mushrooms through a conical sieve, stirring all the time. Leave the sauce to simmer gently for 20 minutes, whisking it frequently.

In a bowl, mix the remaining egg yolks with the cream, then pour this mixture into the sauce. Before it begins to bubble, take the pan off the heat, season the sauce with salt and pepper and keep hot.

ASSEMBLING THE *COQUILLES ST JACQUES*

Increase the oven temperature to 240°C/475°F/gas 9.

Cut the scallop whites into thick slices. Place a layer of mushrooms in each shell, top with the corals and finish with a layer of scallop whites. Cover generously with sauce and sprinkle the top with a mixture of gruyère and breadcrumbs. Melt the remaining butter and pour it over the top of the sauce.

BROWNING AND SERVING

Brown the scallops in the hot oven for 3–5 minutes, until the top of the sauce is lightly glazed and the potato border pale golden. Serve immediately and do not forget to warn your guests that the dish is extremely hot!

NOTES

The scallops can be prepared up to the browning stage the previous day and kept in the fridge. In this case, brown them in a cooler oven (220°C/425°F/gas 7) for 6–8 minutes.

To give the duchesse potatoes a shiny glaze, brush them with a little clarified butter just before serving.

———— • ————

RAIE AU BEURRE NOIR

Skate with black butter

THIS SIMPLE YET DELICIOUS DISH *is found on the menus of many Parisian restaurants. You will find it easy to prepare, but we have just one word of advice – make sure you use the very freshest skate. Serve with plain steamed potatoes.*

PREPARATION

The skate wings: Rinse thoroughly in cold water. Place in a saucepan with the wine, 400ml/14 fl oz water, the thyme, bay leaf, crushed peppercorns and a pinch of salt. Bring to the boil over high heat, then immediately lower the heat so that the liquid simmers at about 90°C/195°F. Cover the pan and cook very gently for 8 minutes. Meanwhile, prepare the croûtons and lemons.

The croûtons: Remove the crusts and cut the bread into 0.5cm/¼in dice. Heat the clarified butter in a frying pan over medium heat and fry the croûtons until golden. Drain and place in a bowl.

The lemons: Using a knife with a flexible blade, pare off the skin, pith and membrane. Slide the knife blade between each segment to remove the segments without their white membrane. Halve each segment lengthways and keep in a bowl.

Preheat the oven to 150°C/300°F/gas 2.

SERVING

Drain the skate wings on a tea towel and lay them, white skin down, on individual plates. Place in the oven for 2 minutes while you cook the black butter.

Heat the butter in a saucepan until it is golden brown and gives off a nutty scent. Ten seconds later, stop cooking, so that you do not burn the butter. Add the capers, then pour a little hot butter and capers over each skate wing. Divide the lemon segments and croûtons between the plates and sprinkle over the parsley. Serve at once.

SERVES 4

PREPARATION TIME: 20 MINUTES

COOKING TIME: 8 MINUTES

INGREDIENTS

4 skate wings, about 200g/7oz each

300ml/½ pt dry white wine

1 sprig of thyme

1 bay leaf

6 peppercorns, crushed

salt and freshly ground pepper

2 slices of white bread

30g/1oz clarified butter

150g/5oz butter

60g/2oz capers

2 lemons

1 tablespoon shredded flat-leaved parsley

In the markets of Île de France there is always a fishmonger offering a smile as well as his or her best fish.

CERVELLES D'AGNEAU AUX CÂPRES

CERVELLES D'AGNEAU AUX CÂPRES

Lambs' brains with capers

THIS TRADITIONAL DISH IS STILL SERVED *in several good bistros around Paris and in families where the art of eating is taken seriously. Calves' or pigs' brains can be prepared in the same way, but will need at least 20 minutes cooking. Our favourite way of eating them is with a potato purée and a garnish of deep-fried parsley. They can be served either as an hors d'oeuvre or as a light lunch.*

PREPARATION

The court-bouillon: Pour 1.5 litres/2½pt water into a saucepan, add the lemon juice, a pinch of salt, the crushed peppercorns, sliced carrot and onion and the bouquet garni. Cook gently for 30 minutes, then pass through a conical sieve and leave to cool.

The brains: Soak for 6 hours in very cold water, changing the water at least 3 times. Hold the brains under a trickle of cold water and carefully pull off the membrane and congealed blood from around them. Keep them in cold water until ready to cook.

The croûtons: Remove the crusts and cut the bread into 0.5cm/¼in dice. Heat the clarified butter in a frying pan and fry the bread over medium heat until golden. Drain and place in a bowl.

COOKING

Preheat the oven to 140°C/275°F/gas 1.

Put the brains in a saucepan and pour over the cooled court-bouillon. Over medium heat, bring the liquid just to simmering point and cook gently at 90°C/195°F for about 8 minutes.

SERVING

Lift out the brains with a slotted spoon, drain them on absorbent paper for 1 minute, then place on individual plates and heat in the oven for 1 minute.

Meanwhile, heat the butter in a small frying pan until it gives off a nutty smell, then immediately pour it over the brains. Deglaze the pan with the vinegar, raise the heat and reduce by half. Add the capers to the pan for just long enough to heat them, then spoon them on to the top of the brains. Sprinkle with the croûtons and chopped parsley and serve at once.

SERVES 4

PREPARATION TIME:
15 MINUTES, PLUS 6 HOURS SOAKING

COOKING TIME:
10 MINUTES

INGREDIENTS

4 lambs' brains

juice of ½ lemon

6 crushed peppercorns

1 carrot, thinly sliced

1 onion, thinly sliced

1 small bouquet garni

2 slices of white bread

50g/2oz clarified butter

100g/4oz butter

2 tablespoons good wine vinegar

50g/2oz capers in vinegar

1 tablespoon chopped parsley

salt

COEUR DE VEAU AUX CAROTTES

Calf's heart with carrots

SERVES 4

PREPARATION TIME:
50 MINUTES

COOKING TIME:
1 HOUR 50 MINUTES

INGREDIENTS

1 calf's heart, about 750g/1½lb

300g/11oz lightly smoked belly of pork

½ calf's foot, split down the middle and cut into 4 pieces

350g/12oz small white onions

350g/12oz small new carrots

50g/2oz clarified butter

2 unpeeled garlic cloves

2 pinches of sugar

50ml/2fl oz cognac or armagnac

200ml/7fl oz Chicken stock (recipe page 15) or water

a pinch of nutmeg

1 bouquet garni, with plenty of thyme

1 tablespoon shredded flat-leaved parsley

salt and freshly ground pepper

THIS IS MICHEL'S FAVOURITE *dish, which our mother still cooks for him. When we were in Paris, we used to treat ourselves to this concierge's casserole. The melting calf's foot and heart combine with the belly of pork and young vegetables to make a sublime dish. Don't forget to dip your bread in the sauce!*

PREPARATION

The heart: Place in a bowl and run under a gentle flow of water for 30 minutes to remove all the blood.

The belly of pork and calf's foot: Place in a saucepan, cover with cold water, boil for 2 minutes to blanch, then refresh in cold water. Drain and place on kitchen paper.

The onions and carrots: Peel, rinse in cold water and pat dry.

COOKING

Lightly salt the calf's heart and cut the pork belly into 4 pieces. Heat the clarified butter in the casserole and put in the heart and pork belly. Lightly brown on all sides over a gentle heat for 10 minutes, then add the onions, unpeeled garlic and a pinch of sugar. Cook for another 5 minutes over gentle heat, stirring from time to time, until everything is golden, then add the pieces of calf's foot and the carrots.

Stir well, increase the heat, pour in the alcohol and flame. As soon as the flames die down, add the chicken stock or water, sugar, nutmeg and bouquet garni. Put on the lid and cook in the oven at 180°C/350°F/gas 4, or lower the heat and simmer on the hob. Turn the heart over every 20 minutes, making sure that it is cooking very gently and that none of the ingredients sticks to the bottom of the casserole. Cook for about 1½ hours.

SERVING

Cut the heart into 8 thin slices and arrange in the centre of a large, shallow dish. Discard the bouquet garni and scatter the rest of the ingredients around the heart. Season the gravy to taste, pour it over the heart and sprinkle with the shredded parsley.

———— · ————

COEUR DE VEAU AUX CAROTTES

NAVARIN D'AGNEAU PRINTANIER

NAVARIN D'AGNEAU PRINTANIER

Lamb stew with spring vegetables

T HIS WAS ONE OF THE ROTHSCHILD FAMILY'S *favourite recipes. It is highly prized by Parisians and is served in many restaurants of the region as well as at home. We prefer to cook the delicate-flavoured lamb without* lardons, *but if we use mutton for the dish, then we do add them.*

Any leftovers can be reheated very successfully, so do not stint on quantities.

PREPARATION

The lamb: If necessary, trim off any excess fat and sinews. Do not bone the neck or breast. Cut each piece into 60g/2oz cubes.

Preheat the oven to 180°C/350°F/gas 4.

COOKING

Heat the clarified butter in a sauté pan over very high heat, put in the lamb and seal on all sides. Sprinkle over the sugar and let the pieces of meat caramelize slightly. Lift the pieces of lamb out of the pan and place in a bowl.

Put the diced carrots and onions in the sauté pan and sweat until soft, then stir in the flour and cook for 2–3 minutes until pale golden, stirring with a wooden spatula. Pour in the white wine and chicken stock, add the chopped tomatoes, garlic and bouquet garni and bring to the boil, still stirring with the spatula.

Return the lamb to the sauté pan, put on the lid and cook in the preheated oven for 45 minutes. Take out the pieces of shoulder and return the neck and breast to the oven for another 20 minutes.

Lift the pieces of neck and breast out of the cooking liquid, put them with the shoulder, cover with a damp cloth and keep warm.

The sauce: Spoon the fat off the surface of the cooking liquid and reduce the liquid until it lightly coats the back of a spoon. Pass the sauce through a conical sieve into a sauté dish, season to taste, then add the lamb, cover and keep warm.

The vegetables: Peel, wash and cook the root vegetables separately in a little lightly salted boiling water until tender. Shell the peas and blanch them for 2 minutes.

SERVING

Drain all the vegetables, put them in the dish with the lamb, simmer for 5 minutes, then pour everything into a deep serving dish. Sprinkle with parsley and serve at once.

——— • ———

SERVES 4

PREPARATION TIME:
35 MINUTES

COOKING TIME:
1 HOUR 10 MINUTES

INGREDIENTS

1 boned shoulder of lamb

500g/1 lb 2oz middle neck of lamb

500g/1 lb 2oz breast of lamb

50g/2oz clarified butter

a pinch of sugar

1 large carrot, finely diced

1 large onion, finely diced

30g/1oz flour

200ml/7fl oz dry white wine

1 litre/1¾pt Chicken stock (recipe page 15)

3 large ripe tomatoes, peeled, deseeded and chopped

3 garlic cloves, crushed

1 bouquet garni

12 small new carrots

12 small new turnips

12 baby onions

12 small new potatoes

300g/11oz peas in the pod

1 tablespoon flat-leaved parsley leaves

salt and freshly ground pepper

SALADE DE CRESSON À LA CRÈME

Watercress salad with cream

SERVES 4
PREPARATION TIME:
15 MINUTES

INGREDIENTS

600g/1lb 6oz river watercress

juice of 2 lemons

100ml/3½fl oz whipping cream

1 shallot, very finely chopped

20 walnut kernels, soaked in a little milk

1 tablespoon chervil leaves

salt and freshly ground pepper

THE ÎLE DE FRANCE ABOUNDS *with watercress beds, which produce some of the very finest watercress in France, and every shelf in the greengrocers' stalls in Rungis groans with boxes of it.*
Our mother often makes this simple and refreshing salad for us; it makes a pleasant change from salads dressed with oil.

PREPARATION

The watercress: Pull off the leaves, leaving 1–2cm/½–¾in stalk still attached. Discard the lower part of the stalks and wash the leaves in several changes of very cold water. Drain and pat dry very thoroughly.
The dressing: Mix the lemon juice with the cream, add salt and pepper to taste and stir in the shallot.

SERVING

Mix the watercress into the dressing and place in a salad bowl. Drain the walnuts and scatter them over the salad. Sprinkle over the chervil leaves, toss the salad and serve.

Freshly picked walnuts are deliciously delicate and milky in the Salade de cresson à la crème.

GALETTE DES ROIS

Traditional Twelfth Night cake

THIS EPIPHANY CAKE IS FOUND *in every pâtisserie on January 6th, when families and friends gather round the table to 'find the king'. The one who pulls out the bean hidden in the cake chooses one of the assembled company to be his or her consort and offers champagne all round. For the people who live in the suburbs of Paris, this provides a good excuse for more evening festivities – while the poor pâtissiers spend sleepless nights rolling out hundreds of galettes des rois; we speak from bitter experience!*

PREPARATION

Rolling out the pastry: With a large knife, cut the pastry into two pieces, 130g/4oz and 220g/8oz respectively. On a lightly floured marble or wooden surface, roll out the smaller piece, giving it a quarter turn every so often, until you have a 22cm/8½in circle about 2mm/1/12in thick. Roll the circle on to the rolling pin, then unroll it on to a baking sheet lightly brushed with cold water.

Roll out the larger piece of pastry in the same way to make a 26cm/10½in circle, 3mm/⅛in thick. Using a knife with a flexible blade, make light vertical slits all round the sides of the pastry; this will help it to rise better and more evenly.

ASSEMBLING THE CAKE

Spoon the almond cream into the middle of the smaller pastry circle. With a palette knife, spread it over the pastry, leaving a 1.5cm/½in border. Brush the border with cold water and place the bean on the almond cream near the edge of the circle. Cover with the second pastry circle and press the edges together with your fingertips to seal them. Leave to rest in the fridge for 30 minutes.

Preheat the oven to 220°C/425°F/gas 7.

DECORATING THE CAKE

Brush the top of the cake with eggwash, then use the point of a knife to draw decorative lines all over the surface, scoring the pastry lightly.

COOKING

Bake the cake in the preheated oven for 25 minutes. Sprinkle the surface with icing sugar, raise the oven temperature to 240°C/475°F/gas 9 and cook for another 5–7 minutes, until the top is beautifully glazed. Immediately transfer the cake to a wire rack and leave to cool.

SERVING

Serve the cake barely warm on a round plate lined with a white or silver doily and cut it at the table in front of your guests.

———— · ————

SERVES 6

PREPARATION TIME:
20 MINUTES, PLUS 30 MINUTES CHILLING

COOKING TIME:
ABOUT 35 MINUTES

INGREDIENTS

350g/12oz Puff pastry
(recipe page 11)

a pinch of flour

80g/3oz *Crème d'amande*
(recipe page 16)

eggwash (1 egg yolk mixed with 1 tablespoon milk)

icing sugar, for dusting

EQUIPMENT

1 ceramic baking bean or a dried haricot bean

paper or silver crown, for crowning the 'king' (optional)

⟞ CRÊPES SUZETTE ⟝

Crêpes with orange sauce

SERVES 6

PREPARATION TIME:
25 MINUTES, PLUS 1 HOUR
RESTING

COOKING TIME:
2–3 MINUTES PER CRÊPE

INGREDIENTS

CRÊPE BATTER

125g/4½oz flour

15g/½oz sugar

a small pinch of salt

2 eggs

300ml/½ pt milk, boiled and
cooled

100ml/3½fl oz double cream

1 tablespoon curaçao

a little clarified butter for the pan

SAUCE

6 sugar lumps

1½ oranges

180g/6oz softened butter

180g/6oz sugar

3 tablespoons curaçao

EQUIPMENT

1 × 16cm/7in crêpe pan

1 bi-metal frying pan (copper
outside with a silvered interior)

spirit stove or fondue heater

THIS CLASSIC DISH *was very much in vogue in restaurants around Paris during the 1960s. Some restaurants like to flambé the crêpes, but this adds nothing to the flavour and simply burns off the alcohol.*

Such is our passion for the delicious orange and curaçao aroma that we always make double quantities of these crêpes, allowing 6 per serving.

PREPARATION

The batter: Put the flour, sugar and salt in a bowl and stir in the eggs, one at a time, with a wooden spatula. Pour in one-third of the milk and mix until smooth and homogenous. Stir in the cream, the rest of the milk and the curaçao, cover the bowl with a plate and leave the batter to stand at room temperature for at least 1 hour before cooking the crêpes.

COOKING THE CRÊPES

Brush the pan with clarified butter and heat it. Ladle in a little batter, tilt the pan to spread it thinly over the base and cook the crêpe for about 1½ minutes, then turn it over with a palette knife and cook for about 1½ minutes more, until golden on both sides. Place the crêpe on a plate and make more crêpes in the same way, until all the batter is used up (you should end up with 18 crêpes).

THE SAUCE

Rub the sugar lumps against the orange skin to absorb as much flavour as possible. With a wire whisk, work together the softened butter and sugar, then add the curaçao and sugar lumps.

SERVING

Squeeze the orange juice into the bi-metal pan, set over high heat and reduce by half. Bring the pan to the table, set it on the heater and beat the butter mixture into the orange juice, bringing the mixture to the boil. As soon as the sauce bubbles, lift one crêpe at a time with a fork and spread it in the sauce, turn it over and fold into quarters. Repeat with all the crêpes; there should be 3 per person.

———— · ————

CRÊPES SUZETTE AND CHAUSSONS AUX POMMES

CHAUSSONS AUX POMMES

Apple turnovers

SERVES 4

PREPARATION TIME:
30 MINUTES, PLUS 20 MINUTES
RESTING

COOKING TIME: 20 MINUTES

INGREDIENTS

3 dessert apples, preferably coxes (about 600g/1lb 6 oz)

1 split vanilla pod

100g/4oz sugar

30g/1oz butter

a pinch of flour

450g/1lb Puff pastry, with 6 turns (recipe page 11)

eggwash (1 egg yolk mixed with 1 tablespoon milk)

30g/1oz icing sugar

EQUIPMENT

10cm/4in round fluted pastry cutter

H OW WELL WE REMEMBER *the apple turnovers which our mother used to make as a teatime treat when we were children. We have equally vivid memories of our days as apprentices, when, in the early hours of the morning, while Paris slept, we would prepare thousands of these pastries for other children to enjoy.*

These chaussons *also make a delicious lunchtime pudding, served with a well-chilled* crème anglaise.

PREPARATION

The apples: Peel, core and chop roughly. Put the pieces in a saucepan with 100ml/3½fl oz water and the vanilla pod, cover and cook gently for about 20 minutes, until the apples have disintegrated. Add the sugar, beat the apple pulp until smooth, then cook for another 5 minutes over very low heat. If the pulp still seems runny, continue to cook over low heat until all the water has evaporated; it should be quite firm.

Remove the vanilla pod, then pass the pulp through a vegetable mill or fine sieve. Beat in the butter, leave the apple to cool completely, then chill in the fridge until almost solid.

ROLLING OUT THE TURNOVERS

On a lightly floured marble or wooden surface, roll out half the puff pastry into a 45 × 15cm/18 × 6in rectangle, 3mm/⅛in thick. Lay 4 spoonfuls of cold apple pulp (about half the total) along the centre of the long side of the rectangle, spacing them 9cm/3½in apart.

Dip a pastry brush in cold water and moisten the pastry round the edge of the mounds of apple. Fold the pastry rectangle over the apple towards you. Place half the pastry cutter over each mound of apple and cut out 4 semi-circles. Press the edges well to seal them so that the filling does not ooze out during cooking. Place on a dampened baking sheet and refrigerate for at least 20 minutes.

Make 4 more turnovers in the same way using the remaining pastry and apple. You will be left with about 100g/4oz pastry trimmings; keep them to use in another recipe.

Preheat the oven to 220°C/425°F/gas 7.

COOKING

Brush the tops of the turnovers with eggwash and use the point of a knife to score decorative lines on the pastry. Bake in the preheated oven for 15 minutes.

Take the turnovers out of the oven. Increase the oven temperature to as high as it will go (260°C/500°F/gas 10). Sprinkle the turnovers lightly with icing sugar and return to the oven for 2–3 minutes, until the tops are highly glazed and look as though they had been varnished, but take care not to burn them. Transfer the turnovers to a wire rack and leave to cool.

SERVING

Arrange the turnovers on a plate lined with a white napkin, or simply serve them straight from the cooling rack.

———— • ————

Île de France

FRESHWATER FISH

Ablette (bleak)
Eel
Small barbel
Bream
Roach
Gudgeon
Perch
Trout

BATRACHIANS

Frogs

POULTRY

Roasting chicken
Chicken

GAME

Thrushes
Partridge

CHARCUTERIE

Andouillette
Pâté en croûte

VEGETABLES

Artichokes
Carrots
Cabbage
Cauliflower
Watercress
Spinach
Lettuce and oak
leaf lettuce
Beans: broad,
flageolet, soissons
Mushrooms: button,
chanterelles, morels
Turnips
Peas
Leeks
Radishes
Tomatoes

CHEESE

Brie
Fromage de
Fontainebleau

FRUIT

Cherries
Chasselas grapes
Strawberries
Raspberries
Peaches
Pears
Apples
Plums

PÂTISSERIE

Allumettes
Beignets
Parisian brioche
Chaussons aux pommes
(apple turnovers)
Eclairs
Puff pastry galettes
Waffles
Macaroons from Crécy
Puits d'Amour
Diplomat pudding
St Honoré

CONFECTIONERY

Fine sweets
Chocolate
Crystallized fruits
from Beauvais
Haricots de Soissons
(pralines)
Marrons glacés
Honey
Barley sugar
from Moret

133

Champagne

A LAND RICH IN GAME, WHOSE NAME STANDS FOR SUCCESS AND CELEBRATION

*C*HAMPAGNE IS GLORIOUS, not only for its famous victories in war, but more especially for its unique and wonderful wines!

Once, this was a region of magnificent forests, which the mediaeval monks demolished in order to build on the land. Two of these forests still remain, however; the picturesque forest of Ders (Celtic for oak) and the forest of l'Orient, which probably took its name from the Knights Templar who had many encampments in the forest (part of it is known as the 'forest of the Temple') and may once have been part of the vast forest of Ders. In 1970, a huge area of 160,000 acres between Ders and Troyes was designated a national regional park and the forest is therefore protected from any man-made destruction. The forest of l'Orient is crossed by small tributaries of the Aube and is a relaxing and peaceful place in which to walk.

Apart from the forests, the plain consists mainly of woods, ponds and rich meadows where horses and cattle graze. Freshwater fish abound in the rivers that flow through the region, among them the Aube, the Seine, the Marne, the Aisne, the Meuse and the Yonne.

Situated to the east of Paris, near the Île de France, Champagne enjoys an identical climate with the same ratio of sunshine and an annual rainfall of 60–70cm/23½–27½in. This is a region of chalky hills; from the summit of the famous Montagne de Reims, the view is of vineyards stretching further than the eye can see. These vineyards can be divided into three main sections: the Côte des Blancs, the Marne hillside (Cumières) and the Montagne de Reims (Bouzy). There are also vineyards in the

Aisne, the Haute Marne and the Aube valley (*rosé des Riceys*) and the Côte St Jacques, which produces *vin gris*. The most commonly used grapes are the chardonnay, the pinot noir and the pinot meunier. Above all, of course, the province is famous for its sparkling wine, which the whole world adores, for it represents celebrations, success and happy gatherings with family and friends.

Unfortunately, these long, vast stretches of vineyards and plains can become rather monotonous, so one can well understand why the natives find it pleasurable to take refuge in their wine cellars! Over the centuries, these cellars have been hollowed out in the chalky hillsides. Some of them are galleried on two or three levels and are quite an amazing sight.

Michel will never forget the seminar of the *Maîtres Pâtissiers* in the cellars at Besserat-Bellefont. For three days, he and his colleagues laboured to produce a dessert based on champagne or *marc de champagne*. His perseverance paid off; his colleagues elected him President of the Jury, which made the acute indigestion and hangover he suffered worthwhile!

Apart from its vineyards, Champagne boasts many historically important sites and towns. For centuries, the region suffered wars, invasions and resistance, for it lies directly on the route of armies marching to Paris. In the thirteenth century, it was invaded by the Barbarians, then, after the turbulent Middle Ages, came the Prussians and their Austrian allies. Parts of the region were later devastated by the Germans, first in 1914, then again during the Second World War.

Through the ages many kings of France and the neighbouring countries were vineyard owners, who celebrated their victories with their own wine – from the rout of the Spaniards at Rocroi by the future *Grand Condé* to the French defeat of the Germans, who signed their capitulation treaty at Reims in 1918.

The cathedral at Reims is one of the great architectural triumphs of the middle ages; here, the pagan king Clovis was baptised and thereafter all French kings were crowned at Reims until the coronation of Charles X. Champagne excels in religious art, with its astonishing proliferation of gothic churches, particularly at Troyes, the ancient capital of the region.

The art of cooking is also important in Champagne, where the natives enjoy such regional specialities as pig's trotters *à la Sainte-Menehould* (rolled in breadcrumbs and grilled or fried), substantial *potée champénoise* and many dishes using game from the Ardennes.

The Ardennes region lies in the north of the Champagne area, its wooded crests straddling the Belgian border. The climate of this austere region is harsh, with an annual rainfall of 1m/39in and a good deal of fog. The river Meuse and its tributary, the Semoy, flow through a deep, winding valley enclosed by sombre hills. Because the ancient Ardennes Massif is only about 500m/1,600ft, trees grow here and the area abounds in game, which we love to hunt. At the southerly end of the foot of the mountain lies an undulating plain, watered by the Meuse and the Sormone. Here, sheep, cows and working horses graze in the meadows.

Ardennes game is made into many fine dishes: pâtés of thrushes and wild boar from Charleville, roast thrushes wrapped in sage leaves from Givet, trout from the Argonne, pike from the Aisne and delectable freshwater crayfish. *Boudin blanc* is a speciality of Rethel and the Ardennes produces delicious beer.

The morning mist hides the secrets of these rolling hills. Here grow the grapes that give us the wine loved throughout the world, champagne.

POTÉE CHAMPÉNOISE

Salt pork and vegetable soup

SERVES 4

PREPARATION TIME:
30 MINUTES, PLUS 12 HOURS
SOAKING

COOKING TIME: 2 HOURS

INGREDIENTS

1 semi-salted blade of pork or half a shoulder of semi-salted pork

300g/11oz lean unsmoked bacon, in one piece

1 tight, hearty green or red cabbage

500g/1lb 2oz potatoes

500g/1lb 2oz leeks

300g/11oz carrots

200g/7oz turnips

1 boiling sausage, about 800g/1¾lb

AROMATICS

2 large onions, each stuck with 1 clove

½ head of garlic, unpeeled and halved

1 large bouquet garni

10 peppercorns, crushed

salt and freshly ground pepper

THIS SUBSTANTIAL SOUP *is traditionally eaten by grape-pickers during the harvest, but it is also much enjoyed even by those not picking grapes! Many regions of France have their own version of* potée, *each one slightly different. In this area, it is based on salt pork with a variety of vegetables; others use different meats, such as beef, lamb, duck, smoked bacon or whole hams.*

PREPARATION

The meats: Soak the salt pork and bacon in very cold water for at least 12 hours.
The vegetables: Peel, wash, quarter the cabbage and halve or quarter the other vegetables, depending on their size.

COOKING

Put the pork and bacon into a large heavy casserole, cover with cold water, bring to the boil and blanch for 5 minutes. Refresh, drain, then put the meats back into the casserole and cover with plenty of cold water. Bring to the boil, immediately lower the heat and simmer gently for 20 minutes, skimming the surface whenever necessary.

Salt lightly and add all the aromatics and vegetables except the cabbage and potatoes. Cook for another hour, then prick the sausage with the point of a knife and add it to the casserole, together with the cabbage and potatoes. Cook uncovered for another 40 minutes.

SERVING

Carefully lift the meats out of the soup. Slice the bacon and sausage and cut the pork into pieces. Arrange the meats in the centre of a large deep platter and arrange the vegetables around them, discarding the aromatics. Pour the soup into a tureen and serve it separately.

Potatoes from the new crop are flavourful and delicate and are an important addition to Potée champénoise.

POTÉE CHAMPÉNOISE

PIEDS DE PORC PANÉS

Pig's trotters in breadcrumbs

SERVES 4

PREPARATION TIME:
30 MINUTES

COOKING TIME: 5¼ HOURS,
PLUS 24 HOURS CHILLING

INGREDIENTS

4 pig's trotters, scraped clean by the butcher

500ml/18fl oz dry white wine

3 litres/5pt Chicken stock (recipe page 15)

1 bouquet garni with plenty of thyme and bay leaves

2 onions, each stuck with 3 cloves

3 carrots, peeled

10 peppercorns, crushed

125g/4½oz lard or butter

120g/4oz fresh white breadcrumbs

salt and freshly ground pepper

2 lemons, a bouquet of watercress and strong dijon mustard, for serving

EQUIPMENT

4 narrow strips of strong material, 40cm/16in long, for tying up the trotters during cooking

THE MOST FAMOUS RECIPE *for pig's trotters is probably* pieds de porc Sainte-Menehould. *In it, the trotters are not split, but are cooked whole for at least 36 hours. They are then rolled in breadcrumbs, baked and served whole. Because the bones have been cooked for so long, they have the same soft consistency as the rind and flesh, so the trotters are eaten bones and all.*

We prefer the classic breaded pig's trotters which our grandfather and father prepared so well; sucking the bones is heavenly – but don't swallow them!

PREPARATION

Put the trotters in a casserole, cover with cold water, bring to the boil, blanch for 5 minutes, then refresh in cold water. Drain and pat dry. With a cleaver, split the trotters lengthways, without cutting right through them. Tie the trotters back into shape by bandaging them tightly with strips of material and tie securely with a knot.

COOKING

Put the wrapped trotters back into the casserole, pour in the wine and chicken stock and add the bouquet garni, vegetables, peppercorns and a pinch of salt. Set the casserole over high heat and bring quickly to the boil, then reduce the temperature so that the liquid is barely trembling (80°–90°C/175°–195°F). Cook for 5 hours, skimming the surface every 30 minutes; it is particularly important to do this during the first 2 hours.

Transfer the cooked trotters into a bowl large enough to hold them and the cooking liquid and strain the liquid through a conical sieve on to the trotters. Leave in a cool place until cold, then refrigerate for at least 24 hours.

FINAL COOKING

Preheat the oven to 240°C/475°F/gas 7, or the grill to very hot.

Take the trotters out of the cooking liquid and carefully unwrap them. Wipe them with a cloth, one at a time, and use a knife to cut through the skin which holds them together so that the 2 halves separate.

Melt the lard or butter and brush some over the half trotters, then roll them in the breadcrumbs, pressing the crumbs so that they stick to the trotters.

Pour a little melted lard or butter into a roasting pan, put in the prepared trotters and place in the preheated oven or under the hot grill for about 15 minutes, until they are piping hot and nutty brown.

SERVING

Put 2 half trotters on each plate, add half a lemon and serve with a little mustard.

NOTES

The most appropriate accompaniment to this dish is a potato purée. However, we often eat trotters with french fries, a béarnaise sauce and a watercress salad with a lemon dressing.

The cooking liquid from the trotters makes a good aspic jelly, or the basis for an excellent veal stock or soup.

FLAMICHE AUX POIREAUX

Leek flan

ORIGINALLY, flamiches *were made from bread dough, but nowadays they are more like a traditional vegetable flan.*

PREPARATION

The leeks: Trim them and discard the greenest parts. Halve them lengthways and wash in several changes of very cold water. Drain and cut into short strips, about 0.5cm/¼in wide.

Melt 40g/1½oz butter in a saucepan, put in the leeks, season with salt and pepper, cover the pan and sweat very gently for 20 – 30 minutes, stirring occasionally with a spatula. The leeks should be very tender and should not have taken on any colour. The precise cooking time will depend on the tenderness and size of the leeks. Leave to cool at room temperature until barely tepid.

The pastry case: On a lightly floured marble or wooden surface, roll out the pastry into a circle about 3mm/⅛in thick. Grease the flan ring with the remaining butter and line it with the pastry, cutting off any excess and pinching up the edges between your thumb and forefinger to make a fluted border. Slide the flan ring on to a baking sheet and refrigerate for 20 minutes.

Preheat the oven to 220°C/425°F/gas 7.

COOKING THE PASTRY CASE

Prick the bottom of the pastry all over with a fork or the point of a knife and line it with a circle of foil or greaseproof paper. Fill it with baking beans and bake blind in the preheated oven for 20 minutes.

Remove the beans and paper and keep the pastry case at room temperature. Reduce the oven temperature to 200°C/400°F/gas 6.

The filling: Lightly whisk together the cream and egg yolks and mix them into the cooled leeks (which should be almost cold), then season to taste.

COOKING THE FLAN

Pour the filling into the flan case and bake at 200°C/400°F/gas 6 for 40 minutes, until the top of the flan is pale golden and the filling set. Lift off the flan ring.

SERVING

Slide the flan on to a round plate and serve it whole, leaving your guests to help themselves.

NOTES

Some people prefer their *flamiche* with a pastry topping, like a pie. Nowadays, it is more often served as an open flan, since it is lighter this way. We sometimes throw classicism aside and add a pinch of curry powder to the leek filling; do give it a try.

SERVES 8
PREPARATION TIME: 25 MINUTES
COOKING TIME: 1 HOUR

INGREDIENTS
1kg/2lb 3oz leeks
60g/2oz butter
300g/11oz *Pâte brisée* (recipe page 10)
a pinch of flour
100ml/3½fl oz double cream
5 egg yolks
salt and freshly ground pepper

EQUIPMENT
1 flan ring, about 22cm/9in diameter, 3cm/1¼in deep
baking or dried beans

TRUITE ARDENNAISE

Ardennes trout with ham

SERVES 4

PREPARATION TIME:
20 MINUTES

COOKING TIME: 8 MINUTES

INGREDIENTS

4 river trout, about 200g/7oz each

1 tablespoon oil

4 tablespoons flour

50g/2oz raw ham fat, finely chopped

30g/1oz clarified butter

2 shallots, finely chopped

150ml/5fl oz dry white wine

350ml/12fl oz double cream

75g/3oz raw Ardennes ham, cut into small batons

1 tablespoon chopped parsley

salt and freshly ground pepper

TROUT ARE STILL ABUNDANT *in the Ardennes and often feature on the menu both at home and in restaurants. This simple recipe tastes wonderful and takes very little effort. Serve it with plain boiled potatoes.*

PREPARATION

The trout: Cut off the fins and gills with scissors and remove the intestines through the gills. Wash the trout in very cold water to remove all traces of intestines, then gently pat dry with kitchen paper. Season lightly with salt and pepper, dip your finger in oil and smear a light film over the fish. Roll them in flour, tap them to remove the excess and lay them on a plate.

COOKING

Melt the ham fat in a frying pan set over low heat, then add the clarified butter and increase the heat. When the fat is very hot, put in the trout and cook for 4 minutes, then turn over the fish with a palette knife and cook for another 4 minutes, until it is golden on both sides. Put the trout on a serving dish and keep warm.

THE SAUCE

Pour off half the fat from the pan. Put in the shallots and sweat over low heat for 2 minutes, then add the white wine and reduce by half. Add the cream and reduce until the sauce is thick enough to coat the back of a spoon lightly. Put in the ham, simmer for 2 minutes, season with salt and pepper and stir in the chopped parsley.

SERVING

Pour the hot creamy sauce over the trout and serve at once.

Flat parsley of this freshness and quality will bring a subtle flavour to Truite ardennaise.

TRUITE ARDENNAISE

BROCHET BRAISÉ AU CHAMPAGNE

Pike braised in champagne

SERVES 4

PREPARATION TIME:
30 MINUTES

COOKING TIME: 25 MINUTES

INGREDIENTS

1 pike, about 1.3kg/2lb 14 oz

200g/7oz small button mushrooms

250g/9oz butter

1 bottle brut champagne

200ml/7fl oz Fish stock (recipe page 14)

3 shallots, finely sliced

1 small bouquet garni

300ml/½ pt double cream

juice of ½ lemon

salt and freshly ground pepper

EQUIPMENT

fish kettle or long, deep ovenproof dish large enough to hold the pike

THIS CLASSIC RECIPE *is served not only in grand restaurants, but is also a popular dish for a family Sunday lunch in this region, which once abounded with pike.*

PREPARATION

The pike: Scale and remove the gills and fins. Make a small incision in the belly and gut the fish. Wash well in very cold running water and pat dry very carefully with a paper towel.

The mushrooms: Peel, wipe with a damp cloth and separate the caps and stalks. Put the caps in a bowl, thinly slice the stalks and put them in another bowl.

Preheat the oven to 220°C/425°F/gas 7.

COOKING THE PIKE

Grease the bottom of the fish kettle or dish with about 100g/4oz butter. Generously season the pike all over with salt and pepper, then place in the fish kettle. Pour over two-thirds of the champagne and the fish stock and add the sliced mushroom stalks, shallots and bouquet garni. Cook the pike, uncovered, in the preheated oven, basting it with the cooking juices every 5 minutes. After 15 minutes, cover the pike with a sheet of well-buttered greaseproof paper and cook for another 10 minutes, still basting with the cooking juices every 5 minutes. After a total of 25 minutes cooking, transfer the pike to a serving dish and keep warm.

THE SAUCE

The mushroom caps: Heat the reserved butter in a saucepan, put in the mushroom caps and lemon juice and sweat for 2 minutes. Season lightly with salt and pepper and keep warm to one side.

Pour all the contents of the fish kettle into a saucepan and add the mushroom cooking juices, the remaining champagne and the cream. Reduce by about half, until the sauce is thick enough to coat the back of a spoon lightly. Pass it through a conical sieve into a food processor or blender and process at medium speed for 2 minutes to make the sauce really smooth and velvety. Season to taste. Put aside 30g/1oz of the remaining butter and whisk the rest into the sauce, a little at a time. Keep the sauce hot.

SERVING

Arrange the mushroom caps around the pike. Pour one-third of the champagne sauce over the fish and serve the rest in a sauceboat.

NOTES

Beware of the bones when you eat the pike; they are fine, but very long. This is the one disadvantage of this most delicate dish.

We like to leave the skin on the pike, as it tastes delicious when it is braised. A rice pilaff or plain steamed potatoes make a fine accompaniment to this fish with its subtle, creamy sauce.

RIS DE VEAU À LA BRIARDE

Veal sweetbreads in a creamy sauce with meaux mustard

THE MEAUX MUSTARD OFFSETS *the richness and creaminess of the sweetbreads in this delightful dish, which is very simple to prepare. We are sure you will enjoy it.*

PREPARATION
Soak the sweetbreads in cold water for at least 24 hours, then blanch them in a saucepan for 2–3 minutes and refresh. If necessary, skin them, drain and carefully pat dry with kitchen paper.

COOKING THE SWEETBREADS
Heat the clarified butter in a sauté pan, add the sweetbreads and sweat gently for 2– 3 minutes on each side, taking care that they do not colour. Pour in the cider and chicken stock, add the bouquet garni, onion and crushed peppercorns, cover the pan and cook gently over low heat for 20 minutes.
The carrots: While the sweetbreads are cooking, peel the carrots and halve them lengthways if they are thicker than your little finger. Place in a saucepan with a little water, 30g/1oz butter, a pinch of sugar and salt and cook gently for about 10 minutes. The carrots should still be slightly firm but not crunchy. Drain thoroughly and keep warm.

THE SAUCE
When the sweetbreads are cooked, drain them and place on a serving dish. Cover with foil and keep warm.

Pass the cooking liquid through a conical sieve into a saucepan, set over high heat and reduce by two-thirds. Pour in the cream and cook for another 10 minutes, until the sauce lightly coats the back of a spoon. Add the mustard, allow the sauce to bubble, then stir in the remaining butter. Season with salt and pepper and keep hot.

SERVING
Arrange the carrots in a border around the sweetbreads. Pour the hot sauce over the sweetbreads, sprinkle with parsley and serve at once.

NOTES
You can use lambs' sweetbreads for this dish. If so, reduce the cooking time by two-thirds.

SERVES 4

PREPARATION TIME:
25 MINUTES, PLUS 24 HOURS SOAKING

COOKING TIME:
ABOUT 30 MINUTES

INGREDIENTS

4 fine veal sweetbreads from the pancreas

30g/1oz clarified butter

300ml/½ pt dry cider

300ml/½ pt Chicken stock (recipe page 15)

1 bouquet garni

1 medium onion stuck with 2 cloves

6 peppercorns, crushed

400g/14oz new baby carrots

60g/2oz butter

a pinch of sugar

200ml/7fl oz double cream

50g/2oz meaux mustard

1 tablespoon chopped parsley

salt and freshly ground pepper

POULARDE POELÉE AU CHAMPAGNE

POULARDE POELÉE
AU CHAMPAGNE

Capon with morels and champagne

SUCCESS IS ASSURED *with this remarkable dish! The smell of the morels as they cook is quite irresistible.*

PREPARATION

The capon: Clean it, remove the wishbone, singe the bird and pull out any feather stumps if necessary. Lightly salt the cavity and cut off the wing tips. Truss the capon and tie the barding fat over the breast with kitchen string. Keep all the giblets.

COOKING

Heat half the butter in a saucepan, put in the capon and cook it over very low heat for 10 minutes on each thigh, then 5 minutes on each breast. Turn the capon over on to its back and cook for a final 5 minutes, making sure that it takes on almost no colour.

Add the bouquet garni, the diced carrots and shallots, the giblets and two-thirds of the champagne, cover the pan and cook for another 30 minutes. Check the cooking by inserting a trussing needle into the thickest part of the thigh; the juices which run out should be shiny and completely clear. If there is any trace of pink, cook the capon for another 10 minutes.

Remove the trussing string and barding fat, lay the capon on its breast on a serving dish, cover with foil and leave to rest in a warm place.

The sauce: Pour the remaining champagne into the saucepan, add the chicken stock and reduce by half over high heat. Add the cream and reduce until the sauce lightly coats the back of a spoon. Season to taste and keep warm.

The morels: Peel the stalks and cut off any earthy or nasty parts. Halve or quarter them lengthways, wash in several changes of cold water to eliminate all traces of sand, and drain. Heat the remaining butter in a frying pan, add the morels, a little salt and pepper and the lemon juice, cover and sweat for 5 minutes. Remove the lid and cook the morels over high heat until all their water has evaporated, then add the chopped shallot and one-third of the sauce and keep warm.

SERVING

Serve the capon whole, surrounded by the morels. Serve the rest of the sauce in a sauceboat and carve the bird at the table in front of your guests.

NOTES

If you use dried morels, soak them in cold water for several hours before using them. Alternatively, if morels are not in season, garnish the dish with some small braised lettuces (see *Arc-en-ciel de légumes angevin* page 48).

———— · ————

SERVES 6

PREPARATION TIME: 30 MINUTES

COOKING TIME: ABOUT 1 HOUR

INGREDIENTS

1 capon, about 1.8kg/4lb

1 thin slice of barding fat, about 14 × 10cm/6 × 4in

80g/3oz butter

1 bouquet garni

2 carrots, diced

3 shallots, diced

500ml/18 fl oz champagne

300ml/½ pt Chicken stock (recipe page 15)

500ml/18fl oz double cream

500g/lb 2 oz fresh morels, or 100g/4oz dried morels, soaked

juice of 1 lemon

1 shallot, very finely chopped

salt and freshly ground pepper

DAUBE DE MARCASSIN

Young wild boar in red wine

SERVES 6

PREPARATION TIME:
50 MINUTES, PLUS 6 HOURS
MARINATING

COOKING TIME: 2 HOURS

INGREDIENTS

2 shoulders of young wild boar, about 6 months old

MARINADE

4 carrots, peeled and cut into 1cm/½in rings

2 onions, 1 finely sliced, 1 stuck with 2 cloves

1 large bouquet garni, with plenty of thyme

10 juniper berries

6 peppercorns, crushed

½ head of garlic, separated into unpeeled cloves

1 bottle red burgundy

2 tablespoons *marc de champagne*

8 tablespoons oil

150g/5oz pork rind

½ calf's foot, blanched

500ml/18fl oz Veal stock (recipe page 15)

1 strip of dried orange zest

salt and freshly ground pepper

A MARCASSIN IS A YOUNG *wild boar, less than 6 months old. The flesh is delicate and full of flavour. Unfortunately, wild boar are becoming rarer; the odds are against them since there are now more hunters than boar!*

PREPARATION

The shoulders: Using a boning knife, lift off the meat from the bones and cut away the nerves and tendons. Cut the meat into cubes weighing about 80g/3oz each and put them into a bowl with the bones, all the marinade ingredients and half the oil. Cover with clingfilm and refrigerate for 6 hours.

COOKING THE *DAUBE*

Preheat the oven to 160°C/300°–325°F/gas 2–3.

Drain all the marinade ingredients and pat the meat dry with kitchen paper. Place the pork rind in a casserole, fat-side down, then put in the calf's foot and the shoulder bones from the boar.

Heat the remaining oil in a frying pan and quickly seal the cubes of meat on all sides until they are a lovely golden colour. Transfer them to the casserole. Put the marinade ingredients into the same frying pan, seal them for 2 minutes, then add them to the casserole.

Pour the strained wine from the marinade into a saucepan, bring to the boil, then pour it into the casserole. Add the veal stock and orange zest, bring to the boil and add a little salt. Cover the casserole and cook in the low oven for 2 hours, or simmer on the edge of a solid fuel hob.

When the *daube* is cooked, skim off the fat from the surface with a spoon.

SERVING

Using a slotted spoon, carefully lift the cubes of meat and the carrots into a deep earthenware or pottery dish. Strain the sauce through a conical sieve into a saucepan and discard all the marinade ingredients, leaving in the calf's foot, if you happen to like it. Reduce the sauce over high heat until it will lightly coat the back of a spoon. Season to taste, pour the boiling sauce over the meat and serve immediately.

NOTES

If you use an older wild boar, cook the *daube* for 3 hours. We often serve a fricassée of *pieds de mouton* mushrooms, which are found all over the Ardennes, with the boar. A purée of two-thirds celeriac and one-third potato also makes an excellent vegetable accompaniment to this winter dish.

CHOU BRAISÉ À L'ARDENNAISE

Braised cabbage

THE REGION ABOUNDS *in white, green and red cabbages so, not surprisingly, this dish often features on the menu. It goes extremely well with game, pork, sausages, our* Daube de marcassin *and* Ris de veau à la briarde *(recipes pages 146 and 143).*

SERVES 4

PREPARATION TIME:
15 MINUTES

COOKING TIME:
ABOUT 45 MINUTES

PREPARATION

Quarter the cabbage, cut out the hardest part of the core and discard the outer leaves if they do not look too healthy. Wash the cabbage in cold water, then put it into a saucepan of boiling salted water and blanch for 5 minutes. Refresh and drain. Use a heavy knife to cut it into thick strips.

Preheat the oven to 200°C/400°F/gas 6.

INGREDIENTS

1 green savoy cabbage

200g/7oz cooking apples

60g/2oz lard or clarified butter

200ml/7fl cz dry white wine

10 juniper berries

100g/4oz pork rind, rolled into a sausage shape and tied with string (optional)

salt and freshly ground pepper

COOKING THE CABBAGE

Peel, core and dice the apples. Melt the lard or clarified butter in an earthenware casserole and immediately put in the apples and cabbage and sweat for 5 minutes, stirring occasionally. Pour in the wine, add the juniper berries, season with salt and pepper and bury the pork rind in the middle of the cabbage. Cover the casserole and cook in the preheated oven for 40 minutes. Check the cabbage at the end of this time; it should be tender and juicy. If it is not, cook it for a little longer.

SERVING

Discard the pork rind, adjust the seasoning and serve the cabbage straight from the casserole or in a vegetable dish.

NOTES

If you like, you can bury a piece of smoked belly of pork in the cabbage, but it will tend to mask the glorious taste of the cabbage.

Red cabbage can be prepared in the same way; simply substitute red wine for the white and, at the end of cooking, add 2 tablespoons wine vinegar.

Cabbage is a most under-rated vegetable, but very popular in this region. Prepare the Chou braisé *when the cabbage is young and at its best.*

SALADE DE PISSENLITS CHAMPENOISE

SALADE DE PISSENLITS
CHAMPENOISE

Dandelion salad with potatoes and bacon

DANDELION SALAD IS FOUND *in various guises all over France, sometimes prepared with hard or soft-boiled eggs, croûtons, herbs or other additions. We think that this version from Champagne is one of the tastiest.*

PREPARATION

The potatoes: Wash them, but do not peel. Place in a saucepan, cover with cold water, add a pinch of salt and cook for about 20 minutes, until you can insert the point of a knife without meeting any resistance. Leave the potatoes to cool in the cooking water, then drain.

The dandelions: Discard the outer leaves and divide each clump into halves or quarters, depending on their size. Wash in several changes of cold water, drain, pat dry and place in a large salad bowl.

The belly of pork: Cut into large *lardons*. Heat the oil in a frying pan, add the *lardons* and cook gently until crisp.

SERVING

Pour the *lardons* and their hot fat over the dandelion leaves. In the same pan, without having wiped it out, cook the chopped shallots and onion for 1 minute over medium heat, stirring with a wooden spatula. Pour in the vinegar, let it bubble, then add the well-drained potatoes, roll them in the shallot mixture for 1 minute and pour the contents of the pan over the dandelions. Grind over 2 or 3 turns of pepper, add a little salt to taste, toss the salad and serve immediately.

NOTES

If the potatoes are not very small and new, peel them after boiling and slice them thickly.

For those who enjoy the taste of *marc*, add a spoonful of *marc de champagne* to the vinegar; no one will be shocked by the addition of alcohol – quite the contrary!

If necessary, you can use frisée or escarole instead of dandelion leaves, but the flavour and appearance will not be as good.

———— · ————

SERVES 4
PREPARATION TIME:
20 MINUTES

INGREDIENTS

200g/7oz small new potatoes

300g/11oz small wild dandelion leaves

200g/7oz semi-salted belly of pork or fat bacon

1 tablespoon groundnut oil

2 shallots, finely chopped

½ onion, finely chopped

3 tablespoons wine vinegar

salt and freshly ground pepper

⤙ SOUFFLÉS À LA VANILLE ⤚

Vanilla soufflés

SERVES 6
PREPARATION TIME:
20 MINUTES
COOKING TIME: 10 MINUTES

INGREDIENTS

CRÈME PÂTISSIÈRE

400ml/14fl oz milk

140g/5oz sugar

2 vanilla pods, split lengthways

10 egg yolks

50g/2oz flour

a little icing sugar, for dusting

8 egg whites, plus a pinch of sugar

40g/1½oz softened butter

70g/2½oz sugar

EQUIPMENT

6 soufflé dishes, about 10cm/4in
diameter, 6cm/2½in deep

H ISTORICAL RECORDS SHOW *that vanilla soufflé originated in the Meaux area – hence its inclusion in the Champagne region. We certainly associate the unique flavour of a vanilla soufflé with that of champagne.*

Michel adores cooking vanilla soufflés; he believes they are the easiest to make! Of course, there are exceptions, such as the amazingly elaborate chocolate and vanilla 'harlequin' soufflé which Michel prepared as his entry in the Meilleur Ouvrier de France *competition in Paris in 1976. Perhaps not everyone could aspire to that!*

PREPARATION

The crème pâtissière: Combine the milk, two-thirds of the sugar and the vanilla pods in a saucepan and bring to the boil. Put the egg yolks in a bowl with the rest of the sugar and work with a balloon whisk for several minutes. Fold in the flour, whisk until the mixture is smooth, then pour on the boiling milk, whisking continuously.

Pour the custard back into the pan, set over high heat and boil for 3 minutes, whisking all the time. Pour the custard into a bowl, sprinkle lightly with icing sugar to prevent a skin from forming and keep in a warm place.

The soufflé dishes: Brush the insides of the dishes with butter, tip the sugar into one dish and rotate it so that the entire surface is covered with sugar. Tip the sugar into the next dish and repeat the operation until all the dishes are coated with sugar.

Preheat the oven to 220°C/425°F/gas 7 and put in a baking sheet.

ASSEMBLING THE SOUFFLÉS

Beat the egg whites in an electric mixer or by hand until they are half-risen. Add a pinch of sugar and beat to fairly stiff peaks.

Remove the vanilla pods from the *crème pâtissière*, then use a whisk to mix in about one-third of the egg whites. Carefully fold in the rest with a spatula. Fill the soufflé dishes with the mixture and smooth the surface with a palette knife. Use the point of a knife to ease the mixture away from the edge of the dishes. This will help the soufflés to rise.

COOKING

Place the soufflés on the heated baking sheet and cook in the preheated oven for 10 minutes. Dust the surface with icing sugar and serve at once.

———— · ————

SOUFFLÉS À LA VANILLE

BEIGNETS DE FROMAGE BLANC

Soft cream cheese fritters

SERVES 6

PREPARATION TIME:
30 MINUTES, PLUS 2–3 HOURS
RESTING AND
15–20 MINUTES FREEZING

COOKING TIME: 2–3 MINUTES

INGREDIENTS

BATTER

7g/1 teaspoon fresh yeast

75ml/3fl oz milk

130g/4½oz flour

60ml/2fl oz pale ale

1 egg yolk

a pinch of salt

2 tablespoons oil

300g/11oz *fromage blanc*, very well drained so that it is firm

80g/3oz mixed candied fruits, diced (cherries, oranges, angelica etc.)

100g/4oz sugar

1 vanilla pod, split lengthways

oil for deep-frying

2 egg whites

caster or icing sugar

EQUIPMENT

deep-fat fryer

U NFORTUNATELY, THESE SWEET TREATS *from Champagne are no longer as widely available as they once were. The fritters take time and a great deal of care to prepare, but you will find they are well worth the attention you lavish upon them.*

PREPARATION

The batter: Make the batter as for *Beignets de pommes à la normande* (page 34).
The fromage blanc: Mix the candied fruits and half the sugar into the cheese. With the point of a knife, scrape the seeds from the vanilla pod into the cheese and mix well. Use 2 teaspoons to shape the cheese into small quenelles and lay them on a sheet of greaseproof paper. Place in the freezer for 15–20 minutes in order to firm up.

Heat the deep-frying oil to 180°–200°C/350°–400°F.
Coating the fritters: Beat the egg whites until half risen, add the remaining sugar and beat until firm. With a spatula, gently fold the egg whites into the batter. You can now coat the cheese quenelles in the batter.

COOKING

Very carefully holding one quenelle at a time on a fork, use a spoon to coat each one with batter, then drop it delicately into the hot oil and deep-fry for 1 minute. You can cook 6–8 fritters at a time. As soon as they rise to the surface, turn them over with a fork and cook for 1 more minute. Drain the fritters on kitchen paper and keep warm while you cook the remainder in the same way.

SERVING

Sprinkle the fritters with caster or icing sugar and serve them very hot, arranging them on individual plates, as they are extremely fragile.

———— . ————

Champagne

FRESHWATER FISH

Eel
Bream
Pike
Carp
Roach
Gudgeon
Perch
Trout

CRUSTACEANS

Crayfish

POULTRY

Cockerel
Rabbit
Goose
Chicken

GAME

Lark
Venison
Pheasant
Thrushes
Wild boar

MEAT

Mutton
Pork
Veal

CHARCUTERIE

Andouillette from
Troyes
Boudin blanc from
Rethel
Hure de porc
(potted pig's head in
jelly) from the Ardennes
Raw Ardennes ham
Stuffed and smoked
tongue
Rabbit pâté

VEGETABLES

Asparagus
Carrots
Cabbage: white, green
and red
Broad beans
Mushrooms: morels,
field mousserons,
pieds de mouton
Onions
Potatoes

CHEESE

Brie
Cendre
Chaource
Coulommiers
Fromage d'Evry
Langre
Marolle
Fromage blanc (made
from ewe's milk)

FRUIT

Strawberries
Cherries
Melons
Bilberries
Walnuts
Pears
Plums
Grapes

PÂTISSERIE

Buchette de Langres
Galette de Paron
Gougère de Bar-sur-Aube
Macaroons from
Bourbonnes-les-Bains
Marzipan
Aniseed bread from
Fère-en-Tardenois
Bilberry and greengage
tarts

CONFECTIONERY

Dragées from Chalon
Honey nougat
Honey

MISCELLANEOUS PRODUCTS

Biscuits from Rheims
Ardennes cider
Croquettes d'or
from Meaux
Plum eau-de-vie
Marc de champagne
Meaux mustard
Gingerbread

Alsace and Lorraine

A CHARMING, PROUD REGION WHERE TRADITION
IN COOKING, AND IN ALL THINGS, STILL HOLDS SWAY

Alsace is a highly unusual region, due partly to its geographical location. Its well-defined boundaries make it profoundly French, despite its pronounced Germanic dialect. It is a welcoming province, smiling and friendly, whose religious tolerance staunched the cruel wounds of war, allowing Catholic churches to be built beside Protestant chapels. The cruel history of the province has made the Alsation people fiercely individual and determined to preserve their cultural heritage. Any event is a cause for celebration – regional and local fairs, pilgrimages, harvests of corn and grapes; all these provide an excuse for merry-making in Alsace, with abundant family feasts, washed down with excellent wines.

Along the Rhine valley, at the foot of the Vosges mountains stretch fields of tobacco, corn, barley, potatoes, sugar beet and hops. There are orchards, too, and woods, with forests to the north and at the foot of the Jura.

The vineyards spread along the entire length of the sunny green Vosges. For centuries, the people of Alsace have treasured their vines, which are the lifeblood of innumerable villages nestling in the plain and on the mountain slopes. The climate and soil favour the cultivation of grapes. The Vosges form a screen from the chill of the wind. The annual rainfall is low, only 45–50cm/18–21½in, and the summers are hot. Autumn is beautiful, but the days are misty and sad in November and December. A cold wind blows on sunny winter days; even Strasbourg does not escape the *bise*.

In this region, the wines often take their names from the grapes they are made from:

sylvaner, pinot noir, muscat and the famous riesling and gewürztraminer. More modest grape varieties, like zwicker, knipperle and chasselas, make light, pleasant table wines.

We often visit Alsace during the grape harvest, which is always an occasion for hard work and intense pleasure. As we follow the wine road which winds through the vineyards for 120 kilometres, we come upon pretty villages, full of flowers, which nestle between the Vosges and the Rhine where we love to stay.

Alsace takes pride in its long history. This pride is coquettishly displayed in its towns and villages, which have retained all their old charm and ancient traditions. Romantic towers, ruined fortresses and a plethora of beflowered dovecotes abound. But some things have changed; the traditional costumes of the region are disappearing and few of the women still wear their hair coiled in a bun. These traditions are now only a part of local folklore, like the storks which used to nest on the village rooftops but have now nearly all deserted their nests, despite recent attempts to reintroduce them to the region.

In the matter of gastronomy, the Alsatian people are still famous for their excellent *charcuterie* and traditional specialities, like sausages and hams from Strasbourg, superbly prepared foie gras, *choucroute* (a meal in itself) and poultry and fish cooked in riesling. Goose and carp make festive eating and many dishes are based on lard, bacon, onions and cabbage. Mirabelle tarts and homely cakes like *kouglof* are very popular. The region boasts a surprising number of original and delicious breads, made from different types of flour and flavoured with cumin, cinnamon and much more. The local café-restaurants (called *wistubs*) serve all these excellent regional specialities.

Bounded by the plains of Champagne and Burgundy on one side and the Vosges mountains on the other, Lorraine is, like Alsace, a meeting point for diverse influences and cultures. It has seen many bitter struggles for freedom. Who has not heard of the village of Domrémy, home of *la Pucelle*, Joan of Arc. It was while she brought her sheep to graze in the meadows near the river Meuse that she heard the voices of saints sending her on her mission to save her country from the English.

This region also saw the bitterest fighting of the First World War. At Verdun, 400,000 French soldiers fell in battle; 300,000 of them lie in unmarked graves, represented only by the tomb of the unknown soldier under the Arc de Triomphe in Paris. The area is full of grim souvenirs of the 1914–18 war, but peace has reclaimed the beautiful Lorraine countryside.

Its imprecisely defined frontiers begin in the area of the Meuse, Champagne and Franche-Comté. The plain of Lorraine has an annual rainfall of 70–80cm/27½–31½in, cold winters which sometimes bring snow and hot summers. It can seem austere, with its vast fields, unbroken by hedges and trees, and its long, ribbon developments of villages.

The cooking of Lorraine is healthy and abundant, although there are few local specialities, apart from the famous macaroons from Nancy, madeleines from Commercy, *potée* – and, of course, *quiche lorraine*. This is unrefined cooking, well flavoured with butter, cream and lard. From the many streams in the region come freshwater crayfish, and fish such as pike and trout. The few regional wines are original; light rosés from Toul and Moselle. The beers are excellent, too, though less well known than those from Alsace, and the *eaux-de-vie*, made from mirabelles and raspberries, are highly prized.

Proud and upright, these rows of vines at Kaysersberg roll on for many kilometres.

SOUPE AU LARD

Bacon soup

SERVES 6

PREPARATION TIME:
30 MINUTES

COOKING TIME:
1 HOUR 40 MINUTES

INGREDIENTS

6 slices of fat smoked bacon, about 180g/6oz each

1 medium savoy cabbage

500g/1lb 2oz haricot beans (preferably from Soisson), soaked in cold water for several hours

6 leeks

6 carrots

500g/1lb 2oz small to medium potatoes

250g/8oz small, round *grelot* onions

1 large onion, halved and stuck with a clove

6 thickish slices of country bread

salt and freshly ground pepper

T HIS SUBSTANTIAL SOUP *is normally served as a main course, particularly in country areas. We like to enrich the broth and bread by adding a good ladleful of cream; believe us, this makes it diabolically delicious. However, you will still enjoy this peasant soup even without the cream.*

PREPARATION

The bacon: Lay it in an earthenware casserole or dutch oven, add 4 litres/7pt cold water and bring to the boil. Skim the surface and leave to simmer gently for 20 minutes, while you prepare the vegetables.

The vegetables: Discard the outer cabbage leaves, cut the cabbage in half and wash in plenty of water. Drain the beans, scrape and wash the leeks, carrots and potatoes and peel the *grelot* onions.

The large onion: Lay both halves directly on the hob or on an electric plate, cook for 3 minutes, then detach them with a palette knife. They should be slightly burnt.

COOKING

Put the onion halves in the casserole with the cooked bacon. Add the beans, cook for 30 minutes, then add the cabbage and carrots and cook gently for another 30 minutes, skimming the surface from time to time. Put in the leeks, potatoes and small onions, season with a little salt and pepper and cook for another 40 minutes.

The bread: Toast until pale golden.

SERVING

Put the toasted bread in a soup tureen and pour over most of the broth. Place the vegetables, bacon and the rest of the broth in a deep dish and serve the 2 dishes together; they must both be piping hot.

———— . ————

SOUPE AU LARD

GRENOUILLES À LA VITELLOISE

GRENOUILLES À LA VITELLOISE

Frogs' legs with mushrooms and herbs

THE PEOPLE OF LORRAINE *are particularly fond of this simple, delicate dish, which everyone will enjoy. It is essential to provide finger bowls, as your friends will no doubt want to lick their fingers.*

PREPARATION

Take the frogs' legs off their skewers and, using scissors, trim them, cut off a little of the upper part of the backs and the 'fingers'. Place in a bowl and pour over the milk. Leave to soak for 2 hours, then drain and pat dry thoroughly on kitchen paper.

Just before cooking, dip the frogs' legs in flour and tap off the excess. Arrange them on a plate and season lightly with salt and pepper.

COOKING

Quickly heat the clarified butter in a deep frying pan, put in the frogs' legs and cook over high heat for 3 minutes, until golden, stirring them gently with a slotted spoon every minute. Add the diced mushrooms and bread, lower the heat to medium and cook for 5 minutes, stirring every minute. Season to taste, cover the pan and cook for another 2 minutes.

SERVING

Scatter the herbs randomly over the frogs' legs and serve them on individual plates. Garnish with chervil sprigs and a lemon quarter, if you like, and serve at once while they are still hot.

SERVES 4

PREPARATION TIME:
20 MINUTES, PLUS 2 HOURS
SOAKING

COOKING TIME: 10 MINUTES

INGREDIENTS

48 medium frogs' legs

500ml/18fl oz milk

3 tablespoons flour

80g/3oz clarified butter

200g/7oz button mushrooms, cleaned and cut into small dice

80g/3oz slightly stale crustless white bread cut into small dice

2 tablespoons mixed chopped or snipped herbs (tarragon, chives, flat-leaved parsley)

salt and freshly ground pepper

1 tablespoon chervil sprigs, to garnish

1 lemon, quartered (optional)

The large Paris mushrooms can be served stuffed or cut into julienne as we do in our Grenouilles à la vitelloise. *They are also excellent raw.*

PÂTÉ LOYAL D'ALSACE EN CROÛTE

Monsieur Loyal's pâté en croûte

SERVES 6

PREPARATION TIME:
35 MINUTES, PLUS 6 HOURS
MARINATING AND 20 MINUTES
CHILLING

COOKING TIME: 1 HOUR

INGREDIENTS

800g/1¾lb boned chine or shoulder of pork, trimmed weight

1 tablespoon groundnut oil

300ml/½ pt riesling

400g/14oz *Pâte brisée* (recipe page 10)

80g/3oz shallots, finely chopped

30g/1oz parsley, finely chopped

30g/1oz dried breadcrumbs

eggwash (1 egg yolk mixed with 1 tablespoon milk)

1 tablespoon clarified butter

salt and freshly ground pepper

THIS SIMPLE ALSATIAN DISH *is highly prized by the local wine makers and country people. It was a great favourite of Monsieur Loyal, Michel's apprentice master, and every Sunday the glorious smell of the pâté would waft out of his pâtisserie, delighting the window-shoppers of Belleville, not to mention Michel himself.*

PREPARATION

Cut the pork into long strips about 1cm/½in deep and wide. Place in a bowl, pour over the riesling and the oil and cover with clingfilm. Place in the fridge and leave to marinate for 6 hours.

ASSEMBLING THE PÂTÉ

On a lightly floured marble or wooden surface, roll out the pastry into a 26 × 40cm/10 × 16in rectangle, 3–4mm/⅛in thick.

Drain the strips of pork and lay them on a baking sheet or plate. Scatter over the shallots, parsley and breadcrumbs and season lightly with salt and generously with pepper. In the centre of the pastry, arrange 6 strips of seasoned pork close together following the line of the longer side of the rectangle and taking the meat to within 7cm/3in of the shorter pastry edge. Make another layer on top of the first and continue to make more layers, one on top of the other, until all the pork is used up.

Brush both ends of the pastry with eggwash. Fold over one long side of the pastry, brush the top with eggwash, then fold over the other long side and brush both ends with eggwash. Fold up both ends to enclose the pork filling. Turn the pâté over and place it on a baking sheet, with the joins underneath. Leave to rest in the fridge for 20 minutes.

Preheat the oven to 220°C/425°F/gas 7.

COOKING THE PÂTÉ

Brush the sides, ends and top of the chilled pastry with eggwash. With the point of a knife, cut out 3 small holes or 'chimneys' at regular intervals in the top of the pastry. Place a small roll of foil in each chimney. Decorate the top of the pastry as you like (with a lattice or pastry leaves, for example). Bake the pâté in the preheated oven for 20 minutes, then reduce the temperature to 200°C/400°F/gas 6 and cook for another 40 minutes.

Use a wide palette knife or fish slice to lift the cooked pâté on to a wire rack, remove the rolls of foil and keep hot.

SERVING

Place the pâté on a long dish, brush with clarified butter and serve very hot. Give your guests a knife to cut their own slices against the grain. It is not necessary to serve any sauce, since the pâté is so moist.

NOTES

You can also serve this pâté cold; pour a little half-set meat jelly into the chimney holes before serving.

TARTE FLAMBÉE

Bacon, cream and onion flan

Originally, this tart *from the northern part of Strasbourg would be filled only with thick cream, without the addition of* fromage blanc. *The cream would be made by the peasants, who would cook the tart at the same time as they baked their bread.*

PREPARATION

The bread dough: On a lightly floured marble or wooden surface, roll out the dough into a circle about 4mm/¼in thick. Roll it round the rolling pin, then unroll it into the lightly oiled flan ring.

Preheat the oven to 220°C/425°F/gas 7.

FILLING THE TART

Whisk together the cream and *fromage blanc*, season with salt and pepper and spread the mixture over the dough base. Scatter over the onions, then strew with the thin slivers of smoked pork. Sprinkle with oil and leave at room temperature for 20 minutes.

COOKING

Bake in the preheated oven for 25 minutes.

SERVING

Slide a palette knife between the tart and the baking sheet and place the tart on a round plate. Serve very hot.

SERVES 8

PREPARATION TIME:
15 MINUTES, PLUS 20 MINUTES RESTING

COOKING TIME: 25 MINUTES

INGREDIENTS

250g/9oz Bread dough (recipe page 13)

a pinch of flour

200ml/7fl oz double cream

150g/5oz *fromage blanc*, well drained

2 onions, very thinly sliced

100g/4oz smoked belly of pork, derinded and very thinly sliced

1 tablespoon oil, plus 1 teaspoon for greasing

salt and freshly ground pepper

EQUIPMENT

1 flan ring, 22cm/8in diameter

Smoked pork for our Tarte flambée *can be easily found in an Alsace or Lorraine* charcuterie *here.*

QUICHE LORRAINE

QUICHE LORRAINE

Savoury bacon and egg flan

THANKS TO THE TALENTS *of his Alsatian apprentice master, Monsieur Loyal, Michel was introduced to the delicious specialities of the region at the early age of fourteen. The tricks of the trade and the recipes of Alsace were revealed to him in next to no time and he soon learned to love them.*

It must be said, however, that the pastry bases in Alsace cooking sometimes tend to be undercooked, so we recommend that you bake the case blind before adding the filling. Sometimes the gruyère is omitted from the recipe; it all depends on family tradition.

SERVES 8

PREPARATION TIME:
20 MINUTES, PLUS 20 MINUTES
CHILLING

COOKING TIME: 1 HOUR

PREPARATION

The pastry case: On a lightly floured marble or wooden surface, roll out the dough into a circle about 3mm/⅛in thick. Butter the flan ring and line it with the dough. Place on a baking sheet. Roll the rolling pin across the top of the flan tin to remove the excess pastry and pinch up the edges with your fingertips to make a smooth, regular border 5mm/¼in above the tin. Chill in the fridge for 20 minutes.

Preheat the oven to 220°C/425°F/gas 7.

BAKING THE PASTRY CASE BLIND

Prick the bottom of the pastry with the point of a knife or a fork. Line the case with foil or greaseproof paper, fill it with baking beans and bake in the preheated oven for 20 minutes. Spoon out the beans, remove the foil or paper and keep the pastry case at room temperature.

Increase the oven temperature to 240°C/475°F/gas 9.

The garnish: Remove the rind from the smoked pork, cut into small *lardons*, blanch in boiling water, refresh and drain. Put the *lardons* in a frying pan and sauté quickly for 1 minute only so that they do not dry out. Scatter the *lardons* and diced gruyère over the bottom of the pastry case.

The filling: In a bowl, whisk together the whole eggs, yolks and cream for 1 minute only; do not overwork the mixture. Season very lightly with salt and add a few turns of pepper, the nutmeg and kirsch if you are using it.

INGREDIENTS

300g/11oz *Pâte brisée* (recipe page 10)

a pinch of flour

a nut of butter, for greasing

200g/7oz lean belly of pork, lightly salted and not too dry

200g/7oz gruyère, 30g/1oz thinly pared, the rest finely diced

3 whole eggs

6 egg yolks

600ml/1pt double cream

a small pinch of nutmeg

2 tablespoons kirsch (optional)

salt and freshly ground pepper

EQUIPMENT

1 flan ring, about 22cm/9in diameter, 3cm/1¼in deep

baking or dried beans

COOKING

Pour the filling into the pastry case (it should come to within four-fifths of the top) and bake in the preheated oven for 20 minutes. Reduce the temperature to 200°C/400°F/gas 6 and cook for another 15 minutes. Lay the gruyère shavings on top and return the quiche to the oven for 5 more minutes. The filling should now have risen to reach the top of the pastry.

SERVING

Remove the flan ring, slide the quiche on to a round china dish or wooden platter and serve it straight from the oven.

——— · ———

CARPE À LA JUIVE

Cold carp in white wine, Jewish-style

SERVES 4

PREPARATION TIME:
35 MINUTES, PLUS 6 HOURS
CHILLING

COOKING TIME: 20 MINUTES

INGREDIENTS

1 carp, about 1.3kg/2lb 14oz

4 tablespoons oil

2 onions, thinly sliced

50g/2oz shallots, finely chopped

3 garlic cloves, finely chopped

30g/1oz flour

500ml/18fl oz dry white wine

500ml/18fl oz Fish stock (recipe page 14) or water

1 bouquet garni

salt

6 peppercorns, crushed

3 tablespoons chopped parsley, for serving

THE JEWISH COMMUNITY *is very important in the Strasbourg area. This dish is traditionally prepared on a Friday so that the Jewish housewife does not have to cook on the Sabbath.*

In one version of this dish, raisins and sultanas are used instead of parsley, but we have always preferred the flavour of the herbs.

PREPARATION

Scale and gut the carp and cut off the fins with scissors. Cut the fish into even-sized cutlets, 3cm/1¼in thick, rinse in cold water and pat dry with kitchen paper.

COOKING

Heat half the oil in a shallow pan, put in the onions and shallots and sweat for 1 minute. Add the garlic and sweat for 1 more minute. Stir in the flour and cook over medium heat, stirring continuously with a whisk, until the flour is a beautiful pale nutty brown. Pour in the wine and fish stock or water and cook, still whisking continuously, for 1 minute. Add the carp cutlets, bouquet garni, a little salt and the crushed peppercorns. As soon as the liquid boils, lower the heat, cover the pan and simmer gently for 20 minutes, skimming the surface halfway through cooking.

SERVING

Carefully lift the carp pieces out of the pan with a slotted spoon and arrange them in a deep dish. Cover with a damp cloth.

Discard the bouquet garni and reduce the cooking liquid by half. Take the pan off the heat and whisk in the remaining oil until well incorporated.

Remove the cloth covering the carp and pour over the cooking liquid. Leave to cool, then chill in the fridge for at least 6 hours.

Scatter the fish with chopped parsley and serve.

CARPE À LA JUIVE

RABLE DE LIÈVRE À LA CRÈME

Saddle of hare with a cream sauce

SERVES 2

PREPARATION TIME:
30 MINUTES, PLUS 8
HOURS MARINATING

COOKING TIME: 15 MINUTES

INGREDIENTS

1 saddle of a fine young hare, aged between 6 months and 1 year maximum

1 small piece of pork back fat, cut into 16 *lardons* 4mm/⅛in × 4mm/⅛in × 4cm/1½ in long

2 tablespoons olive oil

300ml/½pt riesling

1 tablespoon wine vinegar

1 shallot, finely chopped

1 carrot, finely chopped

1 sprig of thyme and 1 bay leaf, coarsely chopped

30g/1oz clarified butter

200ml/7fl oz double cream

1 teaspoon lemon juice

30g/1oz butter

salt and freshly ground pepper

A YOUNG HARE, *aged between 6 months and 1 year, will yield the meatiest and most tender saddle.*

PREPARATION

The saddle of hare: Using a boning knife with a longish, flexible blade, trim off the sinews from the fillets and pare off all the membrane to expose the flesh.

Break the backbone towards the middle by hitting it with a heavy knife from the inside. Using a larding needle, stud the hare with 2 rows of *lardons*, following the line of the fillets.

Lightly season the hare and place it in a long, deep dish. Pour over the oil, white wine and vinegar, stir in the chopped shallot, carrot, thyme and bay leaf, cover with clingfilm and put in the fridge to marinate for 6–8 hours. Turn the hare in the marinade every 2 hours.

Preheat the oven to 240°C/475°F/gas 9.

COOKING THE HARE

Drain the hare and pat dry with kitchen paper. Strain the marinade into a saucepan and reduce by half, skimming the surface from time to time.

Melt the clarified butter in a roasting pan, put in the hare and seal quickly all over. Add the vegetables and herbs from the marinade, place in the oven and roast the hare for 15 minutes, turning it over halfway through cooking. The flesh should still be very pink. Transfer it to a serving dish, cover with foil and keep warm.

THE SAUCE

Spoon off a little of the fat from the roasting pan and pour in the reduced marinade. Reduce again by half, then add the cream and boil until the sauce is thick enough to coat the back of a spoon lightly. Pass the sauce through a conical sieve into a saucepan. Whisk in the lemon juice and butter, season to taste and keep hot.

SERVING

Pour two-thirds of the hot sauce over the hare and serve the rest in a sauceboat. Carve the hare at the table.

NOTES

Fresh noodles or, better still, *Spätzle* (recipe page 170) make an excellent accompaniment to this game dish. If you leave the legs on the hare, the dish is known as *train de lièvre à la crème* and will serve 4 people.

It is not essential to stud the fillets with pork back fat, but this does keep the flesh moister during cooking.

———— · ————

BAECKENOFFA

Beef, pork and lamb stew

THIS ANCIENT RECIPE *is still a family favourite in Alsace, especially in country districts. Originally, the local people took their dish to the baker to cook in his oven. They would arrive early in the morning, usually on the baker's closing day, when the fire had gone out, but was still warm – the perfect temperature to simmer this wonderful family dish very slowly without having to pay for the fuel.*

PREPARATION

The meats: Cut each type of meat into 6 even pieces. Put them into 3 separate bowls and sprinkle generously with white wine. Cover the bowls with clingfilm and refrigerate for at least 12 hours.
The potatoes: Peel and wash. Cut into 1cm/½in slices.
The leeks: Trim, discard the greenest parts, split the leeks lengthways, wash very thoroughly in cold water and dice.
Preheat the oven to 160°C/300° – 325°F/gas 2–3.

COOKING

In a flameproof earthenware casserole, heat the goose fat over low heat, put in the onions and sweat for several minutes. Lay the leeks on top of the onions, then the potatoes. Add the bouquet garni, peppercorns and garlic and arrange the 3 meats separately on top, one type on the left, one in the middle and one on the right. Pour over the wine from the marinade and the remaining wine. Salt lightly, add the chicken stock or water and lay the pieces of calf's foot on top. Put the lid on the casserole.

In a bowl, mix the flour with a little cold water to make a soft paste. Spread this paste between the top of the casserole and the lid to make an airtight seal. Cook in the low oven for 4 hours.

SERVING

Present the casserole at the table just as it is. Break the seal with the back of a knife and lift off the lid. A glorious smell will waft out from the slowly-cooked casserole. Leave your guests to help themselves, starting with the meats. Be sure to remove the bouquet garni when you get to the vegetable layer.

SERVES 6

PREPARATION TIME:
35 MINUTES, PLUS 12 HOURS
MARINATING

COOKING TIME: 4 HOURS

INGREDIENTS

500g/1lb 2oz boned shin of beef, trimmed weight

500g/1lb 2oz boned chine of pork, trimmed weight

500g/1lb 2oz boned shoulder of lamb, trimmed weight

1 bottle dry white Alsace wine

1.25kg/2¾lb potatoes

800g/1¾lb leeks

60g/2oz goose fat or lard

750g/1½lb onions, thinly sliced

1 bouquet garni, with plenty of thyme

10 peppercorns, crushed

2 garlic cloves, crushed

500ml/18fl oz Chicken stock (recipe page 15) or water

1 calf's foot, blanched, split and each piece cut into 3

2 tablespoons flour

salt and freshly ground pepper

CHOUCROUTE À L'ALSACIENNE

Pickled cabbage with pork and sausages

WE SHALL NEVER FORGET *the Rabelaisian feasts of* choucroute *that our father used to prepare for us once or twice every winter. He loved making this dish and would always sing as he uncorked a bottle of riesling. Then there would be a silence as the chef tasted the wine before sacrificing it to the cabbage.*

In our experience, choucroute *needs no accompaniment other than some good strong dijon mustard; it is a meal on its own. When you love it as we do, it becomes a feast and we always have at least 2 or 3 helpings. Serve it with a good riesling or a fine light beer.*

Our friends in Alsace, who certainly know how to eat and drink well, often treat us to this unique dish when we visit their villages.

SERVES 8

PREPARATION TIME:
45 MINUTES

COOKING TIME: 2 HOURS

(recipe ingredients overleaf)

INGREDIENTS

2.5kg/5½lb white *choucroute*, preferably raw

1 onion, chopped

100g/4oz goose fat or lard

1 shin of semi-salted pork, blanched

1 lightly smoked blade of pork, blanched

600g/1lb 6oz semi-salted best end of pork in 1 piece, blanched

4 pigs' tails, blanched

1 small piece of fresh pork rind, rolled into a sausage shape and tied up with string

AROMATICS(*in a muslin bag*)
1 bay leaf; 10 juniper berries; 2 garlic cloves, peeled; 4 cloves; 6 peppercorns

500ml/18fl oz riesling

250ml/9fl oz Chicken stock (recipe page 15)

1.5kg/3lb 5oz potatoes

8 Montbéliard sausages

2 Morto sausages

8 Strasbourg sausages

4 white veal sausages

2 pieces of black pudding

1 tablespoon oil

salt and freshly ground pepper

strong dijon mustard, for serving

PREPARATION

Wash the *choucroute* in plenty of cold water until the water is clear, drain, then squeeze it with your hands, a little at a time, to extract the moisture.

COOKING

In an earthenware or cast-iron casserole, sweat the onion in two-thirds of the goose fat. Spread half the *choucroute* on top, then add all the pork, the pigs' tails and the muslin bag of aromatics. Spread over the rest of the *choucroute* and pour on the wine and chicken stock. Melt the remaining goose fat, pour it into the casserole and put on a tight-fitting lid. Cook over very low heat for 2 hours.
The potatoes: While the *choucroute* is cooking, peel and wash the potatoes. Place in a saucepan and cover with lightly salted cold water. 30 minutes before the *choucroute* is ready, cook the potatoes until tender, then drain.
The sausages and black pudding: 40 minutes before the *choucroute* is cooked, put the Montbéliard and Morto sausages in a saucepan of cold water and poach gently. After 30 minutes, add the Strasbourg sausage. Do not let the water boil, or the sausages will burst.

Smear the black pudding and veal sausages with a little oil and cook them under a medium hot grill for 6–8 minutes.

SERVING

Slice the meats, cut the pigs' tails in half and discard the bag of aromatics and the pork rind. Taste the *choucroute* and adjust the seasoning if necessary.

Put the *choucroute* into a large, deep dish. Slice the grilled sausages and black pudding and alternate them and the sliced meats with the poached sausages on top of the *choucroute*. Arrange the potatoes like a border around the edge.

Put the dish of piping hot *choucroute* on a hotplate in the middle of the table and don't forget the mustard.

———— • ————

POMMES DE TERRE RONCIN

New potatoes with a fromage blanc *sauce*

SERVES 4
PREPARATION TIME: 5 MINUTES
COOKING TIME: 40 MINUTES

INGREDIENTS

750g/1½lb small new potatoes

300g/11oz *fromage blanc*, preferably semi-salted

2 eggs

1 tablespoon double cream

1 tablespoon flour

a small pinch of nutmeg

salt and freshly ground pepper

T HIS MOUNTAIN DISH *from the Vosges, where potatoes are often served with cheese, is a very quick and simple recipe to prepare.*

PREPARATION

Wash the potatoes in cold water, brushing them lightly. Place in a saucepan, cover with cold water, salt lightly and cook for about 30 minutes, until tender. Leave them in the cooking water at room temperature.

THE SAUCE

Drain the *fromage blanc*, put it in a saucepan and heat very gently, stirring occasionally, until it has melted. In a bowl, beat together the eggs, cream and flour. Pour this mixture into the pan containing the melted cheese, stirring all the time. Simmer for 8–10 minutes, beating constantly with a wire whisk to prevent the sauce from sticking. Season with nutmeg, salt and pepper.

SERVING

Drain the potatoes and serve hot in their skins. Pour the sauce into a sauceboat and let everyone peel their own potatoes and help themselves to the sauce.

CHOUCROUTE À L'ALSACIENNE

SPÄTZLE

Alsace noodles

SERVES 4

PREPARATION TIME:
20 MINUTES, PLUS 30 MINUTES
CHILLING

COOKING TIME:
ABOUT 4 MINUTES

INGREDIENTS

250g/9oz flour

4 whole eggs

1 egg yolk

1 tablespoon double cream

a pinch of fine salt dissolved in
3 tablespoons water

a tiny pinch of nutmeg

80g/3oz butter

salt and freshly ground pepper

This is a typical alsatian dish, *which is made in almost every home. These noodles make an excellent accompaniment to meat and game, or they can be tossed in butter and served on their own or with a sauce of your choice.*

PREPARATION

Put the flour in a bowl, make a well in the centre and put in all the other ingredients except the butter. Using a spatula or your hand, draw the flour into the centre, mixing gently as you do so. When all the ingredients are well incorporated, work the mixture more vigorously to aerate it and give it a bit of body. The dough should be soft but not at all liquid. When it begins to come away from the sides of the bowl, stop mixing, cover the bowl with a damp cloth and refrigerate for at least 30 minutes.

COOKING

Fill a saucepan with water, salt lightly and bring to the boil. Spread a little of the dough on to a wooden spatula or a small wooden board and balance it on top of the saucepan. Dip a palette knife in cold water and scrape slivers of the dough into the water, dipping the palette knife into cold water every so often. Cook the *spätzle* in 2 batches for 3–4 minutes per batch, until they rise to the surface. As they rise, use a slotted spoon to transfer them to a bowl of very cold water.

SERVING

Drain the *spätzle* very well. Heat 50g/2oz butter in a frying pan, put in the *spätzle* and toss them over high heat until light golden all over. Season to taste and place in a vegetable dish.

Put the remaining butter in a small saucepan and cook until it is golden and gives off a nutty scent. Pour it over the noodles and serve immediately.

KOUGLOF (*RECIPE PAGE 172*)

⤚ KOUGLOF ⤚

Sweet brioche with raisins and almonds

SERVES 16 (1 × 3.5 LITRE/6PT MOULD OR 2 × 1.75 LITRE/3PT MOULDS)

PREPARATION TIME: 35 MINUTES IN AN ELECTRIC MIXER, 45 MINUTES BY HAND PLUS AT LEAST 4 HOURS CHILLING, AND 2½ HOURS RISING FOR THE DOUGH

COOKING TIME: 50 MINUTES FOR A LARGE MOULD, 35 MINUTES FOR 2 SMALL MOULDS

INGREDIENTS

DOUGH

25g/1oz fresh yeast

120ml/4fl oz milk, boiled and cooled to lukewarm

15g/½oz fine salt

500g/1lb 2oz flour

6 eggs

350g/12 oz butter, at room temperature

75g/3oz sugar

FILLING

200g/7oz raisins

3 tablespoons rum

a nut of butter for the mould

100g/4oz whole almonds, skinned and very lightly toasted

eggwash (1 egg yolk mixed with 1 tablespoon milk)

icing sugar, for dusting

EQUIPMENT

1 *kouglof* mould

TRADITIONALLY, Kouglof, *(also spelt* Kugelhopf *or* gougelhopf*) is baked in a tall, fluted mould. A savarin or baba mould can be used instead.*

PREPARATION

Make a dough following the method for Brioche (page 14) and leave the dough to rest in the fridge for up to 24 hours.

Put the raisins in a bowl with the rum, cover with clingfilm and leave to macerate for several hours.

MOULDING THE *KOUGLOF* (for a large mould)

Generously butter the mould and place one-third of the almonds in the bottom of the ridges.

On a lightly floured marble or wooden surface, roll out the chilled dough into a narrow rectangle long enough to line the bottom of the mould. Chop the remaining almonds and strew them and the rum-soaked raisins over the dough. Roll up the dough into a fat sausage shape, pressing it firmly together. Arrange it round the bottom of the mould and press down lightly. Seal the 2 edges together with a very little eggwash. Leave in a warm place (about 25°C/77°F) for about 2½ hours, until the dough has risen to three-quarters fill the mould.

Preheat the oven to 220°C/425°F/gas 7.

COOKING

Bake the *kouglof* in the preheated oven for 10 minutes, then lower the temperature to 200°/400°F/gas 6 and cook for another 35 minutes. If it is becoming too brown towards the end, cover it with greaseproof paper.

Invert the hot *kouglof* on to a wire rack, carefully remove the mould and return it to the oven for 5 minutes so that the centre finishes cooking and becomes lightly coloured. Leave to cool for at least 2 hours before serving.

SERVING

Lightly sprinkle the *kouglof* with icing sugar. Cut several slices with a serrated knife and serve two-thirds of the dessert uncut for guests to help themselves.

NOTES

Some people brush the *kouglof* with melted butter at the end of cooking and sprinkle it with icing sugar immediately afterwards. However, our recipe is already so rich in butter that we prefer to serve the dessert just as it is, with a simple dusting of sugar.

After 2 or 3 days, the *kouglof* is delicious sliced and lightly toasted or grilled. Sprinkle each slice with icing sugar.

Like brioche, *kouglof* freezes very well once cooked. Wrap in a plastic bag when it is barely cold and freeze; it will keep for several weeks. Be sure to take it out of the freezer 2 or 3 hours before serving.

——— · ———

Alsace and Lorraine

FRESHWATER FISH

Eel
Pike
Carp
Perch
Trout
Zander

SHELLFISH and BATRACHIANS

Crayfish
Snails
Frogs

POULTRY

Cockerel
Turkey
Goose
Pigeon
Chicken
Poussin

GAME

Red deer
Venison
Pheasant
Hare
Wild boar
Partridge

MEAT

Beef
Pork
Sucking pig
Veal

CHARCUTERIE

Andouille
Andouillettes
Boudin de Nancy
Boudin noir
Cervelas
Confit d'oie
Foie gras
Fromage de tête
Smoked ox tongue
Knackwurst
Pig's trotters
with truffles

Stuffed sucking pig
Salaison
(salted bacon, belly and
blade of pork, etc.)
Aniseed sausage
Various sausages
Game and duck
terrines and pâtés

VEGETABLES

Asparagus
Carrots
Mushrooms: ceps,
chanterelles, morels,
mousserons
Kohlrabi
Red cabbage
Chinese artichokes
Chicory
Hops
Turnips
Onions
Peas
Dandelions
Potatoes
Salsify

CHEESE

Carré de l'est
Gérardmer
Gérome
Munster
Recollet

FRUIT

Blackcurrants
Cherries
Quinces
Strawberries
Redcurrants
Mirabelles
Bilberries
Apples
Plums
Greengages
Rhubarb

PÂTISSERIE

Beignets
Pretzels
Christsolle
(yeast cake with fruit
in the shape of a
swaddled baby)
Eierkuchas
(thick pancake)
Waffles from Miremont
Fromage blanc cake
from Lorraine
Kougelhopf
Macaroons from
Boulay and Nancy
Madeleines from
Commercy
Gingerbread from
Remiremont
Stollen
(brioche with raisins)
Truffles from Metz
Tarts made with
local fruit

CONFECTIONERY

Bergamot de Nancy
Bonbons de
Contrexville
'Pebble' sweets from
the Vosges
Cherries in kirsch
Kirsch-flavoured
chocolate
Jams: bilberry,
mirabelle, blackcurrant,
eglantine
Dragées from Verdun
Redcurrant jelly
(whole berries in syrup
from Bar-le-Duc)
Honey from the Vosges
Barley sugar
from Charmes

MISCELLANEOUS PRODUCTS

White eaux-de-vie
made from local fruits
(about 20 varieties)
Smoked eel
Beer
Foie gras
Marc de Gewürztraminer
Fresh pasta
Ratafia de noyau
(made with nut kernels)
from Lorraine

Burgundy

WHERE WATER TURNS TO WINE AND
WILD MUSHROOMS CARPET THE GROUND

BURGUNDY, SET BETWEEN the Morvan and the Jura, is a land of plains, ponds and glades, of springs and undergrowth. The region stretches from the Loire to the Seine, where the Yonne flows almost from one river to the other. The sluggish movement of the rivers echoes the gentle undulations of the hills. Dense forests, spreading in the sun, spawn the wild mushrooms which are a gourmet's delight. The villages have a quaint, old-fashioned charm and benefit from a very sunny climate, with hot cloudless days in summer, few winds and an annual rainfall of only 70–80cm/27½–31½in.

In this region, the water changes into wine and vines grow all along the roads and on the hillsides. Here, bucolic festivals, pagan rituals from time immemorial, take place during grape harvesting – back-breaking work, which ends in a good square meal! Together with Bordeaux, Burgundy produces the finest wines in the world. There are six wine-producing regions: Chablis and Tonnerois (lower Burgundy), Côte de Dijon, Côte de Nuits, Côte de Beaune, Chalonais and Maconnais (or Charollais) – it is impossible to single out one wine, for there are at least a hundred, so here we list only a few of the grape varieties. Most white wines are made from the chardonnay grape; less important are pinot beurrot, pinot blanc and aligoté. The pinot noir is almost the only grape used for red wine, although the gamay is used in the Maconnais region and for wines with the appellation 'Burgundy', *Bourgogne passe tous grains* and 'Macon'.

A few years ago, under the watchful eyes of the mayor and corporation of Meursault, Michel tasted thirty-nine different Meursaults between midday and 6 o'clock the same evening . . . not without something to eat! The all-day tasting is part of a great celebration which takes place in November and lasts for three days; it is known in the wine trade as *les trois glorieuses* ('the three glorious days').

Burgundian cooking relies on wine, pork fat and cream. Many local recipes also include delicious pasta. The markets sell excellent poultry, a match for the chickens from the neighbouring region of Bresse. There are also excellent cattle markets, especially St Christophe in Brionnais. This market, one of the most important in France, specialises in Charollais cattle. When Michel goes further south to make his annual purchase of truffles, he always arranges a little escapade. This begins at 4 o'clock in the morning and ends at 8 or 9 o'clock; before setting off for home, *les maquillons*, the cattle dealers always eat at one of the cafés near the market. Michel is there to join them in a *pot au feu* or a good steak, washed down with a jug of local red wine, even at that ungodly hour of the morning! The market is not far from the Charollais *charcuterie* which our grandfather, Benoit Roux, owned and ran with his wife, Jeanne Lapierre for forty years, serving the families of his village. Our recipes for *jambon persillé* and Charollais oxtail come from our grandparents.

Albert always liked to walk in the rich pastures collecting dandelion leaves, which he proudly brought home to make delicious salads dressed with *lardons* and a trickle of warm vinegar. At Charolles there was a small wood, where he would go to collect baskets of chanterelles. Imagine his amazement when he went back twenty years later and found the mushrooms still growing there! The restaurateur on the corner transformed his last crop into an unforgettably delicious omelette. How sad that London is so far from Charolles!

This picture of Château Corton Andlé would make a perfect label for a great wine.

175

ESCARGOTS À LA CHABLISIENNE

Snails cooked in chablis

SERVES 6

PREPARATION TIME:
40 MINUTES

COOKING TIME: 3–5 MINUTES

INGREDIENTS

6 dozen snails, preferably home-bottled, or tinned

6 dozen snail shells

300ml/½ pt chablis

2 shallots, very finely chopped

1 small bouquet garni

1 unpeeled garlic clove

250g/9oz butter, at room temperature

15g/½oz garlic, very finely chopped

20g/¾oz parsley, chopped

a small pinch of nutmeg

2 tablespoons *marc de bourgogne* (optional)

8g/1½ teaspoons fine salt

freshly ground pepper

50g/2oz fresh breadcrumbs

EQUIPMENT

six 12-groove snail dishes (or twelve 6-groove dishes)

6 snail tongs and forks

AT THE WATERSIDE INN *and Le Gavroche, we use snails which we have bottled ourselves. Since preparing fresh snails is a lengthy and tedious business, we recommend non-professional cooks to use pre-cooked snails, although these will never be as tender or their flavour as full as those you prepare yourself.*

PREPARATION

The snails: In a saucepan, heat the chablis with half the shallots, the bouquet garni and the unpeeled garlic clove. Boil for 5 minutes, add the snails and simmer gently for 5 minutes. Season lightly with salt and pepper, lift out the snails and place in a bowl. Reduce the cooking liquid by half, remove the bouquet garni and garlic, then pour the liquid over the snails, mix with a spatula and set aside.

The snail butter: Cut the butter into small pieces, place in a bowl and work with a spatula until soft and creamy. Add the chopped garlic, the remaining shallots, parsley, nutmeg, *marc de bourgogne*, salt and pepper and work together with a spatula.

Preheat the oven to 240°C/475°F/gas 9.

STUFFING AND COOKING THE SNAILS

Put a small piece of snail butter in each shell, add a snail, then finish with some more butter. Arrange the snails in the dishes and sprinkle each one with a few breadcrumbs. Cook in the very hot oven for 3–5 minutes, until the butter is bubbling.

SERVING

Serve the snails as soon as they come out of the oven and provide lots of soft bread to mop up the sauce.

NOTES

The snail shells can be stuffed the night before and kept in the fridge until ready to cook.

When fresh hazelnuts are in season, we grill them, chop them finely and add them to the snail butter. They add a crunchy texture and a special flavour.

——— · ———

ESCARGOTS À LA CHABLISIENNE

JAMBON PERSILLÉ

JAMBON PERSILLÉ

Cold ham terrine with parsley and white wine jelly

WITH GREAT DELIGHT WE REMEMBER *the wonderful* jambons persillés *made by our* charcutier *grandfather Roux. These were accompanied by dijon mustard, home-pickled gherkins and small white onions in vinegar. There was also a salad of dandelion leaves with garlic croûtons; the supposed consequence of eating these leaves, known as* pissenlits *('wet the bed'), invariably brought a smirk to our childish faces.*

PREPARATION

The ham or shoulder: Soak under a trickle of cold running water for 12–24 hours to remove the salt. Place the ham or shoulder in a large pan and cover with fresh cold water. Bring gently to simmering point; if possible, use a thermometer to check that the water temperature reaches 80°–90°C/175°–195°F (maximum).

Cook very gently for 30 minutes, skimming the surface as often as possible, then add the carrots, onions, bouquet garni, peppercorns, shin of veal and the calf's foot. Simmer for a further 2 hours, then pour in 650ml/1pt white wine and cook for another 30 minutes. The ham or shoulder should now be so well cooked that you can shred it with a fork. Leave in the pan to cool to 30°C/85°F.

Remove the cooled meat from the pan and discard all the aromatics. Strain the cooking liquid through a conical sieve into a saucepan, skim off the fat and reduce by half. Take the pan off the heat and stir in the vinegar. Pour the liquid into a bowl set on crushed ice and leave to cool to a jelly, stirring with a spatula from time to time. Season with salt and pepper.

While the jelly is cooling, take the meat off the bones of the calf's foot, shin of veal and ham. Discard some of the rind and fat, then cut the shin and ham into large cubes and the calf's foot into very small dice.

ASSEMBLING THE *JAMBONS PERSILLÉS*

Pour the rest of the wine into a saucepan, add the chopped shallots and cook for 3 minutes. Take the pan off the heat, add the garlic, then pour into a chilled bowl and leave to cool. When the liquid is cold, add the chopped parsley and tarragon, 1 tablespoon chervil and the diced calf's foot.

Take the terrines or ham dishes out of the fridge and line the bottom and sides of each with a thin layer of half-set jelly. Make a layer of large cubes of veal and ham, then pour on a little more half-set jelly. Spoon in some of the diced calf's foot and herb mixture, pour on a little more jelly, then make another layer of cubed veal and ham. Make 3 or 4 layers in this way, ending with a thin, even layer of jelly. Delicately press some chervil leaves into this layer, then refrigerate the terrines for at least 12 hours.

SERVING

Serve the *jambon persillé* in the terrine and give your guests a large flat knife (such as a boning or *charcuterie* knife) to cut their own portion. Cut off the first outside slice before presenting the terrine at table; this will make serving easier and the dish will look even more appetizing.

NOTES

This dish will keep very well in the fridge for several days, so it is worth making a couple of terrines at the same time; they will disappear very fast!

Serve the *jambon persillé* with a beaujolais nouveau, or, at Easter (the traditional time to eat this dish), a beaujolais villages.

MAKES 2 TERRINES TO SERVE 20 PEOPLE

PREPARATION TIME: 1 HOUR, PLUS AT LEAST 12 HOURS SOAKING AND 12 HOURS SETTING

COOKING TIME: ABOUT 3 HOURS

INGREDIENTS

1 small uncooked salted ham, about 3.5kg/7lb 12oz, or 1 uncooked salted shoulder of ham, about 2.5kg/5½lb

200g/7oz carrots

150g/5oz onions, stuck with 3 cloves

1 large bouquet garni, with plenty of thyme

1 tablespoon crushed peppercorns

½ shin of veal, blanched

1 calf's foot, split lengthways and blanched

1 bottle white burgundy (Aligoté, Saint-Véran or Macon)

1 tablespoon good wine vinegar

150g/5oz shallots, finely chopped

20g/¾oz garlic, finely chopped

3 tablespoons snipped flat-leaved parsley

1 tablespoon snipped tarragon

2 tablespoons chervil leaves (1 for preparing the terrines, 1 for the moulds)

salt and freshly ground pepper

EQUIPMENT

2 terrines or burgundy ham dishes, well chilled (place in the fridge before embarking on the recipe)

cooking thermometer (optional)

OEUFS POCHÉS À LA
~ BOURGUIGNONNE ~

Eggs poached in red wine

SERVES 4

PREPARATION TIME:
20 MINUTES

COOKING TIME: ABOUT 35
MINUTES FOR THE SAUCE

INGREDIENTS

8 eggs

1 bottle pinot noir wine

60g/2oz butter

20g/¾oz flour

1 bouquet garni

6 crushed peppercorns

twelve 5mm/¼in slices from a *baguette*

60g/2oz clarified butter

1 tablespoon groundnut oil

1 large onion, finely sliced

2 tablespoons chopped parsley

salt and freshly ground pepper

THE PERFECT SNACK FOR BURGUNDIAN *restaurateurs returning from market, this dish also makes a pleasant lunch hors d'oeuvre served with a salad of* mâche *(cornsalad). Whatever the occasion or hour, this simple dish is easy to prepare – and typically Burgundian.*

PREPARATION

The eggs: Bring the wine to the boil in a shallow pan, put in the eggs and poach them. Carefully lift them out with a slotted spoon and lay on absorbent paper. Trim off the straggly edges, cover the eggs with a damp cloth and keep at room temperature. Strain the wine through a conical sieve.

The sauce meurette: In a saucepan, heat half the butter, stir in the flour and cook gently for 2 minutes to make a roux. Take the pan off the heat and add the wine in which you poached the eggs, whisking all the time to prevent lumps from forming. Still whisking, return the pan to a low heat and bring the sauce to the boil. Add the bouquet garni and crushed peppercorns and simmer for 30 minutes.

Take the pan off the heat and pass the sauce through a conical sieve, then whisk in the remaining butter. Season to taste and keep warm.

The croûtons: Heat the clarified butter in a frying pan and fry the bread until golden on both sides. Place on a wire rack.

The onion: Heat the oil in a frying pan, add the onions and cook gently for 15 minutes until pale golden. Season to taste.

Preheat the oven to 180°C/350°F/gas 4.

SERVING

Spread the onion over the croûtons. Place an egg on each one and on individual plates, allowing 2 eggs per person. Warm the eggs in the preheated oven for 1½ minutes, then pour the sauce generously over the top and around the edge, sprinkle the top with parsley, and serve at once.

———— · ————

OEUFS POCHÉS À LA BOURGUIGNONNE

GOUGÈRES

Choux puffs with gruyère

MAKES ABOUT 50

PREPARATION TIME:
15 MINUTES

COOKING TIME: 18–20 MINUTES,
DEPENDING ON THE SIZE OF
THE PUFFS

INGREDIENTS

1 quantity Choux paste (recipe
page 12)

100g/4oz freshly grated gruyère

a tiny pinch of cayenne pepper

a tiny pinch of nutmeg

eggwash (1 egg yolk mixed with
1 tablespoon milk)

butter, for greasing the baking
sheet

EQUIPMENT

piping bag with a plain nozzle

IN BURGUNDY, THESE *small* gougères *are often served after wine tastings. They fill the room with their savoury smell and are always much enjoyed. Some people like to fill them with a delicate, cheese-flavoured béchamel. This certainly adds a regal note, but we prefer them plain, simply flavoured with the gruyère.*

PREPARATION

Preheat the oven to 220°C/425°F/gas 7.

Make the choux paste following the method on page 12. As soon as the last egg has been added, fold in three-quarters of the gruyère, taking care not to overwork the mixture. Season with cayenne and nutmeg.

Piping out the choux paste: Fill a piping bag with two-thirds of the paste. Pipe small puffs, about 2.5cm/1in diameter, in staggered rows on to a lightly greased baking sheet. Brush them with a little eggwash and mark them with the back of a fork dipped in eggwash each time. Sprinkle over the rest of the gruyère.

COOKING

Bake in the preheated oven for 5 minutes. Open the oven door, leave it slightly ajar and cook for another 15 minutes. The puffs should be firm and crunchy on the outside, but still slightly moist in the centre. Take them out of the oven and place on a wire rack.

SERVING

Pile the puffs into a pyramid on a plate and serve them slightly warm as an *amuse-bouche* or appetizer.

We often wonder how many gougères *have been consumed during a tasting of such marvellous burgundies.*

⤙ TRUITE À LA BOURGUIGNONNE ⤚

Trout in red wine

W E NEVER TIRE OF THIS CLASSIC DISH. *The sauce will only be as good as the wine you use, so do choose a really decent burgundy.*

SERVES 4

PREPARATION TIME:
30 MINUTES

COOKING TIME 10 MINUTES

INGREDIENTS

4 river trout about 200g/7oz each

80g/3oz butter

1 bottle good red burgundy

1 carrot, thinly sliced

1 onion, thinly sliced

1 small bouquet garni

200g/7oz small button mushrooms

300g/11oz small new *grelot* onions

60g/2oz clarified butter

a pinch of sugar

20g/¾oz flour

1 tablespoon chopped parsley

salt and freshly ground pepper

PREPARATION

The trout: Cut off the fins and gills with scissors and pull out the intestines through the gills. Wash the trout in very cold water, making sure that no trace of intestine remains. Gently pat dry with kitchen paper.

Lightly grease a gratin dish large enough to hold all the trout in one layer. Season the fish all over with salt and pepper and place in the dish. Pour over the wine and tuck the sliced carrot and onion and the bouquet garni between the trout.

The mushrooms: Peel and wipe with a damp cloth. Finely slice the stalks and put them with the trout. Keep the caps for the garnish.

The small onions: Peel, wash and pat dry. Heat the clarified butter in a small shallow pan, put in the onions and a pinch of sugar and cook until pale golden. Add 2 tablespoons water, cover and leave in a warm place.

Preheat the oven to 220°C/425°F/gas 7.

COOKING THE TROUT

Cook the trout in the preheated oven for 10 minutes, basting them with their cooking liquid after 5 minutes. When they are cooked, transfer them one at a time to a serving dish, using a palette knife and draining each one carefully. Cover with foil and keep warm.

THE SAUCE

In a small bowl, mash together with a fork 30g/1oz butter and the flour to make a *beurre manié.* Set the gratin dish containing the cooking liquid from the trout over low heat and whisk in the *beurre manié.* Bring to the boil and let the sauce bubble gently for 5 minutes, whisking continuously with a wire whisk, then pass through a conical sieve into a saucepan. Simmer the sauce for 5 minutes, then add the mushroom caps and cook gently for 3 more minutes. Stir in the remaining butter. Add the small onions to the sauce and heat through for a few moments without letting the sauce boil. Season and keep hot.

SERVING

Pour the hot sauce and garnish over the trout, sprinkle with parsley and serve at once with plain steamed potatoes.

——————— • ———————

CAILLES AUX RAISINS ET CHÂTAIGNES

CAILLES AUX RAISINS
ET CHÂTAIGNES

Quails with grapes and chestnuts

NOWADAYS, MOST QUAILS ARE FARMED *and bought oven-ready. Although they are generally of good quality, we still remember the days when the Morvan region proliferated with wild quail. These delicious birds, still in their attractive plumage, could be found in all the local markets alongside other game birds. They looked so much more beguiling than the naked birds we buy now, and we regret the turning of another page of culinary history.*

SERVES 4
PREPARATION TIME: 1 HOUR
COOKING TIME: 10–12 MINUTES

PREPARATION

The quails: Draw them if the butcher has not already done so and keep the livers. Roughly chop the necks, heads, gizzards and wing tips and set aside.

Truss the quails, then wrap each one in a vine leaf and a thin slice of barding fat and secure these loosely with string.

The chestnuts: Make a light incision in each with the point of a small knife and place under a hot grill or in a hot oven until they open slightly. Peel the chestnuts and put them in a shallow pan with half the chicken stock and the celery. Simmer gently until they are tender but still firm and leave them in the cooking stock.

Preheat the oven to 240°C/475°F/gas 9.

The stuffing: Cut the bacon into julienne. Heat the oil in a frying pan until very hot, then sauté the bacon until golden and crisp. Lift it out of the pan with a slotted spoon and keep the cooking fat in the pan.

Cut the chicken livers into 2 or 3 pieces, put them into the hot fat with the quail livers and sauté quickly for 30 seconds. Pour in the spirit and flame it, strip the thyme leaves over the livers, salt lightly and add the spice. Transfer to a bowl and leave to cool.

Rub the cooled livers through a fine sieve, then work in 30g/1oz butter with a fork. Fold in the bacon julienne taking care not to overwork the mixture and keep at room temperature.

COOKING THE QUAILS

Heat 30g/1oz clarified butter in a roasting pan, put in the quails and seal for 2 or 3 minutes, until light golden on all sides. Add the carrots, shallots and bay leaf, then roast in the hot oven for 8 minutes, turning the birds over after 5 minutes.

Put the quails breast-side down on a serving dish and cover loosely with foil. Lower the oven temperature to 180°C/350°F/gas 4.

Put the chopped giblets in a sauté pan with about 15 of the least attractive grapes, place over medium heat and brown for 2–3 minutes. Deglaze with the red wine, reduce by half, then add the remaining chicken stock. Increase the heat, reduce by two-thirds, then pass the sauce through a conical sieve into a saucepan. It should just lightly coat the back of a spoon; if it is too thin, reduce it for another few minutes. Take the pan off the heat, beat in the remaining butter and keep hot.

The croûtons: Heat the rest of the clarified butter in a frying pan and fry the bread until golden on both sides.

Use a palette knife to spread the stuffing on the croûtons, then heat them in the oven for about 3 minutes. Meanwhile carefully remove the trussing string from each of the quails.

INGREDIENTS

- 8 quails, with their livers if possible
- 16 fresh or tinned vine leaves (if tinned, rinse in cold water before using)
- 8 small, very thin slices of barding fat
- 250g/9oz chestnuts
- 300ml/½pt Chicken stock (recipe page 15)
- 1 celery stalk
- 100g/4oz smoked bacon, derinded and thinly sliced
- 2 tablespoons vegetable oil
- 6 very fresh chicken livers, galls removed
- 2 tablespoons *marc de bourgogne* or cognac
- 1 sprig of thyme
- a pinch of mixed spice
- 60g/2oz butter
- 80g/3oz clarified butter
- 2 carrots, coarsely chopped
- 2 shallots, coarsely chopped
- 1 bay leaf, snipped
- 400g/14oz white or black grapes, peeled and deseeded
- 200ml/7fl oz red burgundy
- 8 thin slices from a *baguette*
- salt and freshly ground pepper

(recipe continued overleaf)

SERVING

Arrange 2 croûtons in the centre of each plate. Place a quail on each croûton, leaving on the barding fat and vine leaves. Drain the hot chestnuts and arrange them around the quails.

Warm the remaining grapes in the hot sauce, taking great care that the sauce does not boil. Space the grapes alternately with the chestnuts around the quails, then pour the sauce over the birds.

Pour the rest of the sauce into a sauceboat and serve separately.

NOTES

Encourage your guests to use their fingers and provide them with finger bowls.

——— · ———

QUEUES DE BOEUF CHAROLLAISES
À LA VIGNERONNE

Charollais oxtail braised in red wine

O UR MOTHER TAUGHT US *to enjoy celeriac, which she often uses in stews and casseroles. We particularly like it with oxtail, which is one of our favourite dishes. Don't forget to provide plenty of bread for your gourmet friends to mop up the delicious sauce. A watercress salad dressed with walnut oil and heavily spiked with mustard and vinegar adds a note of freshness to this robust, country dish.*

SERVES 4

PREPARATION TIME:
35 MINUTES, PLUS 3–4 HOURS
SOAKING

COOKING TIME: 3 HOURS

INGREDIENTS

1.2kg/2¾lb large oxtails, preferably charollais

30g/1oz lard

2 bottles red burgundy, côtes de Beaune or côtes de Nuits

1 pork rind, about 150g/5oz

4 garlic cloves, unpeeled and crushed

8 shallots, peeled and left whole

1 onion, thinly sliced

1 bouquet garni

400g/14oz carrots, peeled and cut into 1cm/½in rounds

300ml/½ pt Veal stock (recipe page 15)

6 peppercorns, crushed

200g/7oz field mushrooms if possible, or button mushrooms

½ celeriac

1 tablespoon flat-leaved parsley leaves

salt and freshly ground pepper

PREPARATION

The oxtails: Soak in cold water for several hours. Cut off any excess fat, then cut the tails into pieces through the joints and pat dry on a tea towel.

COOKING THE OXTAIL

Preheat the oven to 160°C/320°F/gas 2–3.

In a large flameproof casserole, heat the lard, put in the pieces of oxtail and seal for about 6 minutes until well browned on all sides. Bring the red wine to the boil in a saucepan.

Remove the oxtail from the casserole and line the bottom of the casserole with the pork rind, laying it fat-side down. Return the oxtail to the casserole, then add the garlic, whole shallots, onion, bouquet garni and carrots. Pour in the wine and veal stock, salt lightly, add the crushed peppercorns and bring to the boil. Cover the oxtail with greaseproof paper, then with the lid, and cook in the preheated oven for 2 hours.

The mushrooms: Wipe clean and trim off stalks if necessary.

The celeriac: Peel and cut into quarters or into 6 pieces depending on size. Place in a saucepan, cover with cold water, bring to the boil, blanch, refresh and drain.

When the oxtail has been cooking for 2 hours, add the mushroooms and celeriac and cook for another hour.

SERVING

Carefully lift out the oxtail and vegetables from the casserole, using a slotted spoon. Immediately reduce the sauce until it will lightly coat the back of a spoon, then discard the pork rind and bouquet garni. Scatter the oxtail and vegetables into a deep serving dish. Skim off the fat from the surface of the sauce if necessary, season to taste and pour the boiling sauce over the oxtail and vegetables. Sprinkle with parsley and serve at once.

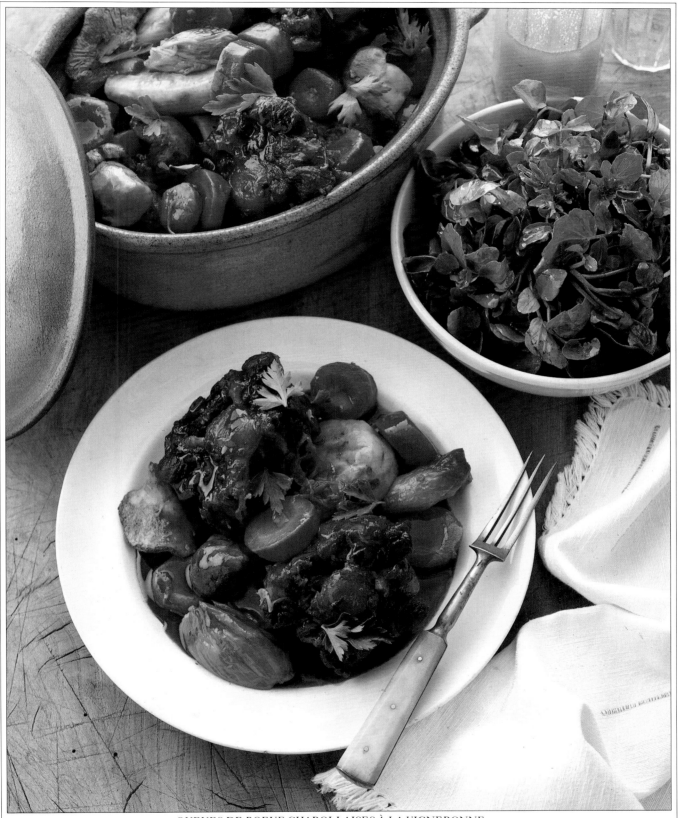

QUEUES DE BOEUF CHAROLLAISES À LA VIGNERONNE

LAPIN SAUTÉ À LA MOUTARDE

Rabbit with dijon mustard

SERVES 4

PREPARATION TIME:
40 MINUTES

COOKING TIME: ABOUT
20 MINUTES

INGREDIENTS

1 wild or farmed rabbit, about
1.5kg/3¼lb, cut into 8 pieces

90g/3oz clarified butter

250g/9oz small button
mushrooms

120g/4½oz butter

juice of ½ lemon

400g/14oz mange-tout or spinach

80g/3oz strong dijon mustard

30g/1oz fresh breadcrumbs

150g/5oz lean bacon, cut into
lardons and blanched

1 tablespoon finely snipped
tarragon or parsley

salt and freshly ground pepper

HERE IS A DELICIOUS *combination of tender rabbit and locally-produced mustard – the mustard coating makes the rabbit especially moist and tasty.*

PREPARATION

The rabbit: Heat 60g/2oz clarified butter in a large frying pan. Lightly season the rabbit pieces, put them in the pan and seal until lightly golden on both sides. Transfer the rabbit to a wire rack and leave to rest at room temperature for 8–10 minutes.

The mushrooms: Trim the stalks and wipe the caps with a damp cloth. Heat 40g/1½oz butter in a frying pan, add the mushrooms and lemon juice and fry until golden. Put the mushrooms on a plate.

The mange-tout or spinach: Top and tail or remove the stalks and wash the leaves. Cook in a pan of lightly salted boiling water for about 6 minutes; the vegetables should still be firm. Refresh in cold water and drain.

Preheat the oven to 240°C/475°F/gas 9.

FINAL COOKING OF THE RABBIT

Grease the bottom of a roasting pan with the remaining clarified butter. Brush the rabbit pieces with mustard, roll them gently in the breadcrumbs and arrange in the roasting pan. Cook in the hot oven for 12 minutes, then remove all the pieces except the legs and keep warm. Cook the legs for another 8 minutes.

The lardons: Sauté in a frying pan with a nut of butter for 3 minutes.

SERVING

Heat 40g/1½oz butter in a saucepan, add the green vegetables and mushrooms and heat through. Finally, add the *lardons* and season to taste. Divide the vegetable mixture between 4 plates and arrange the rabbit pieces on the vegetables.

Melt the remaining butter and pour it over the rabbit, then sprinkle with tarragon or parsley and serve immediately.

NOTES

Vary the vegetables according to the season, but keep them simple, as is the custom in this part of France.

SALADE DE CHOUX AU LARD

Cabbage salad with bacon

THIS DISH IS SOMEWHAT SIMILAR *to the* Salade de pissenlits champénoise *(page 149). The best cabbage is that picked after the first frosts, when it is at its tastiest and is both tender and crisp.*

PREPARATION
Discard the outer leaves from the cabbage if they are too coarse or withered. Quarter the cabbage, wash in cold water and drain. Cut away the core and the largest ribs, then shred the cabbage leaves as finely as possible, using a large heavy knife. Place in a bowl.

SEASONING
In a frying pan, heat the lard with the *lardons* and cook very gently until the *lardons* are crunchy. Take the pan off the heat and add the shallots, then, 30 seconds later, the vinegar. Pour the hot seasoning over the cabbage, add pepper to taste and mix quickly.

SERVING
Serve the cabbage still slightly warm in a salad bowl.

SERVES 4
PREPARATION TIME:
10 MINUTES

INGREDIENTS

1 medium hearty savoy cabbage

2 tablespoons lard

200g/7oz smoked belly of pork, blanched and cut into *lardons*

2 shallots, finely chopped

4 tablespoons red wine vinegar

salt and freshly ground pepper

OMELETTE SUCRÉE AU POTIRON

Sweet pumpkin omelette

WE USED TO EAT THIS OMELETTE *during the depression after the war, since eggs and pumpkin were readily available in the country even in those lean times. It is no less delicious for all that. In these days of plenty, you can flavour the pumpkin with alcohol, such as* marc de bourgogne *or a few drops of orange flower water.*

PREPARATION
The pumpkin: Remove the skin and seeds and cut the flesh into small cubes. Heat the syrup in a saucepan, put in the pumpkin, cover the pan and poach for 5 minutes. Put two-thirds of the pumpkin in a bowl with a little syrup and continue to cook the rest, stirring with a whisk, until it turns to a purée. Transfer to a bowl. Heat the grill or a salamander to very hot.
The eggs: Separate them. Beat the whites until half-risen, then add the sugar and gently stir the whites into the yolks.

MAKING THE OMELETTE
Heat the clarified butter in a frying pan and cook the eggs over high heat for about 2 minutes, stirring with a fork to make an omelette. Fill it with cubes of pumpkin, fold over and turn the omelette on to a serving dish.

SERVING
Mix the pumpkin purée with the cream and pour the mixture over the omelette. Place under the hot grill or salamander until the top is lightly glazed. Sprinkle with icing sugar and serve immediately.

SERVES 3–4
PREPARATION TIME:
10 MINUTES
COOKING TIME: 2 MINUTES

INGREDIENTS

250g/9oz pumpkin

100ml/3½fl oz Sorbet syrup (recipe page 17)

6 eggs

50g/2oz sugar

30g/1oz clarified butter

100ml/3½fl oz double cream

icing sugar, for dusting

⤙ RIGODON ⤚

A creamy dessert with brioche crumbs, nuts and currants

SERVES 6

PREPARATION TIME:
30 MINUTES

COOKING TIME:
ABOUT 50 MINUTES

INGREDIENTS

600ml/1pt milk

2 tablespoons double cream

125g/4oz sugar

½ vanilla pod, split lengthways

½ cinnamon stick, or a pinch of ground cinnamon

6 eggs

2 tablespoons rice flour

120g/4½oz coarsely crumbled Brioche (recipe page 13)

8 walnuts, coarsely chopped

20 hazelnuts, coarsely chopped

50g/2oz currants, blanched

30g/1oz butter

EQUIPMENT

1 charlotte mould, approximately 14cm/6in diameter, 12cm/4in deep

O**UR GRANDPARENTS USED TO COOK** *this traditional Burgundian dessert in the oven when the fire died down at the end of the day. It took longer to cook in this way, but it emerged wonderfully smooth and creamy and cost nothing in fuel. Our mother likes to cover the top of the* rigodon *with barely warm peach jam, or to accompany it with small dishes of strawberries or peaches, lightly poached in red wine and served well chilled. What a feast!*

PREPARATION

Preheat the oven to 150°C/300°F/gas 2.

The mixture: In a saucepan, heat the milk, cream, sugar, vanilla and cinnamon. Boil for 1 minute, then take the pan off the heat and leave the vanilla and cinnamon to infuse until the mixture is lukewarm, stirring occasionally to prevent a skin from forming.

Break the eggs into a bowl and beat them lightly with a fork or wire whisk. Add the rice flour, stir the mixture lightly, then strain the milk through a conical sieve on to the egg mixture. Stir well, but do not overwork the mixture.

Using a spatula, carefully stir in the crumbled brioche, walnuts, hazelnuts and currants.

COOKING

Generously brush the inside of the charlotte mould with butter. Pour in the *rigodon* mixture and cook in the preheated oven for about 50 minutes. To check if it is ready, slide a very fine knife point or a trussing needle into the centre; it should come out smooth and perfectly clean.

SERVING

Leave the *rigodon* to cool in the mould, then carefully turn it out on to a deep round plate. Serve cold but not chilled.

——— · ———

RIGODON

POMME PAYSANNE

Peasant apple tart

SERVES 6

PREPARATION TIME:
25 MINUTES, PLUS 20 MINUTES
CHILLING

COOKING TIME: ABOUT 50
MINUTES

INGREDIENTS

6 not too ripe dessert apples,
preferably coxes

juice of ½ lemon

a pinch of flour

400g/14oz *Pâte à foncer* (recipe
page 10)

100g/4oz butter

100g/4oz sugar

eggwash (1 egg yolk mixed with
1 tablespoon milk)

250ml/9fl oz double cream, for
serving

EQUIPMENT

1 ovenproof china flan dish, about
18cm/7in diameter, 2cm/¾in
deep, or a shallow cake tin, lightly
greased

THIS HOMELY DISH, *both simple and delicious, tastes especially good when made with apples from your own orchard, as it was when we were children.*

PREPARATION

The apples: Peel and core them, leaving them whole, and brush lightly with lemon juice.

Assembling the tart: On a lightly floured marble or wooden surface, roll out two-thirds of the pastry into a circle about 3mm/⅛in thick. Line the flan dish with the pastry, leaving an overhang. Prick the bottom with a fork, then put in the apples. Place a large nut of butter in the cavity of each one and sprinkle thickly with two-thirds of the sugar.

Roll out the remaining pastry into another circle about the same diameter as the top of the dish. Brush the pastry overhanging the dish with eggwash and cover the apples with the second pastry circle. Press the edges of the pastry circles together to seal them, and cut off the excess. Brush the top of the tart with eggwash and, with the point of a knife, cut a small hole or 'chimney' in the centre. Leave the tart to rest in the fridge for 20 minutes.

Preheat the oven to 200°C/400°F/gas 6.

COOKING

Cook the tart in the preheated oven for about 50 minutes. After 20 minutes, sprinkle the top of the tart with the remaining sugar. The apples are done when you can insert a darning needle into the thickest part of the fruit without meeting any resistance.

SERVING

Serve the tart just warm, straight from the dish and serve the cream separately in a sauceboat.

Burgundy

FRESHWATER FISH

Eel
Barbel
Bream
Pike
Carp
Gudgeon
Perch
Tench
Trout
Salmon trout

BATRACHIANS *and* CRUSTACEANS

Crayfish
Snails
Frogs

POULTRY

Duck
Turkey
Pigeon
Guinea fowl
Fat hen
Chicken

GAME

Larks
Woodcock
Quail
Wild duck
Venison
Pheasant
Thrushes
Wild rabbit
Hare
Partridge
Wood pigeon
Wild boar

MEAT

Charollais beef
Mutton
Pork
Veal

CHARCUTERIE

Andouille d'Arnay le Duc
(pork sausage)
Boudin bourguignon
(blood sausage)
Chicken and game
galantines

Jambon persillé
(cold jellied ham)
Jambonneau au macon
(ham in macon)
Judru
(pork sausage
with herbs)
Country sausage
Smoked sausage
Burgundian tripe

VEGETABLES

Asparagus
Celeriac
Chestnuts
Cabbage
Cauliflower
Pumpkin
Mushrooms:
ceps and mousserons
Chinese artichokes
Endive
Sweetcorn
Broad beans
White and
red haricot beans
French beans
Turnips
Onions
Peas
Dandelions
Leeks
Potatoes
White truffles

CHEESE

Abbaye de Cîteaux
Chevroton du
Maconnais and
de Charolles
Chèvre de Vermenton
Epoisses
Fromage blanc
Petit bourgogne or
'bonbon de culotte'
(goat cheese)
Small fresh goat cheese
from Beaune
Rouy

FRUIT

Apricots
Blackcurrants
Cherries
Strawberries
Raspberries
Redcurrants
Melon
Mirabelles
Medlars
Walnuts
Peaches
Pears (many varieties)
Apples
Grapes

PÂTISSERIE

Biscuits from Auxerre
and Avalon
Corniotte de Chany
(triangular pastries)
Duchesse fourée
(Dijon gingerbread
with orange)
Waffles
Gougères
Macaroons from Sens
Nonettes de Dijon
('little nun' iced
gingerbread cakes)
Rigodon
(tart with walnuts
and fruit jam)

CONFECTIONERY

Anis de Flavigny
Orange caramels
Châtelaine
(chocolates from
Semur in the
Auxerre region)

Pears and plums in
sweet wine
Dragées from
Macon
Chocolate snails
filled with praliné or
pistachio cream
Gravier de Sâone
(sweets from
Macon)
Honey
Tonnerois
(sweets from
Tonnerre)

MISCELLANEOUS PRODUCTS

Cassis from Dijon
Pickled gherkins
Sloe liqueur
Marc de bourgogne
Mustard with verjuice
Dijon mustard
Wine vinegar from
Auxerre and Dijon

Lyonnais

FRANCE'S TEMPLE OF GASTRONOMY, LUXURIATING
IN AN ABUNDANCE OF PRODUCE

LYONNAIS COOKING owes its excellent reputation to women, for Lyon is traditionally known as the 'temple of gastronomy' and the chauvinistic men of the region have always expected their women to cook them nothing less than the very finest meals. On the rare occasions when they went out to eat, they demanded the highest standards and only patronised restaurants where the cooking was as good as at home. We can only pay homage to a few of these women, known as *les mères lyonnaises*. Among the first was *la mère* Fillioux, famous for the fat hens *en demi-deuil* and quenelles with crayfish butter which she served at her small tavern. She inspired many more women *chef-patronnes*, like *la mère Guy*, who opened *à la Mulatière* near Lyon in 1870 and whose exquisite fish dishes and desserts were famed throughout the region, and *la mère* Brazier, a former pupil of *mère* Fillioux. All these women and many more helped to contribute to the fame of Lyonnais cuisine.

This is a town of good living, whose inhabitants enjoy laughing, joking and, above all, eating. Here, the onion is king, for it is an essential element in Lyonnais cooking. Everywhere, there are taverns, known as *bouchons*. These are early morning restaurants which serve local specialities like *grattons* (frizzled cubes of pork), good thick pancakes, *cervelles de canut* (a mixture of curd cheese, wine, oil and garlic), tripe *à la lyonnaise* and hot *charcuterie*, all washed down with chilled beaujolais.

For Michel, a trip to this region would not be complete without a wine-tasting at the famous Duboeuf establishment in Beaujolais, to the north of Lyon. Michel chooses the wines for all our restaurants, a pleasure he refuses to share with anyone. Beaujolais contains thirty-nine villages which have the right to the *appellation controllé*, beaujolais villages. Then there are the nine *grands crus*: Brouilly, Chénas, Chiroubles, St Amour, Moulin à Vent, Morgon, Juliénas, Fleurie and Côte de Brouilly. Red beaujolais is made fom the gamay grape; the chardonnay is used for the few white beaujolais.

South of Lyon is the Rhône valley, which grows the syrah grape for classed growth wines. A very small percentage of viognier grapes is used for blending the wines. Among the many great Rhône wines are Condrieu, Château Grillet, Côte Rôtie and Ampuie.

The Lyonnais people are spoilt for choice not only of wines but also of regional produce. Every day, Lyon is submerged in a sea of produce which comes from the surrounding regions – poultry from Bresse, Charollais cattle, Auvergne lamb, trout from the Alps, dairy produce from Bugey and the Dauphiné, whose butter and cream are especially delicious. There are carp and game from the Dombes, truffles from Valréas and Ventoux, fruit, vegetables and wine from the Rhône valley and more wine from Beaujolais and Burgundy – not forgetting the famous Lyonnais *charcuterie*, with its *boudin blanc* which our father prepared in his own special way and to which we often treat ourselves. All this makes Rungis market in Paris pale into insignificance. The quantity and quality of foodstuffs produced in the Lyonnais is unequalled throughout France.

The Lyonnais climate is pleasant and in summer is very sunny and hot. The winds are moderate and the annual rainfall is about 80cm/ 31½in. There are, however important differences in climate between the Rhône valley and the Beaujolais hills. In winter, the snow falls more heavily than in Paris; as children, we loved the snow, for then we were allowed to buy hot chestnuts. Nowadays we feel a twinge of nostalgia when we see the occasional hot chestnut seller on the bridges in Lyon.

A woman of Lyon smiles as she picks cherries ready to make preserves and liqueurs.

BOUDIN BLANC DE VOLAILLE TRUFFÉ

Chicken boudin *with truffles*

SERVES 18 AS AN HORS
D'OEUVRE, OR 9 AS A MAIN
COURSE

PREPARATION TIME:
1¼ HOURS

COOKING TIME:
18 MINUTES POACHING, PLUS 5
MINUTES GRILLING

INGREDIENTS

4 slices of white bread

125ml/4fl oz milk

5 shallots

50g/2oz butter

200g/7oz chicken breast fillets,
well chilled

200g/7oz pork back fat, derinded
and well chilled

5 eggs, well chilled

500ml/18fl oz double cream, well
chilled

75ml/3fl oz port, preferably white

12g/½oz cornflour

20g/¾oz fine salt

100g/4oz truffles, finely chopped
(optional)

50g/2oz slightly stale fine brioche
crumbs, sifted

2.5m/3 yards pork sausage casing

1 litre/1¾pt milk

50g/2oz coarse salt

150g/5oz butter, melted and
cooled

6 leaves of gelatine (optional)

EQUIPMENT

1 large funnel or a sausage filler

food processor

ALBERT PREPARES THIS RECIPE *to perfection; he likes to serve his* boudins *with a port-flavoured veal stock studded with chopped pistachios and a potato* mousseline. *Michel prefers them plain, with an accompanying salad of cornsalad dressed with walnut oil or some apples sweated in butter, which is how our mother serves them. What a pleasurable dilemma this choice puts us in!*

PREPARATION

The panade: Remove the crusts and cut the bread into cubes. In a saucepan, bring the milk to the boil, add the bread and stir with a spatula. Immediately, take the pan off the heat and leave for 30 minutes at room temperature until cold. Rub the mixture through a fine sieve and refrigerate.

The shallots: Peel, chop very finely and sweat gently in the butter for 2 minutes. Keep in a cool place.

The stuffing: Cut the chicken breasts and pork back fat into large cubes, grind finely in a food processor and rub through a fine sieve into a bowl set in crushed ice. Break the eggs into another bowl and beat lightly with a fork as though you were making an omelette, then mix in the cream. Using a wooden spatula, gently fold this mixture into the meats, working continuously until the stuffing is smooth and homogenous. Still using the spatula, work in the *panade*.

Mix together the port, cornflour, shallots and fine salt and stir it all into the stuffing mixture. Finally stir in the truffles, if you are using them, then the brioche crumbs.

FILLING THE *BOUDINS*

Using a funnel and your thumb, or a sausage filler, push the stuffing into the sausage casing. Tie a knot in the casing or tie it with string every 10–12cm/4–4½in. Make about 18 'sausages' in this way. Prick each one in 4 or 5 places with a needle.

POACHING THE *BOUDINS*

Put the *boudins* in a large shallow pan, then pour in the milk and 3 litres/5pt water and add the coarse salt. Set over high heat and heat to 80°–90°C/175°–195°F. Do not let the temperature rise above 90°C/195°F or the *boudins* may burst. Lay a cloth over the *boudins* to keep them immersed and to ensure that they cook evenly and poach for 18 minutes. Leave to cool completely in the cooking liquid. At this stage, you can keep the *boudins* in the fridge for several days before cooking them further; if so, when you take the pan off the heat, add 6 leaves of gelatine to the poaching liquid. Transfer the cooled *boudins* to a large bowl, pour over the liquid and leave in the fridge until needed.

COOKING THE *BOUDINS*

Make a light incision down the length of the *boudins* and peel off the skin. Roll the *boudins* in the cooled melted butter and cook gently in a frying pan or under the grill for 4–5 minutes, turning them over after 2 minutes. They should be pale golden all over.

SERVING

Allow 1 *boudin* per person as an hors d'oeuvre, or 2 if serving as a main course. Serve very hot.

BOUDIN BLANC DE VOLAILLE TRUFFÉ

QUENELLES DE BROCHET

Quenelles of pike

SERVES 10

PREPARATION TIME: 1½ HOURS, PLUS 6–8 HOURS CHILLING

COOKING TIME: 10–12 MINUTES

INGREDIENTS

PANADE

250ml/9fl oz milk

25g/1oz butter

a pinch of salt

85g/3oz sifted flour

1 egg

MOUSSE MIXTURE

320g/11oz pike fillets, skinned

200g/7oz butter, melted and cooled, but not hardened

4 whole eggs

3 egg whites

100ml/3½fl oz double cream

a pinch of nutmeg

salt and freshly ground white pepper

flour, for dusting

60g/2oz clarified butter

Sauce Nantua (recipe page 204), to serve

EQUIPMENT

food processor

10 gratin dishes

ALTHOUGH THESE QUENELLES *can be enhanced with various additions (see notes below), we prefer to serve them as our grandfather did – quite plain, with nothing added. We have been serving them this way at Le Gavroche and The Waterside Inn for over twenty years.*

PREPARATION

The panade: Put the milk, butter and salt in a saucepan and bring to the boil. Take the pan off the heat and beat in the sifted flour with a spatula, mixing well to prevent lumps from forming. Add the egg and return the pan to the heat to dry out the *panade*, stirring continuously for 1 minute. You should have about 220g/8oz *panade*. Transfer it to a bowl and cover with clingfilm to prevent a skin from forming. When the *panade* is cold, refrigerate it for 1–2 hours.

The mousse mixture: Purée the pike fillets in a food processor, then rub through a fine metal sieve. Fold in the chilled *panade* with a spatula and again rub the mixture through the sieve.

The next stage can be done in a bowl with a spatula, or in an electric mixer fitted with a plastic blade. At low speed, mix in the cooled melted butter, taking care not to add any milky deposits from the bottom of the pan. Add the whole eggs, one at a time, then the whites, working the mixture continuously. Stir in the cream and nutmeg and season with salt and 5g/½ teaspoon white pepper.

Increase the speed and beat the mixture more rapidly for 2–3 minutes, until it is very smooth and velvety. Transfer it to a tray or shallow dish, cover with clingfilm and refrigerate for 5–6 hours.

SHAPING AND POACHING THE QUENELLES

Fill a large shallow pan with lightly salted water and bring to a gentle simmer.

Divide the chilled quenelle mixture into 10. On a lightly floured marble or wooden surface, roll each piece into a large oval or sausage shape and poach immediately in the simmering water for 6–7 minutes, until just firm, turning them over very gently after 3–4 minutes. Lift out the quenelles with a slotted spoon and plunge into a bowl of iced water. When they are cold, drain them and carefully pat dry. Place on a dish, cover with clingfilm and refrigerate until you are ready to cook them (they will keep for 2 or 3 days).

COOKING AND SERVING

Preheat the oven to 180°C/350°F/gas 4 and a salamander or grill to very hot. Heat the *Sauce Nantua* until very hot but not boiling.

Brush the gratin dishes with clarified butter, arrange a quenelle on each plate and cook in the oven for 10–12 minutes, until the quenelles have increased their volume by about one-third. Immediately coat them with hot sauce and place under a salamander or very hot grill for about 1 minute, until they have a beautiful light golden glaze. Serve immediately.

NOTES

For an added note of refinement, cut some crayfish tails and mushroom caps into large dice, cook them and scatter them around the quenelles just before glazing them.

The quenelles are also excellent served with *Sauce Normande* (page 31).

QUENELLES DE BROCHET

↬ SAUCISSON LYONNAIS EN BRIOCHE ↫

Lyonnais sausage in a brioche crust

SERVES 4

PREPARATION TIME: 20 MINUTES, PLUS 25 MINUTES RISING

COOKING TIME: 45 MINUTES

INGREDIENTS

1 lyonnais sausage studded with truffles and pistachios, or 1 lightly smoked boiling sausage (about 400g/14oz)

a pinch of flour

250g/9oz Brioche dough (recipe page 14)

eggwash (2 egg yolks mixed with 2 tablespoons milk)

THIS MAKES A GOOD APPETIZER *for a party or an excellent snack, served with a salad of curly endive or cornsalad. Lyonnais sausage is undoubtedly one of the glories of the region. A* charcutier *friend of ours from near Romanèche Thorin, nicknamed 'Bobosse', is a past master at making this sausage and numerous other local specialities.*

PREPARATION

The sausage: Prick it in 5 places with the point of a knife, place in a saucepan, cover with water and bring to the boil. Lower the heat and simmer for 45 minutes; do not let it boil. Remove the sausage, refresh in cold water, make an incision in the skin with a sharp knife and peel off the skin.

The brioche: On a lightly floured marble or wooden surface, roll out the dough into a 14 × 26cm/5 × 10in rectangle, 5mm/¼in thick. Brush the centre of the dough with eggwash. Brush the sausage with eggwash and sprinkle with a dusting of flour. Place the sausage in the middle of the dough and pull up the dough to enclose the sausage completely. Press the edges to seal the dough; the ends of the sausage must not stick out. If necessary, cut off any excess dough. Place the wrapped sausage on a baking sheet, brush with the remaining eggwash and leave at room temperature (20–22°C/68–71°F) for about 20 minutes to allow the dough to rise a little.

Meanwhile, preheat the oven to 220°C/425°F/gas 7.

COOKING

Cook in the preheated oven for 25 minutes.

SERVING

Cut the sausage diagonally into at least 12 slices. Arrange on a long, narrow serving dish, lined with a white napkin. Do not serve the ends of the sausage.

Curly endive is an excellent winter salad and perfect partner to Saucisson lyonnais en brioche.

CERVELLE DE CANUT

Herb-flavoured curd cheese

S ERVE THIS DISH *which is known as 'silk-weavers' brains' – presumably because the brain power of these artisans was not held in high esteem – as an hors d'oeuvre or part of the cheese course, accompanied by a beaujolais nouveau. On no account add garlic – we are not in Provence!*

PREPARATION

Put the *fromage blanc* in an earthenware bowl and beat with a spatula for 2 or 3 minutes to lighten it. Still beating, add the shallot, herbs, olive oil, white wine, vinegar and salt and pepper, adding one ingredient at a time.

In a mixing bowl, beat the cream until the whisk leaves a trail when lifted and fold it into the cheese, using a slotted spoon. Chill in the fridge.

SERVING

Serve well chilled in the earthenware bowl accompanied by country bread.

SERVES 4

PREPARATION TIME:
20 MINUTES

INGREDIENTS

250g/9oz firm, well-drained *fromage blanc*

15g/½oz very finely chopped shallot

1 tablespoon snipped flat-leaved parsley

1 tablespoon snipped chervil

1 teaspoon snipped chives

50ml/2fl oz olive oil

50ml/2fl oz dry white wine

25ml/1fl oz white wine vinegar

50ml/2fl oz whipping cream, chilled

salt and freshly ground pepper

GRAS DOUBLE À LA LYONNAISE

Lyonnais ox tripe

O UR GRANDFATHER PARTICULARLY LOVED *this dish, served with jacket potatoes and a white Macon from his own vineyard. We also adore it, so when you make it, please invite us to join you!*

PREPARATION

Using a sharp knife cut the ox tripe into 2cm/1in cubes.

COOKING

Heat the butter and oil in a flameproof casserole or dutch oven over high heat, then add the tripe and fry for 7–8 minutes, stirring with a spatula, until lightly coloured. Put in the onion, shallots and parsley stalks and season with salt and pepper. Stir gently, then reduce the heat, cover the casserole and simmer for 30 minutes, stirring with a spatula every 10 minutes.

SERVING

Just before serving, increase the heat to high, pour in the vinegar and sauté the tripe for 2 minutes, stirring as you do so. Pour all the contents of the casserole into a deep earthenware or china serving dish and serve immediately.

NOTES

This dish can be reheated very successfully so make plenty.

SERVES 6

PREPARATION TIME:
25 MINUTES

COOKING TIME: 40 MINUTES

INGREDIENTS

1.6kg/3½lb ox tripe equal quantities of each stomach (*panse, bonnet, caille, le feuillet*), blanched

30g/1oz butter

50ml/2fl oz vegetable oil

200g/7oz onion, coarsely chopped

150g/5oz shallots, coarsely chopped

100g/4oz tender parsley stalks, finely chopped

3 tablespoons red wine vinegar

salt and freshly ground pepper

JAMBON AU FOIN AND GRATIN DE MACARONIS AUX TRUFFES

JAMBON AU FOIN

Ham cooked with hay

W E LIKE TO SERVE *this simple yet masterly dish with a madeira sauce made with 50-year-old madeira and our* Gratin de macaronis aux truffes *(recipe below) makes the ultimate accompaniment. Any leftover ham is excellent served cold with toasted country bread.*

PREPARATION
Saw through the ham knuckle bone and bone out the chump end, or ask your butcher to do this for you.

Place the ham in a bowl, cover with cold water and leave to soak for 12 hours, changing the water every 4 hours.

COOKING
Put the ham in a casserole, cover with cold water, then add the hay and seasonings. Place over high heat and watch carefully in the early stages; on no account must the water boil. Skim the surface from time to time. If you are using a thermometer, make sure that the water temperature remains at a constant 80°–90°C/175°–195°F.

Cook for 1¾ hours, then drain the ham, peel off the rind and serve at once.

SERVING
Arrange the hay on a serving dish and lay the ham on top. Carve a few slices and cut the rest at the table.

SERVES 6–8

PREPARATION TIME: 20 MINUTES, PLUS 12 HOURS SOAKING

COOKING TIME: 1¾ HOURS

INGREDIENTS

smoked ham, lightly salted in brine, 2.5–3kg/5½–6lb 10oz

250g/9oz top quality hay, fresh or dried

1 sprig of thyme

2 bay leaves

6 cloves

10 juniper berries

EQUIPMENT

cooking thermometer (optional)

GRATIN DE MACARONIS AUX TRUFFES

Gratin of macaroni with truffles

T HIS RICH AND DELICIOUS *recipe must be the ultimately decadent version of a traditional macaroni cheese!*

COOKING THE MACARONI
Bring to the boil a large pan of lightly salted water and add the oil. Put in the macaroni and cook at a gentle boil for about 10 minutes, until *al dente*, stirring occasionally with a spatula to prevent the pasta from sticking together. Refresh, drain and cut into 5cm/2in lengths. Preheat the grill for 10 minutes.

THE SAUCE
Pour the cream into a saucepan, set over low heat and reduce by half, until it coats the back of a spoon. Add the truffle with its juice and cook for another 2 or 3 minutes. Still over low heat, gently stir in the macaroni and half the gruyère. Season to taste with nutmeg, salt and pepper and give the macaroni another bubble. Grease a gratin dish with the butter and pour in the macaroni mixture. Sprinkle over the rest of the gruyère.

SERVING
Place the dish under a hot grill until bubbling and golden and serve piping hot.

SERVES 6

PREPARATION TIME: 20 MINUTES

COOKING TIME: ABOUT 10 MINUTES

INGREDIENTS

200g/7oz long macaroni

1 tablespoon groundnut oil

500/18fl oz double cream

1 bottled truffle, about 30g/1oz, finely diced, with its juice

100g/4oz grated gruyère

a pinch of grated nutmeg

salt and freshly ground pepper

30g/1oz butter, for greasing the dish

EQUIPMENT

1 gratin dish

❧ POULET AU VINAIGRE ❧

Chicken in wine vinegar

SERVES 4
PREPARATION TIME:
20 MINUTES
COOKING TIME:-20–25 MINUTES

INGREDIENTS

1 × 1.3kg/2lb 14oz chicken, cut into 8 pieces

60g/2oz clarified butter

100g/4oz shallots, finely sliced

150ml/5fl oz verjuice or aged wine vinegar

1 bouquet garni

100ml/3½oz dry white wine

150ml/5fl oz Chicken stock (recipe page 15) or water

beurre manié (30g/1oz butter and 10g/⅓oz flour, mashed together with a fork)

1 tablespoon flat-leaved parsley

salt and freshly ground pepper

THIS DISH ORIGINALLY COMES *from Lyon or Burgundy. It is best made with verjuice (the acid juice of unripe grapes) instead of vinegar, if you can find it. Fresh pasta is the perfect accompaniment to this inexpensive dish, which is very easy to prepare.*

PREPARATION

The chicken pieces: Season lightly with salt and pepper.

COOKING

Heat the butter in the frying pan, then put in the chicken pieces and fry on all sides for 7–8 minutes until golden. Add the shallots, cook for 1 minute, then pour in the verjuice or vinegar. Put in the bouquet garni, cover the pan and cook over gentle heat or in the oven at 170°C/325°F/gas 3 for 10 minutes. Take out all the chicken pieces except the thighs, which will need another 5 minutes' cooking. Keep the chicken pieces warm while you make the sauce.

The sauce: Pour the white wine into the pan and reduce by one-third. Add the chicken stock or water and whisk in the *beurre manié* to bind the sauce. If it seems too thick, add a little more chicken stock or water. Season to taste.

SERVING

Arrange the chicken pieces in a deep white china dish and pour over the hot sauce. Sprinkle with parsley leaves and serve at once.

———— · ————

❧ SAUCE NANTUA ❧

Creamy crayfish sauce

SERVES 4
PREPARATION TIME:
20 MINUTES
COOKING TIME: 12–15 MINUTES

INGREDIENTS

44 cooked freshwater crayfish (reserve the cooking *nage*)

1 medium carrot

2 medium shallots

90g/3oz butter

4 tablespoons cognac

1 litre/1¾pt cooking *nage* from the crayfish

½ bay leaf

500ml/18fl oz double cream

salt and cayenne pepper

THE CLASSIC *SAUCE NANTUA is a creamy béchamel, finished with crayfish butter. Our version is lighter and more subtle. It is delicious served with any poached fish or shellfish, and particularly good with* Quenelles de brochet *(recipe page 198).*

PREPARATION

The crayfish: Separate the heads and tails, shell the tails, wrap the flesh in a damp cloth and keep either to serve with the sauce (warm crayfish by steaming lightly) or to use to garnish in another recipe.

The carrots and shallots: Peel, wash and slice thinly. Place in a shallow pan with 30g/1oz butter and sweat until soft.

COOKING

Crush the crayfish heads, add them to the pan and set over high heat. Flambé with the cognac, add the bay leaf and cooking liquid and reduce by half.

Add the cream, cook over low heat for 10 minutes, then pour the sauce into a food processor or blender and process for a few seconds. Pass through a conical sieve into a saucepan, set over high heat and bring to the boil. Lower the heat and cook until the sauce is thick enough to coat the back of a spoon. Stir in the remaining butter, a little at a time. Season to taste with salt and cayenne pepper.

———— · ————

POULET AU VINAIGRE

GRATIN DE BETTES AUX LARDONS

Gratin of spinach beet with bacon

SERVES 4

PREPARATION TIME:
35 MINUTES

COOKING TIME: 30–40 MINUTES

INGREDIENTS

1kg/2lb 3oz freshly picked tender spinach beet

140g/5oz butter

50g/2oz flour

750ml/1¾pt Chicken stock (recipe page 15)

200ml/7fl oz double cream

2 egg yolks

a small pinch of nutmeg

150g/5oz onions, thinly sliced

200g/7oz smoked streaky bacon, cut into *lardons*

salt and freshly ground pepper

S PINACH BEET IS EXTREMELY *popular in this part of France. It makes an ideal accompaniment to all sorts of meat dishes, including our* Jambon au foin *(recipe page 203) and* Poulet au vinaigre *(recipe page 204).*

PREPARATION

The spinach beet: Cut off the roots, check each stalk separately and cut away any stringy parts. With a small, sharp knife, cut the green part of the leaves from the stalks, as they will need less cooking. Cut the stalks into large sticks, about 4cm/1½in long and 2cm/¾in wide. Wash the stalks and leaves separately in cold water and drain.

THE SAUCE

Melt 60g/2oz butter in a small saucepan, then stir in the flour and cook for 2–3 minutes to make a white roux, stirring with a whisk. Pour in the chicken stock and bring to the boil, whisking continuously. Lower the heat as far as you can and leave to simmer for 20 minutes. Stir in two-thirds of the cream and simmer for another 10 minutes.

Mix the remaining cream with the egg yolks. Take the pan off the heat and whisk in the cream mixture, then season with nutmeg, salt and pepper. Keep the sauce hot, making sure that it does not boil.

COOKING THE SPINACH BEET

Bring a saucepan of salted water to the boil, put in the stalks and cook for 15 minutes. Taste one; it should be firm but not crunchy. Add the green leaves and cook for another 5 minutes. Stand the saucepan under cold running water for 1 minute to stop the cooking, then drain the beet in a colander and pat dry with kitchen paper.

Preheat the oven to 240°C/475°F/gas 9.

The onions: Heat 40g/1½oz butter in a frying pan, put in the onions and sweat over low heat for 20 minutes, stirring occasionally and taking care that they do not colour. Add the *lardons* and simmer them gently with the onions for 5 minutes.

COOKING AND SERVING THE GRATIN

Spread the onions and *lardons* over the bottom of a gratin dish. Mix the spinach beet into the sauce and pour into the dish. Dot the top with a few flakes of butter and cook in the very hot oven for 10 minutes. If the top of the gratin is not yet lightly browned, brown it under the grill for 1 or 2 minutes. Serve straight from the dish.

NOTES

You can make the sauce with milk instead of chicken stock, but the flavour will not be the same. The cooking time of the beet will vary according to its size and the time of year.

BALLES DE NEIGE

Snowballs

THERE IS NOTHING NICER *than these light fritters when they are hot and freshly made. Their airy delicacy gives them their nickname of* 'pets de nones' *('nuns' farts'). Do not be tempted to make them in advance; they really must be eaten the moment they are cooked.*

PREPARATION
The paste: Follow the method for choux paste (see page 12), adding the lemon zest at the same time as the eggs.

Grease a baking tray or line it with baking parchment. Pipe out the paste into even-sized balls, about 2cm/¾in diameter (if you have not got a piping bag, use a spoon).

COOKING
Heat the oil until very hot. Using a palette knife, put 8 or 10 balls into the hot oil; they will puff up and rise to the surface after 2 or 3 minutes. Carefully turn them with a slotted spoon so that they become golden all over. Drain them, place on absorbent paper or a cloth and keep warm. Cook the remaining fritters in the same way.

SERVING
Roll the fritters in the vanilla-flavoured sugar and sprinkle with icing sugar, so that they look like snowballs. Place on a plate lined with a doily or, better still, a napkin, and serve piping hot.

NOTES
The only tricky part of this recipe is the cooking; do not be afraid to let the oil become really hot. Lift the fritters out of the oil from time to time to let them 'breathe' and dry out during cooking. They should be both crisp and melt-in-the-mouth.

———— · ————

SERVES 6–8
PREPARATION TIME: 35 MINUTES
COOKING TIME: 2–3 MINUTES

INGREDIENTS
PASTE
350ml/12fl oz water
50g/2oz butter
2 pinches of salt
180g/6oz sifted flour
4 eggs
grated zest of 1 lemon

butter for greasing
oil for deep-frying
200g/7oz sugar, plus a small pinch of powdered vanilla, or 200g/7oz vanilla sugar
100g/4oz icing sugar

EQUIPMENT
piping bag with a plain 1cm/½in nozzle
deep-fat fryer

GAUFRES À LA LYONNAISE

GAUFRES À LA LYONNAISE

Lyonnais waffles

AS CHILDREN, OUR MOTHER *used to spoil us with these treats, first in the Charollais, then in Vincennes, when we were older but still just as greedy. Children and adults alike will enjoy these waffles topped with redcurrant or quince jelly. Serve some whipped cream separately.*

THE BATTER

Put the flour in a bowl and make a well in the centre. Put in the sugar (reserving a pinch for the egg whites), salt, cooled melted butter and the egg yolks. Gradually add the milk, beating continuously with a whisk until the mixture is very smooth. At the last moment, stir in the flavouring. Cover the bowl with a plate and leave the batter to rest at room temperature for 30 minutes.

THE WAFFLE MIXTURE

Switch on the waffle iron (or heat it over a flame if you have an old-fashioned model).

Beat the egg whites until risen, add a pinch of sugar and beat until fairly firm. Immediately, fold them gently into the batter; do not overwork.

COOKING THE WAFFLES

Lightly brush the plates of the waffle iron with butter. Ladle in just enough waffle mixture to cover the grid. Close the lid and cook for 3–4 minutes (if you are using a non-electric model, turn the iron over after 2 minutes). The cooking time will depend on whether you like your waffles crunchy or soft in the centre, but either way they should be a beautiful golden colour.

Place the cooked waffles on a wire rack and make the rest in the same way; it may not be necessary to grease the grid each time.

SERVING

Arrange the waffles on a plate lined with a napkin or doily. Sprinkle over a little caster or icing sugar and eat them as soon as they are cooked – they are much nicer when absolutely fresh.

———— · ————

SERVES 6

PREPARATION TIME:
10 MINUTES, PLUS 30 MINUTES RESTING

COOKING TIME: 3–4 MINUTES

INGREDIENTS

250g/9oz flour

25g/1oz sugar

a pinch of salt

75g/3oz butter, melted and cooled

3 eggs. separated

400ml/14fl oz cold milk

flavourings of your choice (eg: orange blossom, orange, vanilla or lemon zest)

30g/1oz butter, for greasing the waffle iron

EQUIPMENT

waffle iron

TARTE AU MASSEPAIN DE LUBECK

Marzipan tart from Lubeck

SERVES 8
PREPARATION TIME: 1½ HOURS
COOKING TIME: 30–35 MINUTES

INGREDIENTS

500g/1lb 2oz shelled almonds in their skins

150ml/5fl oz orange flower water

500g/1lb 2oz sugar, sifted

60g/2oz icing sugar, for dusting

rose water

pink or green food colouring (optional)

EQUIPMENT

1 flan ring, about 22cm/9in diameter, 2cm/¾in deep

templates of the shapes of your choice, or pastry cutters

IT IS SAD THAT THIS RECIPE, *once passed on from generation to generation in the Lyonnais, is nowadays forgotten. It does take a long time to prepare, but it is original and delicious – a real taste of the past.*

PREPARATION

The marzipan: Fill a saucepan with water, bring to the boil and plunge in the almonds for 2–3 minutes. Drain, place on a cloth and squeeze them between your thumb and forefinger so that they pop out of their skin. Rinse them in cold water and dry in a cloth.

Grind the almonds in a food processor, adding the orange flower water and sifted sugar, a little at a time, until the mixture has the consistency of a paste. Pour it into a saucepan and dry over very low heat, stirring continuously with a spatula, until the paste comes away from the sides of the pan and no longer sticks to your fingers.

The flan case: Divide the marzipan into 2 equal parts. On a marble or wooden surface dusted lightly with icing sugar, roll out one half to a thickness of 0.5–1cm/¼–½in. Lay the flan ring on the rolled-out marzipan and cut round the edge of the ring with a pointed knife. Keep the trimmings.

Carefully remove the flan ring to leave a round marzipan flan base. Roll this around the rolling pin and carefully unroll it on to a baking sheet lined with a sheet of greaseproof paper. Moisten the edges with rose water.

Roll the trimmings into a rope about 0.5–1cm/¼–½in thick and lay it around the edge of the flan base. Pinch up the top in a regular diagonal pattern, using a pastry crimper or your thumb and forefinger, making it as attractive as possible.

If you have any marzipan left over, you could colour it pink or green and arrange it as a border or lattice around the edge.

Moulding the decorations: Lightly sprinkle a marble or wooden surface with icing sugar and roll out the remaining marzipan to a thickness of 0.5–1cm/¼–½in. Place your templates or pastry cutters on the marzipan and cut out shapes with a pointed knife, taking care not to distort the shape. Discard the trimmings.

COOKING AND SERVING

Preheat the oven to 180°C/350°F/gas 4.

Moisten the flan base with rose water and arrange the shapes on it in an attractive pattern. Cook in the preheated oven for 30–35 minutes, then leave to cool. Serve cold.

NOTES

If you prefer, you can make the marzipan shapes without the flan base. These make delectable little white biscuits, crunchy at the edges and soft in the middle, which are fun to munch at any time. Place the shapes on a baking sheet lined with greaseproof paper and cook at 150°C/300°F/gas 3 for 20–25 minutes. They will keep well in an airtight container.

TARTE AU MASSEPAIN DE LUBECK

TOURTE DES APÔTRES

Apostles' tart

SERVES 8–10

PREPARATION TIME:
45 MINUTES, PLUS 1 HOUR
CHILLING

COOKING TIME: 20 MINUTES

INGREDIENTS

PASTRY

100g/4oz whole blanched almonds

100g/4oz sugar

100g/4oz butter

a pinch of powdered cinnamon

50g/2oz fresh white breadcrumbs, soaked in 2 teaspoons rum and 2 teaspoons Sorbet syrup (recipe page 17)

120g/4½oz flour, plus a pinch for dusting

FILLING

100g/4oz sultanas

6 dried figs

50g/2oz candied orange peel, blanched

50ml/2fl oz rum or madeira

60g/2oz apricot jam

ICING

100g/4oz fondant icing

30g/1oz chopped toasted almonds

EQUIPMENT

24cm/10in flan ring

THIS LYONNAIS TART *is similar to a mince pie, but topped with a fondant icing and toasted almonds.*

PREPARATION

The pastry: Crush the almonds in a pestle with a mortar or in a food processor. Add the sugar and butter and work the mixture for 1 minute. Transfer to a bowl and, using a spatula, stir in the cinnamon, breadcrumbs and flour and work until you have a firm, homogenous dough. Wrap in greaseproof paper and refrigerate for 1 hour.

Preheat the oven to 200°C/400°F/gas 6.

Rolling out the pastry: Divide the pastry into 2 equal parts. On a lightly floured marble or wooden surface, roll out one half to a thickness of 3–4 mm/⅙in. Lay the rolling pin on the pastry, carefully roll the pastry on to the rolling pin, then unroll it on to one end of a baking sheet lined with greaseproof paper; this way, you will not spoil the shape.

Place the flan ring on the pastry and cut round it with the point of a knife. Cut away the excess pastry and carefully remove the flan ring, leaving a 24cm/10in circle of pastry. Repeat with the second piece of pastry, placing it on the same baking sheet beside the first circle. Discard the trimmings.

COOKING

Bake in the preheated oven for 20 minutes. Remove the pastry circles and raise the oven temperature to 250°C/500°F/gas 10.

The filling: Finely chop the sultanas, figs and orange peel, place in a saucepan with the rum or madeira and simmer for 5 minutes, then stir in the apricot jam.

ASSEMBLING THE TART

Using a palette knife, spread the filling evenly over one of the pastry circles and carefully place the other circle on top.

Icing: Heat the fondant icing in a saucepan until barely warm, adding about 2 tablespoons water to give a liquid icing. Brush the icing over the tart, then sprinkle with toasted almonds. Return to the very hot oven for 30 seconds to dry the icing and give it a beautiful shine.

SERVING

Slide the tart on to a round serving plate and present it whole to your guests.

Lyonnais

FRESHWATER FISH

Eel
Carp
Gudgeon
Perch
Pike
Roach
Shad
Salmon
Tench
Trout

SHELLFISH *and* BATRACHIANS

Crayfish
Frogs

POULTRY

Pigeon
Poularde
(roasting chicken)
Chicken

GAME

Woodcock
Quail
Wild duck
Pheasant
Hare
Partridge
Wild boar
Teal

MEAT

Beef
Pork
Veal

CHARCUTERIE

Andouille
Andouillette
Boudin de crèpieu
Cervelas
Tripe
Gratons (crackling)
Jesus de Lyon
(smoked pork liver
sausage)
Petit salé
(salt pork)
Rosette de Lyon
(dry pork sausage)
Sheep's trotter salad
Lyonnais boiling
sausage
Dried sausage

VEGETABLES

Artichokes
Chard
Cardoons
Chicory
Marrows
Mushrooms: boletus,
ceps, chanterelles,
morels
Spinach
Watercress
Green beans
Onions
Extra fine peas
Potatoes
Turnips
Salads: mâche
(cornsalad),
groine d'âne
(dandelion)
Tomatoes

CHEESE

Cervelle de canut
(soft curd cheese
with herbs)
Fresh and half-dried
goat cheese
Mont d'Or

Rigotte de Condrieu
Rougerets

FRUIT

Cherries
Chestnuts
Quinces
Strawberries
Wild strawberries
Raspberries
Hazelnuts
Walnuts
Pears
Plums
Greengages

PATISSERIE

Acacia flower fritters
Lyonnais bugnes
or merveilles
Frangipane
Marrow cake

Matefaim sucré
(sweet pancake)
Shortbread
Tarte lyonnaise
(puff pastry with
almonds and kirsch)

CONFECTIONERY

Chocolate from Lyon
and St Etienne
Marrons glacés
Fruit jellies
from St Etienne

MISCELLANEOUS PRODUCTS

Fruit eaux-de-vie
Marc de beaujolais
Ratafia
(made from nut kernels)

213

Languedoc and Roussillon

AUDACIOUS AND VARIED LATIN FLAVOURS FROM THE
MOUNTAINS AND THE SEA

THIS REGION OF mountains and plains, with its varied geographical features and interesting history, where bloody religious wars raged between Protestants and Catholics, is much beloved of archaeologists.

Roussillon forms the frontier between France and Spain. The mountain range of the Pyrenées, with its abundance of game, both unites and separates the two countries.

The boundary of Languedoc is traced between Provence and Dauphiné by the Rhône, although this is not the only river to flow through this unusually beautiful region. Numerous tributaries of the Rhône, the Ardèche, the Gard and the Garonne and its tributary the Tarn, the Hérault, the Orb, the Aude, the Agly, the Tet and the Tech also flow through the area and offer a rich haul of fish. But the greatest variety of fish comes from the Mediterranean sea, which borders the Roussillon coast and contains those fish which give a special, indescribably wonderful flavour to the famous soups of the region.

This region, so full of culinary riches, was the cradle of many great chefs, including Prosper Montagné. Just as Provençal cooking is Mediterranean in character, the cooking of Languedoc and Roussillon has a Latin flavour, audacious and varied. Snails are prepared in a thousand and one ways, as are cassoulets, each version claiming to be authentic and original. There is poached chicken served with individual plates of seasonings for you to mix yourself, *brandade* of salt cod (Nîmes proudly boasts the best version of this delectable dish), and so many other specialities. Here, goose fat is used for cooking and for potting and preserving goose, duck and pork. The great wooden cupboards in the dining rooms of this region disgorge jars and tins of home-made or farmhouse pâtés, preserved foie gras, truffles, *confits* and much more. When our friends offer us hospitality, we are overwhelmed by an avalanche of local produce, all unique. The wines of this region make excellent drinking – rosés and reds from Banyuls, Pelure d'oignon, Roussillon (from the Tet valley), Clos St Bernard, Clos St Jean, Malvoisie, Muscat (from Riversaltes), Minervois, Narbonnais, red wines from Laviledieu and many others – which so perfectly complement the cooking.

There are fine *premiers crus*, too; from the Rhône come white St Péray, sparkling Blanquette de Limoux and reds like Cornas, St Joseph and les Maures. This region, especially the Aude and Hérault, produces the largest quantity of excellent table wines, using many different grapes, including mauzec, clairette, cinsaut, syrah, malbeck, gamay, negrette, carignan, grenache and mourvèdre.

The climate favours the production of wine, with plenty of sun and an annual rainfall of only 50–70cm/20–27½in. However, there is an important difference between the Hérault and the interior of the eastern Pyrenées. Particularly in the spring, this area is buffeted by winds – the cold north-westerly *tramontane*, the stormy *autan*, the sometimes violent south-westerly *cers* and the south-easterly *marin*, which often brings rain. These winds can spring up very unexpectedly, as we discovered to our cost several years ago when camping there.

These fields of lavender, undulating in the wind, are typical of this area as well as of Provence. The young lavender flower is delicious lightly candied to decorate a dessert.

MOULES DE BOUZIGUE GRILLÉES

Grilled mussels from Bouzigues

SERVES 4
PREPARATION TIME:
30 MINUTES

INGREDIENTS

1 kg/2lb 3oz mussels (preferably from Bouzigues)

200g/7oz softened butter

15g/½ oz chopped parsley

8g/¼ oz chopped garlic

1 small shallot, finely chopped

a pinch of nutmeg

5g/¾ teaspoon salt

1 turn of pepper

30g/1oz fresh white breadcrumbs

THIS IS A SIMPLE AND VERY *popular recipe for stuffed mussels. Allow about 12 mussels per person.*

PREPARATION

The mussels: Place in a little cold water and rub them together. Scrub, debeard and rinse under running water. Place in a casserole without added water, cover and cook over high heat. Stir after 1 minute and stop cooking as soon as the mussels open. Discard any which do not.

Lift off one half of the shells, leaving the mussels attached to the other half. Arrange the mussels in the half shells in one or two gratin dishes. Strain the cooking liquor into a pan and reduce it to a *demi-glace.*

The butter: Put the butter in a bowl with all the remaining ingredients except the breadcrumbs and, using a spatula, work into a paste. At the last moment, add the mussel *demi-glace.* Divide the mixture between the mussels and sprinkle over the breadcrumbs.

COOKING

Just before serving, place the gratin dishes under a salamander or a very hot grill for 4 or 5 minutes, until bubbling and golden.

TO SERVE

Serve the mussels straight from the gratin dish to keep them piping hot.

NOTES

You can assemble the mussels and seasoned butter several hours in advance and cook them at the last minute.

Bouzigues mussels are plump and meaty; if they are hard to find, use Dutch mussels instead.

A fougasse de sète *would be perfect to mop up the delicious juice from the* Moules de bouzigue grillée.

MOULES DE BOUZIGUE GRILLÉES

ESCARGOTS À LA SOMMIEROISE

Snails with salt pork and walnuts

SERVES 4

PREPARATION TIME:
45 MINUTES, PLUS 24 HOURS
PURGING FOR LIVE SNAILS

COOKING TIME: 1¼ HOURS FOR
FRESH SNAILS, 30 MINUTES FOR
PREPARED SNAILS

INGREDIENTS

72 *petits gris* snails or 48 large
snails, preferably live, or tinned
or bottled, with their shells

a handful of coarse salt and
2 tablespoons flour, if you are
using live snails

1 bouquet garni, with plenty of
basil added

120ml/4½fl oz olive oil

10 peppercorns, crushed

150g/5oz semi-salted belly of
pork, blanched and cut into small
sticks

10 anchovy fillets, crushed

4 garlic cloves, finely chopped

150g/5oz shelled walnuts, roughly
chopped

150ml/5fl oz dry white wine

1 tablespoon shredded mixed
basil and flat-leaved parsley

salt and freshly ground pepper

THIS REGION PROLIFERATES *with recipes and different ways of preparing snails, for they are found in abundance here and are greatly enjoyed. We suggest allowing 18 snails per person, unless you have invited Michel to join you; his record stands at 96 snails in one sitting and he has no intention of ever setting out to eat fewer!*

PREPARATION

The snails: Put the live snails into a bucket or basin, sprinkle with coarse salt and flour, cover and leave to purge in a cool place for 24 hours, stirring at least twice. Wash the snails in several changes of cold water and drain them.

Bring a saucepan of water to the boil, plunge the snails and boil for 15 minutes, then drain. Ease the snails out of the shells with a trussing needle and remove the little black twist at the end of the tail. Keep the flesh and shells separately.

The court-bouillon: In a saucepan, put 1.5 litres/2½pt water, the bouquet garni, a tablespoon of olive oil, the crushed peppercorns and a little salt and bring to the boil. Add the snails and simmer for 1 hour. Keep the snails in the court-bouillon.

FINAL COOKING

Put the snails back in the shells and place in a flameproof casserole. Sprinkle over the olive oil, add the salt pork, anchovies and garlic, cover the casserole and simmer gently for 30 minutes, shaking the pan every 10 minutes, as though you were cooking mussels. Add the walnuts after 20 minutes and the white wine 5 minutes after that.

SERVING

Scatter the chopped basil and parsley over the snails and serve them straight from the casserole into deep dishes. Give everyone a snail fork and a soup spoon for the juices.

NOTES

If you use tinned or bottled snails, it is not necessary to purge them or pre-cook them in the court-bouillon. Simply put them back in their shells and do only the final cooking.

———— · ————

PETITS POIVRES LIMOUXIN

Peppery biscuits

THESE LITTLE SAVOURY BISCUITS *are delicious with aperitifs including, of course, the famous sparkling white* blanquette de Limoux.

PREPARATION
Put the flour on a work surface, make a well in the centre and put in the butter, salt, pepper and bicarbonate of soda. Mix all these ingredients with your fingertips, gradually drawing the flour into the well. When the dough resembles fine breadcrumbs, add the water, while continuing to mix with your other hand. Work the dough 2 or 3 times with the heel of your hand until it becomes completely smooth. Do not overwork. Wrap it in polythene or clingfilm and chill in the fridge for 1 hour before using it.

Preheat the oven to 220°C/425°F/gas 7.

SHAPING THE BISCUITS
Lightly flour the work surface and roll one-fifth of the dough into a small sausage shape about 7mm/⅜in diameter. Cut into 5–7cm/2–2½in lengths, depending on whether you want to twist or fold the biscuits; they can be baked just as they are or fashioned into any shape you like. Repeat the operation 4 times, until all the dough is used up.

Brush the biscuits lightly with eggwash, place on a baking sheet and cook in the preheated oven for 10 minutes, until a light golden colour. Place on a wire rack to cool.

SERVING
Arrange the warm biscuits on a plate lined with a doily.

MAKES ABOUT 500G/1LB 2OZ DOUGH (SERVES ABOUT 10)

PREPARATION TIME: 15 MINUTES, PLUS 1 HOUR CHILLING

COOKING TIME: 10 MINUTES

INGREDIENTS

300g/11oz flour, plus a pinch for dusting

100g/4oz softened butter

5g/¾ teaspoon fine salt

5g/¾ teaspoon freshly ground black pepper

2 pinches of bicarbonate of soda

125ml /4fl oz water

eggwash (1 egg yolk mixed with 1 tablespoon milk)

From this selection of herbs, the basil will be used to enhance the flavour of the Escargots à la sommieroise.

∼ POIVRONS ROUGES À LA CATALANE ∼

Catalan red peppers with a rice filling

SERVES 4

PREPARATION TIME:
30 MINUTES

COOKING TIME: 25 MINUTES

INGREDIENTS

4 red peppers

200g/7oz rice

1 sprig of thyme

4 tablespoons olive oil

1 onion, sliced into thin rings

2 tablespoons capers

250g/9oz tomatoes, peeled, deseeded and cut into small diamond shapes

100g/4oz small stoned olives, equal quantities of black and green

2 hard-boiled eggs, sliced

salt

VINAIGRETTE

2 tablespoons wine vinegar

6 tablespoons olive oil

salt and freshly ground pepper

THIS SIMPLE, *inexpensive dish, with its Spanish overtones, is found all over the Roussillon district.*

PREPARATION

Preheat the oven to 220°C/425°F/gas 7.

The rice: Cook with the thyme in boiling salted water for 15 minutes. Refresh briefly in cold water, just enough to stop the cooking, then drain. Discard the thyme and keep the rice at room temperature.

The peppers: Brush them with olive oil, put in a roasting pan and place in the hot oven for 8 minutes, turning them over after 4 minutes. They should be tender and half-cooked, with their shape still intact. Leave to cool at room temperature for about 20 minutes, then halve lengthways. Discard the white membrane, seeds, stalks and cores.

The filling: Make a vinaigrette by mixing together the vinegar, olive oil and salt and pepper. Stir in the rice, onion rings, capers and tomatoes. Reserve 8 black and 8 green olives and stir the rest into the filling. Mix well and adjust the seasoning as necessary.

SERVING

Generously fill each pepper half with the rice mixture. Arrange slices of hard-boiled egg on top and finish with an olive of each colour. Serve the peppers at room temperature, arranged on individual plates or a large serving dish.

NOTES

The peppers are not skinned so that they keep their shape when they are cooked and filled. Chick peas are sometimes added to the rice; fresh ones are quite delicious.

These black olives are amongst the best you can find both on their own and for cooking with.

POIVRONS ROUGES À LA CATALANE

LOUP FARCI EN PAPILLOTE

LOUP FARCI EN PAPILLOTE

Stuffed sea bass in a paper parcel

THE LIGHT VEGETABLE STUFFING *marries wonderfully well with the delicious flavour of the fish in this recipe, while the tomatoes add a splash of colour. This dish will confirm your talent as a true cordon bleu cook.*

SERVES 4
PREPARATION TIME: 1 HOUR
COOKING TIME: 30 MINUTES

INGREDIENTS
1 sea bass, 1.25–1.5kg/2¾–3¼lb
2 red peppers
180ml/6fl oz olive oil
1 sprig of thyme
300g/11oz aubergines
2 medium onions, finely chopped
400g/14oz very ripe but firm tomatoes
juice of ½ lemon
2 tablespoons chopped parsley
salt and freshly ground pepper

PREPARATION

The peppers: Preheat the grill or the oven to 240°C/475°F/gas 9. Smear a little oil over the peppers and place them under the grill or on a baking tray in the oven, turning them over until the skin bubbles and blackens all over. Hold the peppers under cold running water and rub them lightly with your hand to detach the skin. Pat dry with kitchen paper. Leave the oven switched on.

Halve the peppers, discard the white membrane and seeds and cut the flesh into small lozenge shapes. Put them in a saucepan with 2 tablespoons olive oil and the thyme and sweat gently for 15 minutes. Discard the thyme and put the peppers in a bowl.

The aubergines: Wash, dry and cut off the stems. Cut the aubergines into small dice. Gently heat 4 tablespoons olive oil in a frying pan, put in the diced aubergines and sauté for 10 minutes. Place in a bowl.

The onions: Warm 2 tablespoons olive oil in a saucepan, put in the onions and cook gently for 15 minutes. Place in a bowl.

The tomatoes: Peel, deseed and cut into thin strips. Warm 2 tablespoons olive oil in a saucepan, put in the tomatoes, add a little salt and plenty of pepper and cook gently for 5 minutes, then transfer to a bowl and keep hot.

The sea bass: Scale the fish, lay it on its side, then, with a filleting knife, cut along the backbone towards the belly to open it up on one side; do not cut through the belly. Repeat on the other side of the backbone. Use scissors to snip through the backbone near the head and tail and lift out the whole backbone; this will gut the fish at the same time.

Still using the scissors, with your hand inside the fish, cut off the gills, then trim off a little of the tail and cut off the back fins. Quickly rinse the fish in very cold water and dry it well inside and out with kitchen paper. Season the inside of the fish with salt and pepper.

Mix together the peppers, aubergines, onions and lemon juice, season to taste and stuff the fish with this mixture.

Lightly oil the fish on both sides and lay it on a lightly oiled sheet of greaseproof paper. Roll it up in the paper, twist the 2 ends and tie the paper loosely in 3 places with kitchen string, taking care not to tie it too tightly where the paper touches the fish.

COOKING THE SEA BASS

Place the fish in a roasting tin and bake in the preheated oven for 10 minutes, then turn it over. Reduce the oven temperature to 200°C/400°F/gas 6 and cook for another 20 minutes.

Slide the parcel on to a long serving dish, remove the string and keep warm.

SERVING

With the point of the scissors, cut out the top of the paper following the outline of the fish to make a rectangle about 18 × 8cm/7 × 3½in. With the point of a knife, remove the fish skin. Scatter a few of the hot tomatoes over the fish and sprinkle with parsley. Serve the rest of the tomatoes separately in a sauceboat.

CASSOULET DE CASTELNAUDARY

Cassoulet from Castelnaudary

INGREDIENTS

1.2kg/2¾lb small dried white haricot beans

1 unsmoked boiling sausage (about 250g/9oz)

4 coarse Toulouse sausages

400g/14oz salt belly of pork

1 semi-salted knuckle of pork

300g/11oz fresh pork rind, rolled and tied into a sausage shape

200g/7oz carrots, peeled

200g/7oz onions, peeled and halved, 1 half stuck with 2 cloves

1 large bouquet garni

4 garlic cloves

10 peppercorns, crushed

shoulder of lamb (about 1kg/2lb 3oz)

2 tablespoons goose fat or lard

300g/11oz ripe tomatoes, peeled, deseeded and chopped

30g/1oz chopped parsley

60g/2oz dried white breadcrumbs

2 preserved goose legs, home made (see *Confit de canard*, page 107), or tinned

salt

EQUIPMENT

1 large round copper or glazed earthenware casserole

mincing machine or food processor

The origins of cassoulet *are uncertain; it is found all over Languedoc, including Toulouse, Carcassonne and Castelnaudary. The garnishes vary slightly and partridge is sometimes used instead of lamb. Our own undisputed favourite is the one we have given you here, made with pork and lamb.*

PREPARATION

The beans: Soak overnight in cold water.

The sausages and meats: Prick the sausages with the point of a knife and place them in a large saucepan with the belly and knuckle of pork. Cover with cold water and bring to the boil to blanch them. As soon as the water boils, lift out all the sausages with a slotted spoon and put them in a pan of cold water. Leave the pieces of pork to cook gently for 3 minutes, then refresh them in cold water. Drain the pork and sausages.

COOKING THE CASSOULET

Drain the beans and put them in the casserole. Cover with plenty of cold, unsalted water. Add the whole peeled carrots, the onions, bouquet garni, 3 halved garlic cloves and the peppercorns. Bring to the boil, then lower the heat and simmer very gently, skimming the surface as necessary. After 20 minutes, put in the knuckle of pork and the pork rind.

The shoulder of lamb: Bone the lamb and cut away the sinews and fat, then cut the meat into 8 pieces of even weight. Heat the goose fat or lard in a frying pan and quickly brown the pieces of lamb, then drain them in a colander.

The tomatoes: When the beans have been cooking for 1 hour, add the belly of pork and the chopped tomatoes. The beans must be kept covered with liquid; add a little boiling water if necessary.

The lamb and boiling sausage: When the cassoulet has been cooking for 1½ hours, put in the lamb and boiling sausage to cook, skimming the surface from time to time. A glorious smell of cassoulet should start to waft out.

The Toulouse sausages: After another hour, grill the sausages just to brown the surface and add them to the casserole. Simmer the cassoulet for a further 30 minutes.

FINAL COOKING AND SERVING

Preheat the oven to 150°C/300°F/gas 2.

After 3 hours cooking, the beans will be deliciously melting, the meats well cooked and succulent. Taste the beans to see whether they need salt; since the pork and sausages are already salty, this may not be necessary. Discard the bouquet garni, carrots and onions.

Mince or process the pork rind to a purée and, using a spatula, mix in the parsley and breadcrumbs.

Roll the remaining garlic clove in salt and rub it over the bottom of 2 deep serving plates. Pile in the lamb and beans. Slice the belly and knuckle of pork, following the line of the bone, then cut the meat into chunks and mix it with the lamb and beans.

Remove the skins from the sausages and slice them. Arrange them on top of the dish. Shred the goose legs and push the pieces into the middle of the cassoulet. Finally, spread the breadcrumb mixture evenly over the top and cook in the preheated oven for 45 minutes, during which time a lovely crust will form.

(recipe continued overleaf)

CASSOULET DE CASTELNAUDARY

If you like, you can break up this crust with a fork and return the cassoulet to the oven so that a second crust forms. Place the dish under a salamander or a hot grill to brown the crust.

PRESENTATION

Serve the cassoulet straight from the dish. Between the first and second helpings, serve a salad of frisée with garlic croûtons. We like to eat a cassoulet this way, accompanied by a good red Cahors or a mature Corbières.

NOTES

This dish can be successfully reheated and may actually taste better.

———— · ————

CANARD SAUVAGE À LA CATALANE

Catalan wild duck with Seville oranges

SERVES 2

PREPARATION TIME:
25 MINUTES

COOKING TIME: 30 MINUTES

INGREDIENTS

1 wild duck, preferably a mallard, undrawn (about 1.25kg/2¾lb)

6 peeled garlic cloves

30g/1oz clarified butter

2 tablespoons olive oil

60g/2oz raw country ham, cut into julienne

2 Seville oranges (or 1 ordinary orange and ½ lemon), peeled, all pith removed, and cut into thin rings

150ml/5 fl oz dry white wine

200ml/7fl oz Chicken stock (recipe page 15)

1 tablespoon flour

2 tablespoons wine vinegar

30g/1oz butter

salt and freshly ground pepper

THIS IS A CLASSIC *combination of flavours, where the bitter oranges offset the richness of the duck.*

PREPARATION

The duck: Singe over an open flame and, if necessary, pull out any stubble with the point of a knife. Clean and draw the bird and remove the wishbone. Season the cavity with salt and pepper and truss the duck. Chop the neck and wing tips and keep them for the sauce.
The garlic: Blanch for 5 minutes in boiling water, then refresh, drain and crush.

COOKING THE DUCK

Heat the clarified butter and olive oil in a flameproof casserole over medium heat and seal the duck and the neck and wing tips until golden on all sides. Add the ham, crushed garlic and all but the 8 most attractive orange rings (save these for the garnish). Pour in the wine and chicken stock, cover the casserole and simmer for 10 minutes. Transfer the duck to a dish, breast side down, cover with foil and keep warm.
The sauce: Vigorously boil the duck stock for another 10 minutes. Mix together the flour and vinegar, then, with a wire whisk, stir the mixture into the stock. Cook for another 10 minutes, then adjust the seasoning. Pass the sauce through a conical sieve into a saucepan and, with the pan off the heat, beat in the butter and keep the sauce hot.

SERVING

Cut off the duck legs, place them under a hot grill and cook for 2 minutes on each side. Carve the breast into thin slices; they should be very pink. Reassemble the breasts on 2 plates, place a leg beside each breast and arrange 4 orange rings around the edge. Pour the hot sauce over the oranges and around the duck and serve immediately. Serve the rest of the sauce separately in a sauceboat.

NOTES

Wild mushrooms or mousserons, cooked in butter with a touch of parsley added at the last moment, make a wonderful accompaniment to this dish. A less classic partner would be aubergine fritters.

———— · ————

⤙ PINTADEAU BRAISÉ TARNAISE ⤚

Braised guinea fowl

THE RUSTIC STUFFING *in this dish enhances the delicate flavour of the guinea fowl. The Languedoc region abounds in lentils; simply cooked with aromatic herbs, they make an ideal accompaniment.*

PREPARATION

The stuffing: Cut the poultry livers and heart of the guinea fowl into small pieces. Heat half the goose fat in a frying pan and, over high heat, sauté the livers and heart for 10 seconds. Immediately, add the pork, cook for 2 minutes, then add the salami and raw ham and cook quickly for another 2 minutes.

Take the pan off the heat and add the garlic, parsley and olives. The texture of the stuffing should be rather coarse. Season with salt and pepper and keep the stuffing in a cool place until needed. It should still be warm when you stuff the guinea fowl.

COOKING THE GUINEA FOWL

Take out the wishbone and season the inside of the bird. Fill the cavity with the stuffing, then truss the bird.

In a flameproof casserole, heat the remaining goose fat, put in the guinea fowl and brown lightly on all sides. Add the carrot, shallots and bouquet garni and pour over one-third of the chicken stock. Cover the casserole and cook very gently for 30 minutes.

Turn the guinea fowl over, add another third of the stock, cover and cook gently for a further 20 minutes. Transfer the guinea fowl to a serving dish, untruss it, cover with foil and leave in a warm place for 20 minutes.

The sauce: Spoon off the fat from the surface of the cooking broth and pass the broth through a conical sieve into a saucepan. Add the remaining chicken stock and boil briskly to reduce the liquid to a light juice. Season to taste.

SERVING

Carve the bird at the table and spoon a little stuffing on to each plate. Serve the sauce in a sauceboat.

NOTES

You can use a 1.6kg/3½lb chicken instead of guinea fowl; prepare it in exactly the same way.

SERVES 4

PREPARATION TIME:
55 MINUTES

COOKING TIME: 50 MINUTES,
PLUS 20 MINUTES RESTING

INGREDIENTS

1 guinea fowl, about 1.3kg/
2lb 14 oz, with its heart

3 guinea fowl or chicken livers

4 tablespoons goose fat or lard

100g/4oz unsmoked neck or belly of pork, very finely diced

80g/3oz salami, finely diced

50g/2oz raw ham, finely diced

2 garlic cloves, finely chopped

1 tablespoon chopped parsley

80g/3oz olives, stoned and finely diced

1 carrot, cut into large dice

2 shallots, finely sliced

1 bouquet garni

400ml/14fl oz Chicken stock (recipe page 15)

salt and freshly ground pepper

⤙ TOMATES FONDUES À L'HUILE D'OLIVE ⤚

Tomatoes stewed in olive oil

USE VERY LARGE *good-quality tomatoes that are bursting with flavour for this fresh-tasting southern dish.*

COOKING THE TOMATOES

Put the olive oil, bouquet garni and garlic in a flameproof casserole or earthenware pot and heat gently for 2 minutes. Put in the whole skinned

SERVES 4

PREPARATION TIME:
10 MINUTES

COOKING TIME:
ABOUT 45 MINUTES

(recipe ingredients overleaf)

227

AUBERGINES ET TOMATES NÎMOISES

tomatoes, season lightly with salt and pepper, cover and cook gently for 30 minutes. Carefully turn over each tomato separately, cover and cook for another 15 minutes. By now, the tomatoes should have absorbed most of the oil and still keep their shape, but be very soft. Depending on how ripe they are, you may need to cook them for a little longer.

SERVING
Discard the bouquet garni and garlic cloves, sprinkle the tomatoes with parsley and serve straight from the casserole.

NOTES
This recipe brings out the full fruitiness and scent of the tomatoes. Some people add breadcrumbs and chopped garlic to the parsley garnish, but we disapprove strongly of this practice, unless the tomatoes are of poor quality.

INGREDIENTS

1kg/2¼lb ripe but firm local or Marmande tomatoes, skinned

150ml/5fl oz top quality olive oil

1 bouquet garni, with plenty of basil added

4 unpeeled garlic cloves

2 tablespoons finely chopped flat-leaved parsley

salt and freshly ground pepper

---·---

⌁ AUBERGINES ET TOMATES NÎMOISES ⌁

Aubergines and tomatoes from Nîmes

T HIS IS A VERY SIMPLE RECIPE *that makes the most of the wonderful flavour of the vegetables of this region.*

PREPARATION
The aubergines: Wash, dry and cut off about 1cm/½in from the stem end. Halve lengthways. Using a sharp knife, cut round the inside of the flesh about 1cm/½in inside the skin, tracing round the contours of the aubergine. With the point of the knife, score the flesh into squares, sprinkle with salt and lemon juice. Set aside for 20 minutes to draw out the bitter juices.

Pat the aubergines dry and fry in 100ml/3½fl oz olive oil, flesh side downwards, for 10 minutes, until golden. Grease a gratin dish with olive oil and put in the aubergines, skin-side down.
The tomatoes: Halve and deseed with the handle of a teaspoon. Salt lightly and alternate them with the aubergines in the gratin dish, arranging them skin-side down.
The topping: Cut the ham into very fine dice, mix in the chopped garlic, onion, parsley, breadcrumbs and 2 tablespoons olive oil. Season generously with pepper but no salt. Spread the filling as evenly as possible over the aubergines and tomatoes.

COOKING
Preheat the oven to 220°C/425°F/gas 7. Cook the vegetables for about 20 minutes, until the topping is well browned. Remove from the oven and immediately scatter the aubergines with the chopped olives. Sprinkle a few drops of olive oil over the tomatoes.

SERVING
Serve piping hot, straight from the dish or leave for 30 minutes and serve warm.

SERVES 4

PREPARATION TIME: 45 MINUTES

COOKING TIME: 20 MINUTES

INGREDIENTS

2 medium aubergines (total weight about 600g/1lb 6 oz)

salt

juice of 1 lemon

150ml/5fl oz olive oil

4 firm ripe tomatoes (total weight about 600g/1lb 6oz)

200g/7oz unsmoked raw ham

3 garlic cloves, finely chopped

1 small white onion, finely chopped

3 tablespoons chopped parsley

75g/3oz fresh breadcrumbs

freshly ground pepper

50g/2oz small nîmoise olives, very finely chopped

---·---

TARTE AUX RAISINS

Grape tart

SERVES 8

PREPARATION TIME:
20 MINUTES, PLUS 20 MINUTES
CHILLING

COOKING TIME: 30 MINUTES

INGREDIENTS

360g/12oz *Pâte sucrée* (recipe page 11)

2 tablespoons flour

a nut of butter, for greasing

750g/1½lb black or white local grapes

2 tablespoons sugar

100ml/3½fl oz whipping cream

150g/5oz *Crème pâtissière*, well-flavoured with vanilla (recipe page 17)

EQUIPMENT

22cm/9in flan ring, 2cm/¾in deep

baking or dried beans

THE LANGUEDOC AND ROUSSILLON *region abounds in a variety of excellent quality grapes. Local cooks have many different ways of using them, particularly in tarts and tartlets.*

PREPARATION

Preheat the oven to 220°C/425°F/gas 7.

The pastry case: Grease the flan ring. On a lightly floured marble or wooden surface, roll out the pastry to a thickness of about 3mm/⅛in. Place the flan ring on a baking sheet and line with the pastry. Leave to rest in the fridge for 20 minutes, then prick the bottom of the pastry with a fork and line with greaseproof paper. Fill with baking beans.

Bake blind in the preheated oven for 25 minutes. Use a spoon to lift out the beans and remove the greaseproof paper. Reduce the oven temperature to 200°C/400°F/gas 6 and return the pastry case to the oven for 5 minutes. Carefully slide it on to a wire rack and keep at room temperature.

The grapes: Wash, take them off the stalk, peel and remove any large pips. Put 150g/5oz of the least attractive grapes into a hard sieve and press the juices into a saucepan. Add the sugar and cook for 3 minutes to make a light syrup. Keep warm.

The filling: Lightly whip the cream, then mix it delicately into the *crème pâtissière* without overworking the mixture.

Filling the tart: Spread the filling evenly over the bottom of the pastry case. Arrange the grapes on top and brush them with the syrup to make them shine.

SERVING

Slide the tart on to a round plate and present it whole to your guests.

NOTES

The pastry case can be cooked and the grapes peeled the day before, but do not fill the tart until just before you serve it.

If you can manage it, by all means use *pâte sablée* instead of the *pâte sucrée*; it is finer and more delicate, but difficult to work with. However, gourmets will not fail to notice the difference!

—————— · ——————

TARTE AUX RAISINS

LE SUISSE DE VALENCE

'Swiss guard' biscuits from Valence

MAKES ABOUT 12

PREPARATION TIME:
20 MINUTES, PLUS 30 MINUTES
CHILLING

COOKING TIME: 20 MINUTES

INGREDIENTS

150g/5oz butter, at room
temperature

125g/4½oz granulated sugar

a pinch of salt

1 egg, at room temperature

65g/2oz candied orange peel,
chopped

grated zest of 1 lemon

250g/9oz wheat flour and 65g/3oz
wholemeal flour, sifted together

2.5g/½ teaspoon baking powder

a pinch of flour

EQUIPMENT

1 Swiss guard template (or any
shape you choose)

L EGEND HAS IT THAT *a detachment of the Vatican Swiss Guard was garrisoned at Valence for a long period. The picturesque uniform of the soldiers was a familiar sight and inspired a local pâtissier looking for new ideas. These delicious, exquisitely-shaped orange-flavoured* sablés *have now become the trademark of Valence.*

PREPARATION

The dough: Cut the butter into small pieces, place in a mixing bowl and work with your fingers until very soft. Add the sugar, salt, egg, orange peel and lemon zest and work all these ingredients until completely incorporated. Add the sifted flours and baking powder and mix thoroughly. Lightly knead the dough 2 or 3 times with the palm of your hand to make it completely smooth, but do not overwork it at this stage. Roll the dough into a ball, wrap in greaseproof paper and refrigerate for 30 minutes.

Preheat the oven to 180°C/350°F/gas 4.

SHAPING THE DOUGH

On a lightly floured wooden or marble work surface, roll out the dough to a thickness of 3–4mm/⅙in. Place the template on the dough and cut round it with the point of a knife to make a Swiss guard (or whatever shape you have chosen). There should be enough dough to make 10 or 12 soldiers. Using a palette knife, transfer the shapes to a baking sheet, taking care not to spoil the shape.

COOKING

Bake in the preheated oven for 20–25 minutes (a 'guard' 10cm/4in high and 4cm/1½in wide, weighing 30g/1oz, will need about 20 minutes).

The market in Valence, a city which is the gateway of Provence.

SPECIALITIES OF

Languedoc and Roussillon

FRESHWATER
FISH

Shad
Eel
Pike
Lamprey
Perch
Trout
Salmon trout

SEA FISH

Anchovy
Monkfish
Scorpion fish
Conger eel
Sea bream
Gurnard
Lemon sole
Sea bass
Mackerel
Whiting
Hake
Cod
Rockling
Grey mullet
Red mullet
Sardine
Sole
Tuna
Turbot

SHELLFISH,
CRUSTACEANS,
MOLLUSCS
and
BATRACHIANS

Spider crab
Squid
Clovisses (small clams)

Crab
Crayfish
Snails
Frogs
Bouzigue oysters
Lobster
Langoustine
Mussels
Sea urchins
Clams
Octopus
Praires (warty Venus)
Cuttlefish
Tellines (flat clams)

POULTRY

Duck
Goose
Pigeon
Guinea fowl
Chicken

GAME

Larks
Becfigues (figpeckers)
Quail
Hazel grouse
Thrushes
Wild rabbit
Hare
Macreuse (scoter duck)
Ortolan
Partridge
Plover
Teal
Wood pigeon
Wild boar

MEAT

Lamb
Beef
Venison
Pork
Veal

CHARCUTERIE

Bougnette de porc de
Cabarde (pork sausage)
Cerdagne ham
Raw, salted
mountain ham
Melzat
(large blood sausage)
Poultry liver pâté
Truffled hare pâté
Dried sausage
Toulouse sausage
Pig's liver sausage
Mountain sausage

VEGETABLES

Artichokes
Asparagus
Aubergine
Carrots
Chard
Mushrooms: ceps,
coutives, morels,
mousserons, oronges
Chestnuts
Cauliflower
Spring cabbage
Courgettes
White haricot beans
Lentils
Onions
Green and black olives
Red, green
and yellow peppers
Peas
Chick peas
Potatoes

CHEESE

Cantal
Andorran ewe's cheese
Picodon from
St Agreves
Roquefort Rouergat

FRUIT

Apricots
Almonds
Cherries
White grapes
(moissat and muscat)
Figs
Strawberries
Raspberries
White melons
Medlars
Watermelon
Peaches
Vineyard peaches
Pears
Apples
Greengages

PÂTISSERIE

Biscotin de Montpellier
Bunyète
(a type of merveille)
Croquant de Nîmes
Fouace de
gratillons sucrée
(tart with frazzled pork
and eggs)
Almond cake from
Amélie-les-Bains
Gâteau de Limoux
(citron cake)
Waffles
Sugared millas
(flat oat cakes)
Oreillettes
(sweet fritters)
Rosquillas
(almond biscuits)

CONFECTIONERY

Aniseed tart from
Villefranche
de Conflans
Berlingot de Nîmes
(boiled sweets)
Biscotin from St Paul
de Fenouillet

Crystallized fruits
from Castelnaudary
Crystallized violets
from Toulouse
Galichoux
(pistachio-flavoured
almond paste)
Honey
Jams: fig, raspberry,
bilberry
Liquorice from Uzès
Marrons glacés
Marzipan from
Montauban
Nougat from Limoux
Touron catalan
(soft nougat)

MISCELLANEOUS
PRODUCTS

Aniseed
Banyuls (aperitif)
Byrrh (aperitif)
Coriander
Gherkins
Eau-de-vie from Beziers
Truffled foie gras
Juniper berries
Olive oil
Muscat de Frontignan
(aperitif and
dessert wine)
Orange ratafia
Sea salt
Truffles from
Montferrier, Bagnols-sur-
Ceze and Uzes

233

Provence

HOMELY COOKING THRIVING ON AN ABUNDANCE OF
FRESH HERBS, VEGETABLES AND SHELLFISH

THE NATURAL BEAUTY of this area gives it a certain magic; the coastline and horizon are beyond compare. The vibrant Provençal sky, the ancient mountain crags, the plains, the sunny valleys dotted with olive groves, almond and cypress trees, vineyards and pine forests all combine in a dramatic landscape which is at once harmonious and yet full of violent contrasts.

During the hot summer days, the air is filled with the intoxicating song of the cicadas and perfumed with the scents of wild thyme, bay, fennel, basil and the great profusion of herbs which sprout from the crevices and cling to the stony, sun-scorched rockface of the Garrigue. This is the land of *santons*, colourful clay figurines made by local people. In December, these *santons* decorate the Christmas cribs, filling our heads with childhood dreams.

Every village in the region has its market, each offering an unparallelled choice of sweet fruits bursting with flavour and fresh, tasty vegetables. The market squares are usually near the town hall or church and are shaded from the sun by ancient plane trees. When your shopping is done, the shady terrace of a nearby café tempts you to spin a few yarns with the locals while you quench your thirst with a refreshing *pastis*.

The vines, too, flourish in the sun and yield rich, full-bodied wines like the celebrated classics from the Rhône valley – Châteauneuf du Pape, Côte Rôtie, Château Grillet. There are also naturally sweet wines like Beaumes de Venise and more ordinary wines that make pleasant spring or summer drinking – red or

white Bellet, Côte de Luberon, Côte de Provence, Côte de Ventoux, Muscadet de Sospel, Rasteau, Bandol, white wine from Cassis and rosé and white from des Maures. The grape varieties most commonly used are syrah, mourvèdre, grenache, carignan, cinsaut and some cabernet sauvignon.

This is the birthplace of one of the greatest chefs of all time, Auguste Escoffier; there is even a museum dedicated specifically to him at Villeneuve-Loubet.

Michel first discovered the region at the age of twenty, when he came to spend the summer months in St-Raphael-Valescure as chef to Mlle Cécile de Rothschild. Here, he fell in love with Provençal cooking and has never tired of it – quite the contrary! Provençal cookery is essentially homely, based on olive oil, tomatoes, garlic and herbs. Vegetables often stuffed or simply sweated in olive oil are king, and fruit is emperor. Omelettes filled with all sorts of vegetables are also very popular. Interestingly, tomatoes, which now play the most important rôle in Provençal cooking, were not introduced into France from tropical America until the sixteenth century.

As for fish, they grace every table, made into soups or simply grilled, stuffed with a scented stick of fennel and brushed during cooking with a sprig of thyme dipped in olive oil.

Michel was totally seduced by the region and decided to spend all his holidays there. Thus, over a period of thirty years, he has explored almost all the towns along the coast as well as the charming, picturesque hilltop towns and villages and those on the banks of the Rhône.

This river, and its tributaries the Durance and the Verdon, together with the Var, which rises at Gros-de-Cagnes and the Ardens which rises near Fréjus, divides Provence from Languedoc.

Seven years ago, Michel indulged his love of the area and bought a small shepherd's cottage near Gassin. The cottage is surrounded by a vineyard, an orchard full of fruit trees, an olive grove and a wooded area of bay trees, chestnuts and oaks. Each morning, after a visit to the market at St Tropez or Cogolin, he savours in his imagination the rustic Provençal meal he will prepare for himself, his wife and friends. At the end of each day, he works in his vineyard, which produces a white wine made by the neighbouring Château Minuty.

He loves the climate which is kind and dry all through the year; even in winter, the temperature never falls below 2°C/36°F. He prefers to be there in spring or autumn, writing his books, absenting himself in the hot months of July and August, when the temperatures soar to 30°C/86°F and there is a danger of forest fires. Occasionally, the dry spells are broken by sudden torrential rains. Many winds blow in the region – the *fahen*, *levant* and *marin*, which generally bring rain, the *grec*, which can be cold and dry over Provence, but humid on the Côte d'Azur and, of course, the violent *mistral* which can blow at any time of year, bringing clear skies, sunshine and an intense luminosity.

Michel loves the quality of life in this little paradise of natural beauty and he looks confidently ahead to his future semi-retirement in this wonderful region.

Each morning the harbours of Provence are thriving with baskets of fresh fish. Even in St Tropez there is still a corner of the harbour where the locals await the arrival of the fishing boats laden with an abundant catch. The variety of flavours and colours immediately makes one think of Bouillabaise.

SOUPE AU PISTOU

Vegetable soup with pistou

SERVES 6
PREPARATION TIME:
1 HOUR 10 MINUTES
COOKING TIME:
1 HOUR 10 MINUTES

INGREDIENTS

500g/1lb 2oz fresh haricot beans in the pod

200g/7oz tender young broad beans in the pod (optional)

300g/11oz french beans

200g/7oz carrots

250g/9oz potatoes

1 leek, about 75g/2½oz

1 tender celery stalk, about 75g/2½oz

100g/4oz baby turnips

400g/14oz courgettes

300g/11oz very fleshy tomatoes

150g/5oz pumpkin (optional)

1 onion, about 100g/4oz, peeled and stuck with 2 cloves

1 bouquet garni

100g/4oz thick vermicelli or elbow macaroni

salt and freshly ground pepper

PISTOU

4 garlic cloves

18 large basil leaves

250g/9oz freshly grated parmesan

150ml/5fl oz olive oil

T HIS SOUP, *which originally came from Genoa in Italy, is best made between spring and autumn, when the vegetables are at their peak of flavour. It will fill your house with the scents of Provence.*

PREPARATION

The vegetables: Shell the haricot and broad beans. Top and tail the french beans, wash and cut into 7mm/¼in lengths. Peel the carrots, potatoes, leek, celery and turnips. Top and tail the courgettes. Wash all these vegetables and cut into 5–7mm/¼in dice.

Peel, deseed and roughly chop the tomatoes. Peel the piece of pumpkin and roughly chop it. Keep all the vegetables separately.

PRE-COOKING

Put the clove-stuck onion in a casserole with the shelled haricot beans and 4 litres/7pt unsalted water. Bring to the boil and cook for 30 minutes.

COOKING THE SOUP

Add to the casserole the bouquet garni, leek, carrots, pumpkin, tomatoes and celery and simmer gently for 15 minutes. Add the potatoes, french beans, turnips and broad beans. As soon as the liquid boils again, put in the courgettes and vermicelli or macaroni. Add salt to taste and cook for about 15 minutes, until the pasta is tender. Discard the onion and bouquet garni.

THE *PISTOU*

Peel the garlic, put it in a pestle or blender with a pinch of salt and crush to a purée. Add the basil and crush until smooth. Add 100g/4oz of the parmesan then pour in the oil in a steady trickle, stirring continuously with a fork. Season generously with pepper.

SERVING

Put the *pistou* in a tureen and pour in the piping hot soup, stirring all the time with a ladle. Serve the remaining parmesan separately.

NOTES

Vary the quantities of vegetables as you like.

The pumpkin disintegrates as it cooks, giving the soup a lovely melting texture.

Serve a mixture of parmesan and mature Dutch cheese with the soup, as they do in the area around Marseille.

For a more full-bodied soup, make a larger quantity of *pistou* and serve the extra separately.

——— · ———

SOUPE AU PISTOU

PANIER DE LÉGUMES À L'ANCHOÏADE

PANIER DE LÉGUMES À L'ANCHOÏADE

Basket of raw vegetables with anchovy paste

THIS SUMPTUOUS BASKET *of the very freshest, most healthy and natural Provençal vegetables is a wonderful informal dish to share with friends.*
Have a plate of dried Arles sausage on the table and some slices of delicious ham from the Camargue. A variety of olives is also essential to complete this feast. Bon appétit!

PREPARATION
The vegetables: Scrape those that are very fresh, young and tender; peel any which are not. Wash in very cold water and pat dry. Divide the cauliflower into large florets and cut the cucumbers, fennel and celery into 4 or 6 pieces.
The anchoïade: Soak the anchovies in cold water for 30 minutes to remove the salt, then pat dry and crush in the mortar with the garlic to make a smooth purée. Gradually add the olive oil, a little at a time, working the mixture all the time until all the oil is incorporated. Stir in the vinegar and season to taste.

SERVING
Arrange the vegetables in a large willow basket or on an earthenware platter, composing them like a bouquet of flowers. Marry the colours and shapes harmoniously so they are as pleasing to the eye as to the palate. Cover the vegetables with a damp cloth and keep in a cool place until ready to serve.

Put the *anchoïade* into small stoneware bowls around the table. Leave your friends to help themselves to their favourite vegetables and let them shell the broad beans directly on to their plates.

SERVES 6
PREPARATION TIME: 45 MINUTES

INGREDIENTS
12 small new violet artichokes
2 small bunches of radishes
500g/1lb 2oz young broad beans in the pod (optional)
1 small very white cauliflower
300g/11oz young carrots, with their tops
12 large firm mushrooms
2 green and 2 red peppers, deseeded and sliced lengthways
12 small new onions, with their green tops
2 small Provençal cucumbers
6 small very tender fennel bulbs
1 head of young celery
ANCHOÏADE
250g/9oz fresh lightly salted anchovies
1 garlic clove, peeled
150ml/5fl oz olive oil
2 tablespoons wine vinegar
salt and freshly ground pepper

L'AÏOLI

Garlic mayonnaise

THIS IS THE RECIPE *for the* aïoli *that we serve with our fish soup at The Waterside Inn. Although potato does not appear in the classic recipe, we find that it gives the sauce a smooth, mellow quality. We also prefer to serve* aïoli *with* bouillabaisse *instead of the traditional* rouille, *as the red pepper can be overpowering.*

PREPARATION
Infuse the saffron in a cup with the boiling water or stock.

In a bowl or mortar, combine the sieved potato pulp, garlic, cooked and raw egg yolks and a pinch of salt and work with a wire whisk or pestle until smooth.

Beat in the olive oil, one drop at a time, adding the occasional few drops of hot liquid from the infusion of saffron. Once you have added about one-third of the oil, you can pour in the rest in a thin, steady trickle, still beating and adding a few drops of hot liquid every so often to prevent the *aïoli* from separating.

Lastly, add the saffron threads, cayenne and salt to taste. The *aïoli* should have the consistency of a firm mayonnaise, but be less smooth and shiny.

SERVING
Serve the *aïoli* in the mortar or in a bowl made of pottery or Provençal stoneware.

SERVES 8
PREPARATION TIME: 20 MINUTES

INGREDIENTS
a pinch of saffron threads
3 tablespoons boiling water or Fish stock (recipe page 14)
180g/6oz pulp from a baked potato, sieved and kept at room temperature
4 garlic cloves, peeled and crushed
2 hard-boiled egg yolks, sieved
1 raw egg yolk
200ml/7fl oz olive oil
a small pinch of cayenne pepper
salt

DAUBE DE SUPIONS

Braised baby cuttlefish

SERVES 4

PREPARATION TIME:
30 MINUTES

COOKING TIME: 50 MINUTES

INGREDIENTS

1kg/2lb 3oz baby cuttlefish or small squid

100ml/3½fl oz olive oil

1 medium carrot, finely diced

4 shallots, finely chopped

1 garlic clove, peeled and crushed

2 tablespoons concentrated tomato purée or 4 large tomatoes, peeled, deseeded and chopped

50ml/2fl oz cognac

300ml/½pt dry white wine

20g/¾oz chopped parsley

a small pinch of cayenne pepper

salt and freshly ground pepper

W E HAVE OFTEN ENJOYED *this delicious dish at our friends at Mouans-Sartoux. Be sure to give your guests soup spoons and plenty of bread to mop up the sauce.*

PREPARATION
Remove the ink and spines from the ink sac of the cuttlefish or squid, peel off the membrane and wash the fish very thoroughly in cold water. Drain and dry well with kitchen paper.

THE SAUCE
Heat half the oil in a casserole, then add the carrot, shallots and garlic and sweat without colouring for 5 minutes. Stir in the tomato purée or chopped tomatoes and simmer for another 5 minutes. Keep hot.

COOKING THE CUTTLEFISH
Heat the remaining oil in a frying pan until very hot, put in the cuttlefish and sauté over medium heat for 5 minutes. Drain, then add them to the casserole containing the vegetables. Set over high heat and quickly heat the contents of the casserole for 2 minutes, then flame with the cognac. Pour in the white wine, add the parsley, cayenne and a little salt, cover, and simmer for 40 minutes more. Season to taste with salt and pepper and keep hot.

SERVING
Pour the cuttlefish into a deep serving dish and serve very hot.

NOTES
If the sauce seems a little too liquid, lift out the cuttlefish with a slotted spoon, place them in the serving dish and reduce the sauce over high heat for 5 minutes, stirring frequently. Pour the boiling sauce over the cuttlefish and serve immediately.

BRANDADE

Creamed salt cod with olive oil

SERVES 8

PREPARATION TIME:
30 MINUTES, PLUS 24 HOURS SOAKING

COOKING TIME:
6 MINUTES FROM BOILING

D URING THE SEASON, *the inhabitants of the truffle-producing regions add slivers of raw truffle to the* brandade *at the last moment. Served this way, the dish acquires succulent and sophisticated overtones.*

PREPARATION
The salt cod: Place in a shallow pan, cover with cold water and heat until the water just begins to boil. Lower the heat to just below boiling point (90°C/195°F), so that the water is barely trembling, and cook for 6 minutes. Drain the cod and cover with a damp cloth.

Dip the garlic in salt and rub it over the inside of an enamelled casserole. Discard the skin and bones from the cod, flake the fish into the casserole and set over very low heat. Crush the cod with a spatula, without making the texture too dense, then add one-third of the olive oil in a thin, steady trickle, stirring it in as though you were making mayonnaise. Now add a little of the lukewarm milk in the same way to loosen the mixture.

Continue to add a little more oil, then a little more milk until the mixture is malleable but firm. When it will absorb no more liquid, season to taste and add the lemon juice.

SERVING
Put the *brandade* in a deep dish and serve it just warm, with the toasted bread arranged around the edge.

NOTES
Any leftovers are delicious served cold on rounds of toast. Sprinkle with freshly grated parmesan and serve with a salad of *mesclun* (bitter salad leaves).

INGREDIENTS

1kg/2lb 3oz fillet of salt cod, soaked in very cold water for at least 24 hours to remove the salt; change the water every 4 hours

1 garlic clove, peeled

400ml/14fl oz olive oil

300ml/½ pt milk, boiled and cooled to lukewarm

juice of 1 lemon

salt and freshly ground pepper

24 thin slices of french bread, toasted, for serving

PISSALADIÈRE

Provencal pizza

THIS DISH IS FOUND *all over the region, especially around Nice, where it has its origins. It makes an excellent hors d'oeuvre or snack and can be served with a salad of bitter* mesclun *leaves as a light Provencal lunch.*

PREPARATION
The onions: Peel and slice as thinly as possible. Gently heat the olive oil in a flameproof casserole, put in the onions, garlic and bouquet garni, cover and cook over very low heat for 2 hours. Stir the onions every 30 minutes, making sure that they do not colour at all. After 2 hours, they should be cooked and melting and lightly *confits* or candied. Remove the garlic cloves and bouquet garni, salt the onions very lightly and add a touch of pepper. Put the onions in a bowl and keep warm.

ROLLING OUT THE DOUGH BASE
On a lightly floured marble or wooden surface, roll out the dough into a 20cm/8in circle, about 3mm/⅙in thick. Roll the dough round the rolling pin, then unroll it on to a lightly oiled baking sheet. Pinch up the edges with your fingers to make a small rim to hold in the onions when the dough is cooked. Leave the dough base at room temperature for about 15 minutes to allow it to rise slightly.

Preheat the oven to 220°C/425°F/gas 7.

COOKING
Bake the empty dough base in the preheated oven for 10 minutes, then take it out of the oven and quickly put in the onions, draining off the oil if necessary. Spread the onions over the base, arrange the anchovies on top and strew over the olives. Return to the oven for another 20 minutes.

SERVING
Slide the *pissaladière* on to a pottery or brightly coloured china dish or a wooden board. Serve it piping hot, leaving a pepper mill and a little olive oil spiced with chillies on the table for those who like extra zest to help themselves.

SERVES 4

PREPARATION TIME: 35 MINUTES

COOKING TIME: 2 HOURS FOR THE ONIONS, PLUS 30 MINUTES FOR THE *PISSALADIÈRE*

INGREDIENTS

250g/9oz Bread dough (recipe page 13)

1kg/2lb 3oz onions

100ml/3½fl oz olive oil, plus a few drops for greasing

3 garlic cloves, unpeeled

1 bouquet garni, with a little added fennel and oregano

a pinch of flour

12 salted anchovy fillets, soaked to remove the salt

36 small black niçois olives

salt and freshly ground pepper

A SELECTION OF FISH USED TO MAKE *BOUILLABAISSE*

⤚ BOUILLABAISSE ⤙

Provencal fish soup

O NE HELPING IS NOT ENOUGH! *Let lovers of this divine dish enjoy as much as they want. Do not be put off by the apparently long preparation involved; it is not too onerous, especially if you can persuade your fishmonger to prepare the fish for you. However, it really is not worth the effort to make this soup for fewer than 8 people.*

There are many versions of this dish; some people like to add langoustines or crayfish, but we think this is gilding the lily.

PREPARATION
The fish: Scale, gut, trim off the fins, wash in very cold water and keep the fish for the soup separately from those for the garnish.

The soup: Gently heat the olive oil in a saucepan, add the leeks, onions, garlic, tomatoes, bouquet garni, the fish for the soup, crabs and the conger eel heads or tails and sweat over low heat for about 15 minutes, stirring with a wooden spatula as often as possible.

Pour in 3.5 litres/6pt boiling water and bring to the boil. Leave to bubble gently for 40 minutes, then pass the soup first through a vegetable mill, then through a conical sieve. Season to taste.

The garnish: Peel the potatoes and cut into 3mm/¹⁄₁₆in slices. Wash in cold water and drain. Lay them in the bottom of a casserole, then put in all the firm-fleshed fish, such as John Dory, conger eel, scorpion fish and monkfish. Pour over the boiling soup, then the olive oil and saffron threads. Bring to a brisk boil and cook quickly for 10 minutes. Add the fish with delicate flesh, boil briskly for another 5 minutes, then stop cooking. The fish should still be firm and the potatoes well done, but not disintegrating

SERVING
Quickly lift out the pieces of fish with a slotted spoon and immediately remove the skin and bones from the large fish, leaving the smaller fish whole. Put all the fish into a serving dish, the potatoes into a vegetable dish and pour the soup into a tureen.

Arrange the bread on a plate and put the *aïoli* into 2 or 3 bowls. Give your guests deep soup plates and place the various dishes on the table so that they can help themselves (and take second helpings . . .).

NOTES
Remember that *bouillabaisse* will not wait! Treat it as you would a soufflé – seat all your guests at the table and make them wait. The soup should be piping hot, with a rich aroma, but not too full-bodied.

———— • ————

SERVES 8

PREPARATION TIME: 1½ HOURS

COOKING TIME: 40 MINUTES FOR THE SOUP. 20 MINUTES FOR THE GARNISH

INGREDIENTS

SOUP BASE

1kg/2lb 3oz assorted small rock fish (wrasse, rainbow wrasse, comber, perch, scorpion fish, blenny, sea bream, weever fish, mediterranean prawns), or firm white fish such as monkfish, John Dory, sea bass etc., cut into chunks

3 tablespoons olive oil

white parts of 2 leeks, thinly sliced

100g/4oz onions, thinly sliced

3 garlic cloves, crushed

500g/1lb 2oz very ripe tomatoes, roughly chopped

1 bouquet garni, with a little dried orange peel and a branch of fennel

10 *favouilles* (small green crabs) (optional)

2 heads or tails of conger eel

salt and freshly ground pepper

GARNISH

500g/1lb 2oz potatoes

2kg/4½lb assorted fish (John Dory, conger eel, sea bream, gunard, scorpion fish, monkfish tails, weever fish, sea bass, royal sea bream), cut into chunks if large, otherwise left whole

100ml/3½fl oz olive oil

3 pinches of saffron threads

12–15 thin slices of slightly stale country bread

1 quantity *Aïoli* (recipe page 239)

EQUIPMENT
vegetable mill

DAURADE ROYALE À L'OURSINADO

Sea bream in a sea urchin sauce

SERVES 4
PREPARATION TIME:
50 MINUTES
COOKING TIME: 20 MINUTES

INGREDIENTS

1 sea bream, about 1.2–1.5kg/
2¾–3¼lb (preferably a royal sea
bream)

20 sea urchins

3 tablespoons double cream

4 egg yolks

2 tablespoons shredded flat-
leaved parsley

salt and freshly ground pepper

COURT-BOUILLON

500ml/18fl oz dry white wine

150g/5oz onions, chopped

200g/7oz carrots, thinly sliced

1 bouquet garni

5 peppercorns, crushed

T HE SEA URCHINS *give this dish a deliciously delicate flavour. Michel loves to serve it when he entertains friends at his shepherd's cottage in Provence.*

PREPARATION

The court-bouillon: Pour 1 litre/1¾pt water into a saucepan and add the wine, onion, carrots, bouquet garni, crushed peppercorns and a small pinch of salt. Bring to the boil and simmer for 20 minutes, then pass through a conical sieve and leave to cool completely.

The bream: Scale it and remove the gills with the point of a pair of scissors. Make a small incision in the belly and use the handle of a small ladle to empty the fish. Trim off the fins, rinse the fish in very cold water and pat dry with kitchen paper.

The sea urchins: Open them with the point of the scissors and remove the corals with a coffee spoon. Save 8 of the best corals and put them on a plate. Put the rest in a bowl and beat in the cream and egg yolks. Keep in a cool place.

POACHING THE BREAM

Place the fish in the oval casserole, add the cold court-bouillon and set over high heat until the liquid begins to bubble. Reduce the heat so that the liquid is just trembling (90°C/195°F) and cook for 15 minutes, then turn off the heat but leave the bream in the court-bouillon for another 5 minutes.

SERVING

Drain the bream and transfer it to a deep serving dish. Pour about 400ml/14fl oz of the court-bouillon into a saucepan and boil fiercely for 3 or 4 minutes. Take the pan off the heat and stir in the sea urchin mixture, then return to the heat, stirring with a wooden spatula. Do not let the sauce boil. As soon as it thickens slightly, take the pan off the heat and pass the sauce through a conical sieve, pouring two-thirds over the fish and the rest into a sauceboat. Arrange the 8 reserved sea urchins around the bream, sprinkle with parsley and serve at once.

NOTES

Tender young spinach sweated in butter and a few steamed potatoes mashed into the sauce make a marvellous accompaniment to the bream.

ARTICHAUTS BARIGOULE

Baby Provencal artichokes in olive oil and white wine

SERVES 4
PREPARATION TIME:
20 MINUTES
COOKING TIME: 20–30 MINUTES

T HESE ARTICHOKES ARE *particularly tasty and succulent when served as an accompaniment to baked fish. They also make a marvellous warm hors d'oeuvre.*

PREPARING THE ARTICHOKES

Take off the outer layer of hard leaves. With a sharp knife, cut off all but 2cm/ ¾in of the stalks and trim off about 1cm/½in from the tips of the leaves. Wash the artichokes under cold running water and drain.

(recipe ingredients overleaf)

244

DAURADE ROYALE À L'OURSINADO

INGREDIENTS

16 small violet artichokes

200ml/7fl oz olive oil

150g/5oz carrots, finely diced

250g/9oz baby onions, finely diced

200ml/7fl oz dry white wine

3 garlic cloves, peeled

2 sprigs of thyme

2 bay leaves

a small bunch of parsley stalks

6 peppercorns, crushed

salt and freshly ground pepper

COOKING

Pour the oil into a casserole and heat gently. Add the carrot, onion and artichokes and cook for about 5 minutes, stirring occasionally with a spatula, until the vegetables have turned a very pale golden. Moisten with the wine and 100ml/3½fl oz water, add the garlic, thyme, bay leaves, parsley stalks, crushed peppercorns and a little salt, cover and simmer gently for about 20 minutes. Test the artichokes with the point of a knife; they should be tender but still just firm. Cook for a little longer if necessary.

SERVING

Arrange the artichokes in a deep dish with the garlic, carrot and onion. Discard the thyme, bay leaves and parsley from the casserole, reduce the cooking liquid by one-third, then pour it over the warm artichokes. Serve at once.

NOTES

The real success of this dish depends on the quality of the artichokes, which must be small and very tender, otherwise the choke and outside leaves will be hard and inedible. Only use the long violet artichokes from Provence; green globe artichokes are not suitable for this recipe.

———— · ————

GARDIANE D'AGNEAU

Lamb cutlets with olives and potatoes

SERVES 4

PREPARATION TIME: 10 MINUTES

COOKING TIME: 1 HOUR

INGREDIENTS

4 best end lamb cutlets, trimmed and bones scraped

4 slices of neck of lamb, each 1.5cm/¾in thick

4 tablespoons olive oil

750g/1½lb potatoes

1 onion, thinly sliced

4 garlic cloves

1 bouquet garni, containing plenty of thyme

a pinch of savory

750ml/1¼pt boiling Chicken stock (recipe page 15) or water

75g/3oz small niçois black olives, stoned and blanched

2 tablespoons shredded flat-leaved parsley

salt and freshly ground pepper

THIS CLASSIC DISH *from Provence and the Côte d'Azur is very simple to prepare. It is particularly delicious in autumn or winter, served with a dandelion leaf salad.*

PREPARING THE POTATOES

Peel, wash, cut into 0.5cm/¼in slices and wrap in a damp cloth.

COOKING

Put the oil in a flameproof earthenware or cast-iron casserole and heat over medium heat. Put in the lamb cutlets and neck and seal on both sides until pale golden. Add the onion and garlic, cook for 2 minutes, then add the bouquet garni, savory and potatoes.

Pour in the boiling chicken stock or water, bring back to the boil, then lower the heat so that the liquid barely trembles. Season lightly, put on the lid and simmer for 45 minutes. Add the olives and parsley and cook gently for another 10 minutes.

SERVING

Discard the bouquet garni and serve the lamb straight from the casserole into deep dishes, so that everyone can enjoy the delectable cooking broth.

———— · ————

RATATOUILLE

I N A PERFECT *ratatouille, the vegetables should be well cooked, but not to a pulp, so that the individual flavour of each vegetable is clearly defined.*

SERVES 4

PREPARATION TIME:
35 MINUTES

COOKING TIME:
ABOUT 1 HOUR 40 MINUTES

PREPARATION

The aubergines and courgettes: Wash and trim the ends. Cut the aubergines into rings 1cm/½in thick, place in a bowl, sprinkle with fine salt and leave to disgorge for 30 minutes. Cut the courgettes into 1cm/½in cubes and place in a bowl.
The peppers: Smear with a little olive oil, then place under a very hot grill or in a very hot oven until they are blackened on all sides and the skin begins to blister. Rinse in cold water, then carefully peel off the skin. Halve lengthways and remove the seeds and white membrane. Cut the flesh into 1cm/½in squares and place in a bowl.

INGREDIENTS

400g/14oz aubergines

400g/14oz courgettes

200g/7oz green peppers

200ml/7fl oz olive oil

200g/7oz onions, diced

1 bouquet garni

½ bulb of garlic

1kg/2lb 3oz tomatoes, peeled, deseeded and chopped

salt and freshly ground pepper

COOKING THE RATATOUILLE

Heat one-third of the olive oil in a casserole, put in the onions, bouquet garni and garlic and sweat for 5 minutes without colouring. Add the tomatoes and simmer gently for 15 minutes, stirring with a spatula every 5 minutes.

Meanwhile, cook the aubergines. Drain them and pat dry with kitchen paper. Heat the remaining oil in a frying pan, put in the aubergines and cook over medium heat for 20 minutes, turning them over every 5 minutes. Add them to the casserole, cover and cook gently for 30 minutes, stirring every 10 minutes.

Now add the courgettes and peppers to the casserole, cover and cook for another 30 minutes, stirring every 10 minutes. Remove the bouquet garni and garlic and season the ratatouille with plenty of pepper and salt to taste.

SERVING

Put the ratatouille in an earthenware dish or serve it straight from the casserole. It must be piping hot.

NOTES

Ratatouille is also delicious served cold, with cold roast chicken, for example. It can be used to fill an omelette, too, or served as an hors d'oeuvre.

Provençal aubergines are the vital ingredient of ratatouille.

247

PETITS FARCIS PROVENCAUX

PETITS FARCIS PROVENCAUX

Stuffed Provencal vegetables

THESE VEGETABLES ARE EQUALLY *delicious served as an hors d'oeuvre or vegetable accompaniment (they are particularly good with local kid or simple roast lamb). They can be eaten cold, to stimulate the appetite, or hot, topped with a little freshly grated parmesan. We like to pour on a dribble of olive oil just before eating the vegetables.*

PREPARATION

The vegetables to be stuffed: Peel the onions and cut off one-third from the top. Wash all the other vegetables, halve lengthways and cut off a sliver from the bases so that the vegetables stand firmly. Use a soup spoon and, if necessary, the point of a knife, to hollow out the vegetables, leaving a 0.5cm/¼in thickness of pulp and skin so that they keep their shape when they are filled and cooked. Keep the different types of pulp separately. Blanch the fennel in boiling water for 2 minutes, refresh and drain.

Preheat the oven to 200°C/400°F/gas 6.

The stuffing: Keeping the different varieties separate, finely chop the vegetable pulp, chopping the onion and fennel particularly finely.

Heat two-thirds of the olive oil in a roasting pan or casserole. Add the onion and cook over medium heat for 5 minutes. Add the fennel, then add the rest of the vegetables at 2 minute intervals and in the following order: ceps or mushrooms, aubergines, summer squash or courgettes, spinach, tomatoes and finally the garlic, savory and parsley. Season lightly with salt and pepper and cook gently for 30 minutes, stirring occasionally with a wooden spatula.

Add 120g/4½oz breadcrumbs, let the mixture bubble for 1 minute and adjust the seasoning.

COOKING THE STUFFED VEGETABLES

Lightly salt the insides of the vegetables. Spoon in the stuffing. Lightly oil 1 or 2 gratin dishes and put in the stuffed vegetables. Sprinkle over a few drops of the remaining oil and the rest of the breadcrumbs. Bake in the preheated oven for 40 minutes, then place the vegetables under a hot grill to brown the tops.

SERVING

Arrange the vegetables on a plain serving platter to show off their glowing colours and serve immediately, while they are very hot.

NOTES

The vegetables can be prepared in advance, in the morning or even the night before – most useful if you are entertaining guests.

———— · ————

SERVES 4

PREPARATION TIME: 1¼ HOURS

COOKING TIME: 30 MINUTES FOR THE STUFFING, PLUS 40 MINUTES FOR THE VEGETABLES

INGREDIENTS

8 medium white onions

4 small aubergines

4 medium very firm tomatoes

4 round summer squash or courgettes

4 small fennel bulbs

STUFFING

100ml/3½fl oz olive oil

150g/5oz Provençal ceps or button mushrooms, peeled, washed and chopped

150g/5oz spinach, blanched and chopped

150g/5oz onions, finely chopped

300g/11oz tomatoes, peeled, deseeded and chopped

3 garlic cloves, peeled and crushed

10g/¾oz savory, finely chopped

30g/1oz flat-leaved parsley, finely chopped

150g/5oz fresh breadcrumbs

salt and freshly ground pepper

TARTE AU POTIRON ET
✦ AUX AMANDES ✦

Pumpkin and almond tart

SERVES 8

PREPARATION TIME:
25 MINUTES, PLUS 20 MINUTES
RESTING

COOKING TIME: 35 MINUTES

INGREDIENTS

300g/11oz pumpkin

120g/4oz whole almonds,
blanched and skinned

120g/4oz sugar

30g/1oz dried orange zests

1 coffee spoon orange flower
water (optional)

a pinch of flour

300g/11oz Puff pastry (recipe
page 11)

eggwash (1 egg yolk mixed
with 1 tablespoon milk)

granulated sugar, for serving
(optional)

THIS DIVINE PROVENÇAL TART *was traditionally served at Christmas. It is a very old recipe, which is nowadays found only in the remoter parts of the region.*

PREPARATION

The pumpkin: With a sharp knife, cut off the skin and seeds, then cut the flesh into small pieces and place in a saucepan with 3 tablespoons water. Cover the pan and cook over low heat, stirring occasionally with a wooden spatula until you can crush the softened pumpkin with the spatula.

Purée the pumpkin in a food processor or blender, return it to the pan and cook over low heat, stirring continuously, until thick and smooth. Transfer the purée to a bowl.

The almonds: Spread on a grill pan and grill until pale golden. Put in the food processor with the sugar and orange zests and crush into small pieces. Stir these into the pumpkin purée and add the orange flower water if you are using it.

The pastry case: On a lightly floured marble or wooden surface, roll out 250g/9oz puff pastry into a circle 2–3mm/⅛in thick. Brush a baking sheet with water and lay the pastry circle on the sheet. Brush a 1cm/½in border with eggwash, roll it over and pinch up the edge to make a small rim to hold in the filling.

Filling the tart: Using a palette knife, spread the pumpkin and almond filling evenly over the pastry. Brush the outer rim of the pastry with eggwash.

Roll the remaining pastry into a long rectangle and cut into strips to make a lattice on top of the tart. Lay these strips in a criss-cross pattern on the tart and brush with the rest of the eggwash. Chill in the fridge for 20 minutes.

Meanwhile, preheat the oven to 220°C/425°F/gas 7.

COOKING

Bake the tart in the preheated oven for 35 minutes, then immediately slide it on to a wire rack.

SERVING

Sprinkle the tart with a little granulated sugar, if you like, and serve it whole on a round china plate.

——— • ———

TARTE AU POTIRON ET AUX AMANDES

Provence

FRESHWATER FISH

Eel
Trout

SEA FISH

Shad
Anchovies
Chapon (scorpion fish)
Conger eel
Sea bream
Girelles (rainbow
wrasse)
Gurnard
Monkfish
Sea bass
Whiting
Mostelles
(rockling)
Mullet
Murène
(moray eel)
Pageot
(pandora sea bream)
Rascasse
(scorpion fish)
Red mullet
Rambous
(brill)
John Dory
Sar
(similar to sea bream)
Sardines
Turbot
Vives
(weever fish)

SHELLFISH *and* CRUSTACEANS

Cigale de mer
(flat lobster)
Clovisses
(small clams)
Crab
Favouilles
(small green crabs)
Spiny lobster
Mussels
Sea urchins
Palourdes
(large clams)
Octopus
Poutines
(larval sardines
and anchovies)
Praires
(warty Venus)
Cuttlefish
Violets
(sea figs)

POULTRY

Chicken

GAME

Duck
Wild rabbit
Hare
Wood pigeon
Partridge
Venison
Wild boar
(recently)

MEAT

Mutton
Kid
Rabbit

CHARCUTERIE

Caillettes
Herb boudin from Nice
Tripe from Marseilles
Camargue ham
Thrush pâté from
Dignes and Nyons
Pieds et paquets
Arles sausage

VEGETABLES

Garlic
Violet artichokes
Lauris asparagus
Aubergines
Chard
Carrots
Cardoons
Cabbage
Pine forest mushrooms
Marrows and their
flowers
Courgettes
Spinach
Fennel
Broad beans
Green beans
Sweetcorn
Mesclun
(bitter salad leaves)
Turnips
Chick peas
Dandelions
Potatoes
Leeks
Peppers
Pimentoes
Radishes
Tomatoes
Jerusalem artichokes
Onions

HERBS

Basil
Thyme
(also known as
farigoulette and
serpolet)
Bay
Rosemary
Sage

CHEESE

Banon
Brousse
Cachat
Picardon
Pèbre
(donkey, goat or cow,
according to the season)
Rigotte
Tôme
All these cheeses are
made from goats' and
ewes' milk

FRUIT

Apricots
Almonds
Arbutus berries
Cherries
Chestnuts
Lemons
Quinces
Figs
Strawberries
Raspberries
Jujubes
Melons from Cavaillon,
Cantaloupe, Verdon
Medlars
Watermelon
Table grapes
Peaches
Plums
Pears

PÂTISSERIE

Chichi-frégi
Gâteau de St Blaise
Pet de none
Pompe d'Aix en
Provence

CONFECTIONERY

Soft boiled sweets
from Marseilles
Boiled sweets from
Carpentras
Calissons from
Aix en Provence
Crystallized fruits from
Nice, Apt, Grasse
Lavender honey
White and dark nougat

MISCELLANEOUS PRODUCTS

Anisette from Marseilles
Anchoïade
Capers from Toulouse
Olive oil from Menton,
Marseilles, Nice, Aix en
Provence, Valréas
Green and black olives
Fresh and commercially-
produced pasta
Grilled peppers
Poutargue
(dried pressed mullet
roe)
Rice from the Camargue
Saffron
Tapénade
Truffles from Tholoneu,
Riez, Valréas, Marche,
Apt, Richerenches,
Carpentras

Index

PHOTOGRAPHIC ACKNOWLEDGMENTS

All the photographs were taken by Martin Brigdale with the exception of the following: Bruce Coleman page 116 and Denis Hughes-Gilbey pages 38, 56, 96, 194 and 234.

THE *Roux* BROTHERS

FRENCH COUNTRY COOKING